The Complete Guide to Bicycling in Canada
Revised Edition

The Complete Guide to Bicycling in Canada

Revised Edition

Elliott Katz

Doubleday Canada Limited, Toronto

Maps by Bo Kim Louie
Cover photo © by Alec Pytlowany
Back cover photo reproduced with the permission of
The Grey-Bruce Tourist Association
Jacket design by Dragon's Eye Press
Typesetting by Compeer Typographic Services Limited
Printed and bound in Canada by Gagne Printing

Canadian Cataloguing in Publication Data
Katz, Elliott
   Complete guide to bicycling in Canada

Includes index
ISBN 0-385-25220-X

1. Bicycling touring - Canada - Guide-books.
2. Canada - Description and travel - 1981 -   -
Guide-books.   3. Cycling paths - Canada - Guide-books.
I. Title.

GV1046.C3K37 1987   917.1'04644   C86-094927-3

For Marsha

Contents

Preface

You get on your bike and start riding. As you pedal, you feel the immediate exhilaration of freedom. You're beginning an adventure. Gliding gently down a winding country road, you breath the spring air in deeply. The wind blows in your face and through your hair. The sun peeks over the horizon, and there is a soothing silence.

On a bicycle you see, feel, hear, and smell the land intimately. You can explore peaceful wooded valleys, tree-framed riverbanks, picturesque villages, rustic islands, snow-capped mountains, and ocean beaches. You're traveling slowly enough to hear the birds, smell the pungent pine forests, and absorb the tranquility of Canada's natural areas—yet going fast enough to cover distance. Scenery that flashes by a motorist is savored from a bicycle. Because you're on a bike you're open to experience the world, and local people take an interest in your journey. You'll return from a bicycle trip with unforgettable memories.

Canada has some of the world's most spectacular scenery, and a bicycle is the best way to discover and experience it. Canada also has some of the best bicycle touring in the world, whether you ride for a day, a weekend, a week, a month, a summer, or longer. Cycling, according to a Canada Fitness Survey, is the country's most popular summer recreation activity.

Take your bicycle with you on vacation, as a part of your vacation, or as the entire vacation itself. You can load your bike onto your car or onto a train, an airplane, a ferry, or a bus. When you arrive at a tour's starting point, unload the bike and start riding.

Facilities for those who want to tour on a bicycle are provided in many magnificently scenic regions. Along quiet roads with little traffic are campgrounds and accommodations within an easy day's ride of each other. Registries reserve accommodation in bed-and-breakfasts or inns a day's ride apart.

Bicycle touring is for everyone. You can ride as little or as far as you wish. Cover a leisurely 32 km (20 miles) or a challenging 160 km (100 miles) per day. It's up to you. You can also plan a bicycle trip to fit every budget. It can be an inexpensive camping vacation or you can spend more on luxury accommodation. The bicycling, however, is free.

Touring on a bicycle lets you appreciate just how few things a person needs to be comfortable, and develops self-reliance. Take only the essentials. Anything more becomes a burden.

Not only is the bicycle the most efficient way of using energy to transport the body, it can also improve the quality and appreciation of life. The health and fitness benefits of bicycling are well known. Cycling is invigorating. It benefits your cardiovascular system and uses large muscle groups continuously. Bicycling is graceful and quiet. As you achieve a steady pedaling rhythm, you feel the tension rolling off your body. You can think clearly and ideas come to you as you glide by fields and forests. A bicycle ride is an enjoyable outing to share with friends and family. And bicycling is a lot of fun.

For some, a bicycle trip can be a personal journey of self-discovery. The experiences and encounters of the voyage become an education in life.

Cyclists have been exploring Canada since the nineteenth century, whether pedaling their bikes to the next town or to another part of the country. I was fascinated to discover the book *The Cyclists' Road Guide of Canada*, published by the Toronto Bicycle Club in 1894. The book, which went through several editions, guided cyclists to routes linking Canadian towns and cities at a time when there were no cars and few roads and the thoroughfares that did exist were dirt cart-tracks.

In 1876, when the first bicycle was brought to Montreal, the excitement was so great that a half-day holiday was declared and Montrealers watched the owner pedal his high-wheeler up and down the city streets. During bicycling's first golden era in Canada in the

1880s and 1890s, bicycles were ridden mainly by adults, many of them members of bicycle clubs, which had an air of exclusiveness.

This book is your guide to enjoying Canada's best bicycle tours. The first part, "Getting Ready," offers some tips on safe cycling, buying a bicycle, what to take with you, and planning a tour. The second part, "Where to Bicycle in Canada," is a guide to Canada's most scenic and enjoyable bicycling. The book is a useful guide for everyone, from beginners going on their first tour to experienced cyclists looking for new and interesting tours.

Each chapter includes a number of tours, varying in length from one day to ten days or more. Both well-known bicycling routes and lesser-known routes are included. For cyclists who want to ride across Canada, each chapter has an across-the-province tour. These link together to form a continuous route, generally following scenic roads with light traffic.

Each route description tells you the tour's approximate length, where to start the tour, and how to reach the starting point by bicycle, car, train, bus, or ferry. Transporting bicycles on public carriers is discussed in the chapter on planning your tour. The description guides you along the route, pointing out details of scenery and topography, sites of general and historical interest, national and provincial parks, and accommodations and campgrounds. The chapter's reference maps help you plan your tour. Provincial road maps are available from each province's tourism department (addresses and telephone numbers given at the beginning of each chapter).

You can use the tours as a base to plan your own tour. For an extended trip, you can join two or more tours. Or you can do part of a longer tour for an exciting day-long or overnight trip. Don't let this book sit on the shelf. Get on your bike and experience the pleasures of cycling!

Foreword

Canada's reputation as an internationally renowned cycle touring destination is well earned. More and more Canadians are discovering that one of the best adventures of their lives is waiting on their own doorsteps. The pleasures of cycle touring include Gulf Island-hopping on British Columbia's west coast, exploring the Canadian Rockies along Alberta's Icefields Parkway, enjoying the autumn colors in the Ottawa Valley, or sampling Atlantic-style hospitality in Quebec's Gaspé region or on Nova Scotia's Cabot Trail.

Many of Canada's roads carry light traffic and have sufficient width for enjoyable cycling. A growing number of towns and cities are providing cyclists' route maps and developing special cycling facilities such as recreational bicycle paths. In the country, many campgrounds and youth hostels cater to the long-distance cyclist.

The bicycle tourist in Canada also enjoys the services of the non-profit Canadian Cycling Association, an organization founded in 1882 to promote organized cycling across Canada. Although primarily a competitive organization at its inception, the CCA has grown to encompass the needs of the recreational cyclist as well. Today, the CCA is recognized as the governing body of organized cycling in Canada. It promotes the growing use of bicycles for transportation, exercise, adventure, and competition.

The Recreation and Transportation Commission of the CCA endeavors to promote a better environment for cyclists through the activities of three major sub-committees: The Advocacy and Safety Committee, the Education Committee, and the Touring Committee.

The Advocacy and Safety Committee encourages higher bicycle equipment safety standards and lobbies for cyclists' continued right to the road. This committee also recommends changes to existing legislation that will benefit safe cycling practice.

The Education Committee is responsible for developing and delivering the Canbike programs that train cyclists in proper and effective cycling technique. The programs fall into three major categories: roadcraft, touring skills, and bicycle maintenance.

The Touring Committee is responsible for developing the touring skills stream of the Canbike program and for the general promotion of bicycle touring in Canada. To this end, the CCA wishes to acknowledge Elliott Katz's significant achievement in the compilation of this important resource for touring cyclists in Canada.

For more information about the CCA and its programs, write to: Canadian Cycling Association, 333 River Road, Vanier, Ontario K1L 8H9.

Don Hollingshead
Touring Chairman
Recreation and Transportation Commission
Canadian Cycling Association

Acknowledgements

This book was a joint effort with the Canadian Cycling Association (CCA). Rose Mercier, CCA Director General, set up the CCA involvement in this project. Charles Laframboise, CCA Director of Recreation and Transportation, worked tirelessly, contacting resource people in every region of Canada who shared their knowledge of the best bicycle tours in their area.

British Columbia: Gary Janovick, Stephen Hinde, and Ruby Gretchen of the Nanaimo Bicycle Club; John Mandryk of Prince George Cycling Club; Bob Boomstra of Kamloops Bicycle Club; Len Christianson of Kootenay Bicycle Club.
Alberta: Gail Helgason and John Dodd, authors of *The Canadian Rockies Bicycling Guide* and *Bicycle Alberta*; Marc Beaumont of the Elbow Valley Cycling Club; Victor Dorion of the Edmonton Bicycle and Touring Club; Don Hollingshead of the Alberta Cycling Association.
Saskatchewan: Bill and Virginia Stewart, Saskatchewan Cycling Association.
Manitoba: Howard Skrypnyk, Manitoba Cycling Association.
Ontario: Dennis Szilvasy of the Toronto Bicycling Network; Frank Fogelin of the Ontario Cycling Association; Les Humphries of the Ottawa Bicycle Club.
Quebec: Louise Roy and Michel Labrecque of Vélo-Quebec.
New Brunswick: Carl White of Vélo Nepisiquit Cycling Club.

Nova Scotia: Dave Dermott, Bill Silvert, and D.J.B. Watts of Bicycle Nova Scotia and their publication *Bicycle Tours in Nova Scotia*.
Prince Edward Island: T. Susane MacPhee-Manning, Prince Edward Island Cycling Association.
Newfoundland: Tom Sandland, Newfoundland and Labrador Cycling Association, and their publication *Newfoundland by Bicycle*.

Part One: Getting Ready

1   Buying a Bicycle

The best bicycle for your tour is the one that suits your specific needs. A large variety of bikes are now available and many new models are brought out every year. If you want to go on an overnight or longer trip on paved roads, you will need a multi-speed touring bike. If you want to explore backcountry trails, old logging roads, or other off-road areas, you should shop for an all-terrain (mountain) bike.

On a cycling trip you are dependent on your bicycle for transportation. Buy the best bike you can afford. You want a bicycle that will make touring a pleasure and not break down and ruin your trip. Worse, a breakdown could leave you stranded in a remote area.

If you have bought this book, it probably means you want to do touring. The multi-speed touring bicycles have a large range between low and high gears to let you ride steadily up steep hills, pedal against the wind, or cruise over level terrain at a good pace. Touring bikes now come in ten, twelve, fifteen, or eighteen speeds. Racing bicycles are similar in appearance to touring bikes but are not meant for riding with any extra load. Touring bicycles have lower pressure tires and more durable rims and wheels.

The lighter your touring bicycle, the better. Even a small amount of weight makes a big difference on a tour. The more expensive lighter bikes usually have higher-quality components which are not only lighter but more reliable.

The touring bike with dropped handlebars is best suited to long distance cycling. Dropped handlebars put your body in the best

3

position to pedal. By leaning forward you also cut down on wind resistance. This dropped position may initially give you a stiff neck, but as your neck muscles strengthen this feeling will go away. You may also find it takes some time for your hands to adjust to dropped handlebars. One way to make dropped handlebars more comfortable on your hands is to put a foam-padding covering on them, or wear cycling gloves with padded palms.

Three-speed, five-speed, and six-speed bicycles are also suitable for day-long or overnight tours. Some have dropped handlebars but most come with upright handlebars and spring saddles. Both are easier to get used to than dropped handlebars and a hard seat. If you plan a leisurely tour, covering only a small distance each day, and don't want the dropped handlebars, one of these bicycles should be fine. Sitting upright does mean you have more wind resistance. However, if you're not interested in covering distance but rather in savoring short tours of less than 40 or 50 km (25 or 30 miles) per day, and if you want to sit upright, by all means get one of these bikes. Several around-the-world cyclists have done their multi-year tours on these kinds of bikes.

All-terrain bikes (also known as mountain bikes) are designed to withstand the rough handling of backcountry dirt roads and trails. They combine the best features of the one-speed coaster-brake bicycle and the multi-speed touring bike. These all-terrain bikes have fat tires that are usually 6.5 cm (2½ inches) wide, wide-range gears — up to eighteen speeds — to get up and down hills, upright handlebars for better control, and heavy-duty brakes. I have found that all-terrain bikes are an advantage when you are riding on the gravel shoulder of a highway with heavy traffic. With the all-terrain bike's fatter tires you can easily ride on the unpaved shoulder a good safe distance from the trucks. However, for regular riding on paved roads, all-terrain bikes tend to be slower and heavier than most touring bikes. It's a trade-off — your choice depends on the kind of riding you're going to be doing.

The best place to buy a bicycle is at a reputable bicycle shop that guarantees its bikes and has trained mechanics who service the bikes on the premises. The sales staff are usually knowledgeable and can help you choose the best bike for your needs in your price range. Bike shops usually sell only quality makes. Bikes are like most consumer products: you get what you pay for. The cheaper brands carried by discount stores may give you problems soon after they're out on the road.

Shop around and compare bicycles and prices. When you've decided on a bicycle, try to purchase it from a shop near your home. Even if it costs a few dollars more, the extra convenience may be worth it. When the bike needs adjustment it's a lot easier to take it a few blocks than to haul it across town.

Getting the Right Size

Most important when buying a bike is that it fits you properly. Frame size is your first consideration. The standard adult bicycle frame ranges from 58 to 66 cm (19 to 26 inches). This is the distance between the top of the frame where the seat post slides into the frame, and the center of the crank where the pedals revolve. Your frame size is roughly 28 cm (11 inches) shorter than your inseam measurement.

Get on the bicycle. With both feet flat on the ground you should be able to straddle the top tube of the frame of a men's bike with about 5 cm (2 inches) to spare.

The saddle or seat is the proper height when you can sit on it with one foot touching the ground. When the middle of your foot is on the pedal in the down position, your knee should be slightly bent. With one elbow touching the tip of the saddle, the handlebars should be no more than 25 mm (1 inch) from your fingertips. If the handlebars are too far forward, too low, or too high, ask the shop to adjust them. It may be necessary to change the handlebar extension for one of a different size. (The handlebar extension is the piece that connects the handlebars and the stem.) The handlebar should be a bit lower than the saddle. Neck pain and soreness in the upper arm and lower back can be symptoms of a badly adjusted saddle.

Secondhand Bicycles

Ads for used bicycles can be found in daily and weekly newspapers, as well as on bulletin boards in supermarkets, universities, and some bike shops. The old saying that buying a used car is buying someone else's troubles is sometimes true for bicycles, so you have to be careful. Buying a secondhand bicycle is like buying other mechanical devices. Know what you are buying or it may end up costing you a lot more than you anticipated. Some bike shops sell used bicycles, usually bikes that were traded in by their owners to purchase a new bike. If the bike shop overhauls these used bikes there probably is little risk in buying one.

When you are looking at a used bicycle, ride it and see how it handles at slow and fast speeds. If the bike fits you and is comfortable, do the safety check described in the chapter on safe cycling, and examine it carefully for mechanical defects. Here are some things to look for.

☐   Look at the bicycle from the front and back to see that the frame is straight and the wheels are in line. Turn the bike upside down, letting it rest on the seat and handlebars. The wheels should spin freely and be centered between the forks. Spin the wheel and hold a pencil beside the brake shoe to measure side to side movement; it should be no more than 3 mm (1/8 inch).

☐   Hold the wheel and push it from side to side. The wheel should be firmly secured at the dropouts and should not move sideways. Pluck each of the spokes; they should be tight and have the same twanging sound.

☐   Turn the pedals. When the wheels spin there shouldn't be any clicking noises. Put on the brakes; the wheels should stop instantly. Brake shoes should hit the rim squarely and release it without sticking.

☐   Examine the frame carefully, particularly the forks and where the tubes of the frame join. Wrinkled paint may indicate that the bicycle was in an accident. A fresh paint job may also indicate this.

☐   The pedals and cranks should turn freely with little or no sideways play. Cranks should be straight. Bent cranks may be a sign that the bike was in an accident.

☐ Gears should change smoothly, without slipping and without a chunking noise. Try the gears both with the bike upside down and during your test ride.

☐ With the bicycle right side up, put the front brake on and try to move the handlebars back and forth. If there is a lot of play, the headset — the part that connects the handlebar stem with the frame — may be worn or in need of adjustment.

The used bicycle you look at may not be in perfect condition. Before you actually purchase the bike, bring it into a repair shop and find out how much repairs will cost.

Renting a Bicycle

In a lot of cities, as well as in national and provincial parks and other areas offering good cycling, many bike shops now rent touring bicycles. If you're traveling to an area and find it too difficult to transport your bike, or if you don't own one, contact a bicycle rental outlet in advance and reserve a bike for your trip. Some rental outlets will also rent helmets, panniers, and other accessories. To find out about shops which rent bicycles, contact the provincial tourism departments or the provincial cycling associations.

2 *What to Take with You*

The exhilarating freedom of bicycle touring comes from traveling and living comfortably, even luxuriously, with just your bike and what you're carrying on it. To travel freely means bringing only the essentials and cutting every unnecessary gram. If you weigh down your bike with non-essentials, you'll probably be tempted to mail home all the extras after a day of pedaling against the wind or up a mountain.

The amount of gear you need depends on your touring plans. If you're cycling from motel to inn and planning to eat only in restaurants, you can travel very light. Just pack some clothing and toiletries and you're off. Not having to carry a sleeping bag, tent, and cooking gear leaves you with a fairly light load.

Camping out and cooking your meals requires more gear, but can give you a greater sense of freedom. You are self-sufficient. You can stop anywhere and discover your ability to be self-reliant with just a few essentials.

Panniers

The bags that attach to a carrier and hang alongside the wheel are called panniers (sometimes referred to as saddlebags). Both front and rear panniers are available. Front panniers are generally smaller and are used only when the extra capacity is needed for a very long camping tour.

Shop around before you buy. The cheaper panniers tend to be smaller and less sturdy than the better quality bags. They might be good enough for doing errands around town, but for touring you'll have fewer problems with a better quality pannier.

Get panniers with a capacity of around 41 liters (approximately 2,500 cubic inches). Each pannier usually consists of one large main pocket and smaller outside pockets.

The better pannier bags are made of a sturdy and waterproof material such as Cordura, and come with safety reflectors. Inside each pannier there must be a stiff frame or strong backing, so the panniers won't get caught in the rear wheel spokes.

The panniers' suspension systems should attach very securely to the carrier. Some of the cheap systems don't. If the panniers are loose, they can get caught in the spokes or fall off the carrier. Bring your bike with you when you're shopping and try the panniers on. If you have cantilever brakes, make sure the panniers don't interfere with their operation.

You should be able to remove panniers from your bicycle fairly quickly so you don't have to leave them unattended. When off the bike, some pairs of panniers can be attached together with snaps or Velcro and have an adjustable shoulder strap for easy carrying when you're walking.

Carriers

To attach panniers to the bike you need a carrier (also called a rack). Get the best you can afford. Quality rear carriers attach to both seat stays and have two or more supports on each side to support the weight of the panniers. Among the best known rack makers are Blackburn, Minoura, and Vetta. Most quality carriers are made of aluminum.

Front carriers attach to the front forks and some are designed to lower the center of gravity to keep your bike more stable. Try to keep your baggage to a minimum so you use only rear panniers and don't weigh down your bike with attachments to both front and rear.

The lower the weight on the bicycle, the lower the center of gravity and the easier and safer the riding. Pack heavy items such as stoves and canned food in the bottom of the pannier. Put light items such as sleeping bags on top of the carrier.

Handlebar Bags

A handlebar bag is handy for items that you want to reach quickly without dismounting from your bike. A clear plastic map case on the top of the handlebar bag lets you refer to the map while riding. Handlebar bags range in volume from 8 to 11.5 liters (500 to 700 cubic inches). The handlebar bags designed for all-terrain bikes are generally smaller, in the 2-liter (130-cubic-inch) size.

Strong shock cords running from the bottom of the handlebar bag to the front wheel forks prevent the bag from bouncing around when you go over bumps. Buy a bag made of sturdy material so that it won't sag when it's full and rub your front wheel. Handlebar bags should be easily removable from the bike. Some come with a shoulder strap to convert them to shoulder bags.

Put light items only in the handlebar bags. Heavy gear raises the bike's center of gravity, which makes steering difficult.

Water Bottles

The plastic bottles designed for cyclists come with wire frames that attach to the handlebars or the frame of the bicycle. Their double caps have a small opening which lets you drink while pedaling. Most bike frames now have built-in bolts for mounting water bottle holders.

Tools and Spare Parts

Always carry a small tool kit when you're touring. If you don't have the tools needed to fix a flat, or some other problem, you may have a long walk to a bike shop. Get a dependable pump that can inflate your tire hard enough for you to be able to ride on it. Many of the cheap pumps can't do this.

A suggested kit contains: Tire irons • Spare inner tubes • Tire pump • Tire patch kit • Pressure gauge • Extra spokes and spoke tool • Spare brake and gear cables • Bicycle wrenches • Adjustable wrench • Allen keys needed for your bike • Screwdriver • Pliers • Small knife or scissors • Chain tool and spare links • Freewheel removal tool • Spare bulb and batteries for your lights.

Locks

Every time you leave your bicycle, even for a few minutes, lock it against something secure — like a lamp-post, bicycle rack, or other immovable object. Take your panniers and handlebar bag with you. If your gear is stolen from your bike, the trip is ruined.

Lock the frame and both the front and rear wheels, or, if you have quick-release wheels, take the front wheel with you. Never lock your bicycle by the front or rear wheel alone.

If you do use a cable with a regular lock, position it so that the lock is high off the ground. That way, bike thieves can't put one side of their bolt cutters on the ground, and they will have less leverage to cut the lock.

You may think you're only going to be gone for a moment but it takes less than a minute for a thief to make off with your bicycle or panniers. You've probably spent a fair amount of money on your bicycle so protect it with a dependable lock. There's nothing worse than the empty, sinking feeling you get when you walk out of a store to discover a thief has made off with your bike. I once came out of a shop in the middle of the day on a busy street and found two thieves with bolt cutters trying to cut the cable lock on my bicycle. None of the passersby did anything. Fortunately when I yelled at them they ran. I immediately bought one of the large U-shaped locks.

It's definitely worthwhile to invest in one of those virtually indestructible heavy duty U-shaped locks, such as the Kryptonite, Citadel, or Bike Guard. All of them include a guarantee of several hundred dollars if your bike is stolen because a thief was able to break the lock.

To overcome the inconvenience of having to take off your front wheel every time you lock the bike with one of these U-shaped locks, use a cable and lock to lock the wheels to the frame while using the U-shaped lock to lock the frame to an immovable object.

Here are some other measures you can take to safeguard your bike:

☐   Record the bike's serial number and register the bike at a police station.

☐   Scratch your name and telephone number on the frame.

☐   Take a color photo of your bicycle so you can identify it in case it is stolen.

☐   Get theft insurance for your bicycle. It can be included in your household policy. Bring the receipt for your bike to your insurance agent and have him add it to your policy.

Clothing

Bring the least amount of clothing possible. Choosing the right clothing lets you do more with less. For most bicycle touring on summer days you'll probably be most comfortable wearing a T-shirt and shorts. Even in cool weather, shorts are usually more comfortable than long pants which can constrict knee movement. If you do wear long pants, choose a light cotton pair. Avoid jeans as they have thick, folded-over seams that can chafe your skin. Use pant clips to keep cuffs out of the chain.

On your torso wear layers of light clothing. This lets you regulate your comfort by adding or removing layers as the weather changes. A cotton T-shirt is the first layer. Cotton absorbs perspiration without feeling clammy. The next layer can be a shirt, followed by a wool sweater and then a nylon windbreaker for cool temperatures. As you warm up, stop and remove a layer of clothing.

In case of rain, pack a poncho or rainsuit. During spring or fall, or at high elevations, the weather can be cool and windy, and your hands can get cold. Bring a pair of gloves or mitts.

Keeping your head protected is also important. Always wear a helmet. On cold days wear a wool hat under your helmet. On hot days, you can wear a cycling cap under your helmet and dampen it to keep your head cool.

To pack your clothes, put each item in a plastic bag. Roll up the bag and slip it vertically into the pannier. This way, when you want to retrieve something, you can see the top of each bag and won't have to dig to the bottom of the pannier to find it.

Sun and Insects

In hot weather make sure you wear a sun-hat with a visor that fits under your helmet. You may also want to wear sunglasses to protect your eyes from wind and insects. If your skin tends to burn in the sun, use a sunscreen to block the harmful effects of the sun's rays. Use a suntan lotion if you want to tan.

The mosquito, according to an Indian legend, was created by the nature spirit Gitchi Manitou, who was angered one day when all the men married all the women of the tribe and a universal honeymoon began. There was nobody to harvest the corn. Gitchi Manitou sent swarms of the maddening bugs to the world, bringing an end to the honeymoon.

Mosquitoes and blackflies can be a problem for cyclists, especially when you stop for a break or to camp. Insect repellents block the sensors on the mosquitoes' antennae and prevent the bugs from landing and biting. Use a repellent with a high percentage of active ingredient. In most repellents, M-diethyl-meta-toluamide (diethyl toluamide or DEET for short) is used.

Floral scents attract bugs, so don't use colognes, scented soaps, or shampoos while in the outdoors. Do wash, though, as mosquitoes like warmth and humidity, and are more attracted to people who perspire a lot.

When choosing a campsite, look for a dry and open area that has a breeze to keep insects from clustering. Tall grass and thick woods should be avoided as they break the wind. Most important, stay away from areas with stagnant water where mosquitoes breed.

Food

Bicycle touring enables you to shop at local stores every day for fresh food. Not having to carry a lot of food saves a lot of weight. Of course, the easiest way to get your daily nourishment when bicycle touring is to stop at restaurants. But this can be expensive, and you miss the pleasure of eating in the outdoors.

When you shop, buy the foods you like and determine your needs from experience. How you feel is the best measure of how well you are eating.

Carbohydrates are quick-energy foods. Snacks consumed during rest stops should be high in carbohydrates. Good snacking foods are granola bars, fruit bars, raisins and other dried fruits, chocolate, nuts, and shredded coconut. Some stores sell "trail mix," which contains a variety of dried fruits, raisins, and nuts.

Fat, found in meat, margarine, and nuts, is another source of energy. The body stores fat and can convert it into heat energy very quickly when needed. On cold days, adding extra margarine to your morning oatmeal will help keep you warm.

Protein, found in meat, fish, eggs, milk, and cheese, produces energy that lasts longer. However, protein consumes calories in its conversion into energy.

Water is the best liquid to drink to prevent dehydration. Your body loses moisture in perspiration and urine. When you exert yourself cycling and perspire more than usual, you should drink water regularly.

If you're touring through the backcountry or in a remote area where you will not be able to buy food, stock up on non-perishables, such as dehydrated soup mixes, canned meat or fish, and macaroni.

It's a good idea to bring along small amounts of salt, pepper, spices, sugar, tea, coffee, peanut butter, and jam in tightly closed plastic containers. These items are usually sold in volumes larger than you need for your trip, and if you buy them on the road they will add extra weight and volume.

To get an early start in the morning, eat a quick and simple breakfast such as eggs, oatmeal, granola, or peanut butter and jam on bread, with juice or fruits.

Quick lunches can be made with bread and cheese, salami, canned meat or fish, or peanut butter and jam, with fruit or juice.

Supper is usually a bigger meal. After riding all day you're hungry, and you have more time to prepare the meal. Try to plan a meal that takes about half an hour to prepare so you can cook and set up camp while it's still daylight. Cook fresh meat, fish, or anything else that you can buy at the local grocery store.

Stoves

The lighter your cooking gear, the better. Butane stoves are the simplest to operate. The cartridges contain pressurized butane gas that vaporizes instantly when vented to atmospheric pressure. Just open the valve and light. The cartridges weigh more than white gas for the same amount of heating energy, but they're more convenient.

The Bleuet S200-S stove is the most widely available butane stove. It costs about $25 and weighs 420 g (15 ounces). A butane cartridge lasts about three hours, weighs 190 g (7 ounces), and costs about $2.50.

White gas stoves burn hotter than butane stoves and the fuel is cheaper. The most popular of the white gas stoves are: the Coleman Peak 1, which weighs 800 g (1 pound, 12 ounces) and sells for $60; the Svea 123 which weighs 510 g (1 pound, 2 ounces) and sells for $60; and the Optimus 8R which weighs 670 g (1 pound, 8 ounces) and also costs about $60. The MSR WhisperLite uses the Sigg fuel bottle as the stove's reservoir and is very light, weighing in at only 350 g (12 ounces). It sells for about $70. White gas is very flammable and should be carried in a metal, leak-proof container such as a Sigg fuel bottle.

Practise operating the stove at home so you won't have any problems when you're out on the road. Avoid using the stove inside a tent. Make sure it's stable and that there is adequate air circulation.

For cooking and eating, get a lightweight aluminum cooking set consisting of a pot with a lid that doubles as a frying pan and a dish. Sigg offers sets of nesting pots designed to fit a Coleman Peak 1 or Svea 123 stove inside the cooking set, which will save space in your panniers. Don't forget a knife, fork, and spoon.

Tents

The lightest shelters are plastic tube tents or coated rip-stop nylon tarps measuring approximately 2.7 by 3.6 meters (9 by 12 feet), with grommets along the edges. Both protect you from rain and sun, but not from biting mosquitoes and blackflies. For complete protection, get a tent. In recent years, tents designed for bicycle touring have come out. They're lighter, usually under 2 kg (4.4 pounds), and smaller than most lightweight tents. They fit into panniers where space is at a premium.

Pack the tent and pegs at the bottom of a pannier. If the tent poles don't fit in the panniers, secure them with shock cords to the carrier or the top tube of your bicycle.

Sleeping Bags

Don't scrimp on a sleeping bag. There is nothing worse than a miserable night lying awake and shivering in a bargain basement sleeping bag. Buy a bag that will keep you warm at the coldest temperatures that you're likely to encounter in the region and time of year you will be cycling. But don't go overboard either. A winter sleeping bag is too much weight and is too hot for the summer.

Get a quality bag from a good camping equipment store. Mummy bags are generally warmer and lighter than rectangular bags. Synthetic filled bags cost less than down bags rated to the same temperature, but down has the advantage of compressing to a smaller size for packing—a definite advantage in the very limited space on your bike.

On the other hand, the top-quality synthetics, such as PolarGuard, Hollofill II, and Quallofill, dry faster when wet. But if you're careful with a down bag you should be able to keep it dry. When you are riding, always cover your stuff-sack with a large plastic bag in case you get caught in a sudden downpour.

Backpacking hammocks are light, compact to pack, and comfortable to sleep in. Just find two trees spaced the correct distance apart and tie one end of the hammock to each tree. If there's a possibility of rain, rig a tarp over the hammock.

Checklist

Here's a suggested checklist. You can modify it to suit your plans and needs.

Bicycle gear:
Bicycle • Helmet • Panniers and carrier • Handlebar bag • Battery-operated light to double as flashlight • Cycling gloves or wool gloves • Water bottle • Tool kit and spare parts (see list on page 10).

Clothing:
T-shirt • Long-sleeved shirt • Sweater • Nylon windbreaker • Shorts • Long pants • Underwear • Socks • Shoes • Swimsuit • Towel • Sun hat • Wool hat • Poncho or rain suit.

Toiletries:
Toothbrush and toothpaste • Soap.

Cooking gear:
Stove, fuel, and matches • Pot and pan set • Dish and cup • Knife, fork, and spoon • Food containers • Can opener.

Shelter:
Tent • Sleeping bag.

Miscellaneous:
Insect repellent • Sun screen • Candles.

3 Planning Your Tour

To start enjoying the independence of bicycling, begin with daytrips and overnight or weekend tours. A shorter trip helps you learn what equipment you need and what is just extra weight. Chances are that on your first trip you'll burden yourself with too much gear. After a few short tours you'll know how to operate all your equipment, and will be able to decide exactly what you need to bring for a weekend, a week, or a month.

Another reason for starting with short trips is to get an idea of how far you can journey in a day. Don't try to cover too much distance. A good average for your first trip is 65 to 80 km (40 to 50 miles) each day. This allows you enough time to stop for a swim or lunch and still arrive at your overnight destination in time to cook supper and—if you're camping—to put up the tent in daylight.

When you've chosen a tour, take out the provincial road map, available from the province's tourist office, and choose an objective for each day of your tour. The tour description gives a suggested plan, but design your tour to suit your own tastes.

On a weekend trip, you don't want to spend your precious time looking for accommodation. Reserve ahead. Many campgrounds accept reservations for a number of their campsites, with the remainder given out on a first-come, first-served basis.

Reservations can be more important for cyclists than for motorists. If it's late in the afternoon and there's no room at the campground, a motorist won't mind driving 100 km (60 miles) to another. For a cyclist, it's not that easy.

When making reservations, say what time you expect to arrive if it will be late in the day. If you see you're not going to make it to your reserved accommodation, call and tell them. If you don't call, and you arrive the next day expecting a place, you may find they don't have one for you.

Camping

This type of touring means filling your panniers with gear to camp and cook on your own, but it is worth the effort. You are totally self-sufficient on your bike, living in the outdoors.

The tours in this book generally have an abundant selection of campgrounds in national or provincial parks. Start your day early, so you can arrive at your campground early. It's much more pleasant to set up in daylight. With your site set up and your bike unloaded, you're free to explore the area. At night, a campfire and singing can be wonderful. Carry a harmonica if you know how to play one.

A guide to each province's campgrounds, including those in national parks, provincial parks, and private campgrounds, is available from each provincial tourist department.

Bed-and-Breakfasts

Bed-and-breakfasts are popular with all manner of travellers, and cyclists are no exception. One of the joys of cycling is exploring the country and getting to know its people. Staying at bed-and-breakfasts can be part of this experience. Bed-and-breakfasts are cozy, generally cost less than hotels, and are operated from private homes, so you can get to know your hosts. You can find bed-and-breakfasts in rural towns and villages, and in cities.

In some areas, a central registry takes reservations for the bed-and-breakfasts in the area. This is a good way to plan and reserve accommodation for a multi-day tour in which you can stay at a different bed-and-breakfast each night. Information on bed-and-breakfast places is available from provincial tourist departments.

Hostels

Canadian hostels offer not only inexpensive accommodation, but also an opportunity to meet people of all ages from all over the world, many of whom are cyclists. Hostels are not limited to young people.

Along the spectacular Icefields Parkway through the Canadian Rockies is a chain of hostels within a day's ride of each other. As well, there are hostels available in cities and in other national and provincial parks.

If you intend to use hostels regularly, get a membership in the Canadian Hostelling Association; if you're traveling to Canada, get a membership in the hostelling federation of your country. Non-members pay a slightly higher fee to stay at a hostel. Advance reservations are recommended during the summer season. The address and telephone number of each provincial hostel association is given at the beginning of each chapter. The national office of the Canadian Hostelling Association is: 333 River Road, Vanier, Ontario K1L 8H9. Telephone (613) 748-5638.

Motels and Hotels

If you want more comfort and privacy at night, and if you can afford it, you may want to stay at motels or hotels. Economical motels offering comfortable rooms are widely available. The safest place to keep your bike is in your room with you. Just make sure your bike isn't dripping with mud. The accommodation guides available from the provincial tourism offices give details on prices and facilities.

Backcountry Touring on an All-Terrain Bike

Using an all-terrain bike on backcountry trails combines the best of cycling and hiking. You're free of having to deal with cars and trucks and can get closer to nature — which is the joy of hiking. But on your bike you can cover greater distances. Some people use an all-terrain bike to cover a long stretch of relatively uninteresting country to reach an isolated hiking area that is too steep for an all-terrain bike.

When you're touring the backcountry, you need to carry all your food. If you want to camp overnight in the backcountry, you'll need, in addition to camping equipment, freeze-dried and other lightweight foods containing little or no water, such as rice, noodles, oatmeal, or beans.

Transporting Your Bicycle

Many people take their bikes with them on vacation. That way, they can cycle some of these tours for a day, a weekend, a week, or longer, to experience the country intimately. Others want to bicycle just outside their own city and don't want to ride half a day to get out of the city and suburbs. Whatever your plans, you're faced with the question: how do you transport your bicycle?

Cars

More and more people are loading their bicycles onto their cars to do some cycling for all or part of their vacation. They drive themselves and their bikes to the tour's starting point, park the car, and cycle for a day or a week before returning to the car.

The easiest way to transport your bike is to have a van or station wagon that allows space to put bicycles inside, although you may have to remove one or both wheels to get it in. However, even if you do have a van or station wagon (and not everyone does), you probably need the space inside for passengers and luggage. To transport bicycles, then, you need a bicycle carrier that mounts outside your car or van. Three designs are available: bumper-mounted carriers, trunk-mounted carriers, and car-top carriers.

When shopping for a bike carrier, make sure the carrier fits the design of your vehicle. Also, consider the number of bicycles you want to transport. The bumper-mounted carriers can only carry one or two bikes safely. The trunk-mounted carriers and the car-top carriers can usually hold up to four bicycles.

Make sure that the parts of the carrier that come in contact with your bicycles are coated with vinyl or another material that protects the bicycle's paint. A rack with rust-resistant, galvanized, or plasti-cized steel will last longer.

When loading the bikes on a carrier, remove items that can fall off such as pumps, panniers, and handlebar bags. The car's exhaust can melt bicycle tires, so position the bikes so that the exhaust pipe is not aimed at a tire. When transporting bicycles with the bumper-mounted or trunk-mounted carriers, be careful that the wheels are not so low that they hit the ground when you drive over a dip or up a steep road. Always keep in mind the car's extra bulk, especially when parking.

Trains

To transport your bike overland in Canada by public transport, the easiest way is by train. Trains that have a baggage car will take your bike without being boxed or disassembled. You can just hand it to the baggage attendant, and there will be no extra charge. Most train routes in Canada have at least one train per day with a baggage car. VIA Rail operates most of the railway services throughout Canada and provides access to most of the bicycle tours described in this book. Check a current schedule or call VIA Rail. The telephone numbers in each province are given at the beginning of each chapter. If a train doesn't have a baggage car, they probably will not take your bike.

VIA Rail recommends that you disassemble your bike and put it in a box. It sells bike boxes for a few dollars. If you have the tools, you can remove the front wheels and pedals, turn the handlebars sideways, and pack it into the box. VIA Rail accepts bicycles at your own risk. Boxed or not, VIA Rail will not accept responsibility for damage.

Buses

Check with bus companies in advance. Some take bikes but require them to be disassembled and boxed. Bus companies don't supply boxes; they can be bought from bike shops. Dismantling a bike so that it fits in a box usually involves removing the front wheel and the pedals, and turning the handlebars sideways. Put the pedals and any loose bolts in a sturdy bag and store them in your panniers.

If the bus company will transport your bike, it may be a good idea to ship your bike a few days ahead to make sure it's there when you arrive. Some bus companies won't guarantee that the bike will travel on the same bus as you or even on the same day. On a long weekend or in high travel season your bike may get bumped to a later bus. Also, some bus companies may say the bus you want to take will transport your bike—but the bus they use that day may have a small baggage compartment that won't accommodate your bike.

Airlines
Regulations vary with the airline. Some allow a bicycle as your first piece of checked luggage. Others consider it excess baggage and charge a flat fee. Call a few airlines and compare.

On some airlines you can buy extra insurance for your bike when you buy your ticket. Some sell bicycle bags for a few dollars in which you can pack a disassembled bike. If you plan to transport your bike regularly on public carriers, you can buy a good quality bicycle bag made of heavy-duty nylon. Airlines require than you turn the handlebars and remove the pedals. Always secure the handlebars after turning them.

Keep all the parts you have removed from your bike together in a sturdy bag and put them in your panniers. Remove the panniers from the bike and check them separately or take them as carry-on luggage. They will fit in a large lightweight duffle bag. One tip: your bicycle tools may trigger the airport's metal detectors. Mine did. Tools are not permitted on board aircraft. Keep them in a separate case that you can check with your bike.

Ferries
You can walk on ferries with your bike. Almost all ferries charge for bicycles. The addresses and telephone numbers of ferry services are given at the beginning of each chapter if you must take the ferry to reach a province. If the ferry is part of a specific tour only, the address is given within the description of the tour.

4 Safe Cycling

As bicycle touring becomes more and more popular, the safety of cyclists on the road has become an important issue. Learning defensive cycling skills is vital. This chapter can help you prepare to handle potentially dangerous cycling situations safely.

The safest situation for cycling is when both cyclists and drivers are aware of and respect each other's place on the road. Fortunately, drivers are becoming more accustomed to bicycles. However, there are still many drivers who aren't used to thinking of cyclists. These drivers, although they may seem to be looking right at you, are not used to considering the cyclist's place on the road and will drive as if they had not seen you at all.

With the growing number of cyclists, there has been an increase in the number of cycling accidents, not all of which are the driver's fault. The most common causes of accidents in which motorists are at fault are: failing to yield the right of way, making turns in front of cyclists, or opening car doors into them. On the other hand, riding on the wrong side of the road or on the sidewalk, turning without looking behind, riding without lights at night, and failing to yield the right of way are the usual causes of accidents in which the cyclist is at fault.

The tours described in this book generally follow roads that have light traffic and offer pleasant cycling. Wherever you ride, proper precautions by both cyclists and drivers can help prevent accidents.

Rules and Regulations

Ride as far to the right of the road as possible. Groups should bicycle in single file. Obey stop signs and traffic lights, even if it means losing momentum. And though you may think it's perfectly safe to go through a red light or ignore other traffic regulations, you are simply giving all cyclists a bad name when you do.

When you stop to check your map or to adjust something on your bicycle, move your bike and yourself completely off the road. Don't block any part of the road for cyclists or car traffic.

Ride defensively. Be aware of the road directly in front of you, as well as a long distance ahead. Always grasp the big picture by looking well ahead. Defensive bicycling lets you plan what to do in each situation so you won't be taken unawares by a merging road, or by obstacles such as a pothole, broken glass, or a storm sewer that can make you fall.

If there is a pothole or similar hazard in your path, check for oncoming traffic and traffic behind you to see if you can safely swerve around it. Otherwise stop or, if you continue over it, slow down and lift yourself out of your seat to prevent your spine from absorbing the bumps.

Roads with wide, paved shoulders make the best touring routes. Riding well onto the paved shoulder keeps you safely away from the main flow of traffic. On a narrow road without a paved shoulder, ride where you will be visible. This may mean that at times you are claiming the lane.

Riding a touring bike on a gravel shoulder is slow going. If you're going to tour roads with unpaved shoulders, consider using an all-terrain bike which can easily handle gravel. It's slower than a touring bike on paved roads, but you're farther from the traffic and not limited to the edge of the pavement.

When you're riding, put yourself in the motorist's shoes. Or if you drive, think about the occasions when you yourself have had to pass cyclists. When I'm driving I get nervous about getting too close to bicycles, so I veer left — and then I worry about the car being too close to the oncoming lane. Experience teaches that sharing the road requires courtesy and effort from both cyclists and drivers. Some tips for motorists are at the end of this chapter.

City Bicycling

When you're riding in a city, try to choose a route on side streets that parallel the heavily traveled main streets. City traffic can be frightening when you are distracted by looking for street names. When choosing a route from one point to another we often think of the city's main arteries, but that's thinking like a car driver. It's usually easy to avoid these streets. Take out a map and plan a route through quieter residential streets. They're safer, have less car exhaust to inhale, and are usually more scenic.

Sidewalks

The safest place to ride your bike is on the road, *not* on sidewalks. When you're bicycling in a town or city, stay off the sidewalks and be courteous to pedestrians. Bicycles are a vehicle and belong on the road.

Just as cyclists can feel persecuted by hostile drivers, pedestrians often feel their safety threatened by cyclists zooming by on a sidewalk. "Inconsiderate boors!" wrote one irate pedestrian to a newspaper. "Silent menaces that threaten life and limb," wrote another.

Riding on the sidewalk, or riding on the wrong side of the road and surprising pedestrians when they step off the curb, can make pedestrians hostile to cyclists and can even injure people walking. If the street has heavy traffic, don't ride on the sidewalk. Take a less traveled road.

Some people think that riding on the sidewalk is safer, but it can actually be more dangerous than riding on the road. Consider this: pedestrians average 5 km (3 miles) per hour, while a cyclist travels about four or five times that speed. Bicycles are not as maneuverable as your own two feet, and they take more time and distance to stop or to turn. Accidents can occur when a car backs out of a driveway and hits a cyclist on the sidewalk who was hidden by hedges, fences, or other obstructions.

The problem of cyclists riding on sidewalks is not new. During the bicycling boom of the nineteenth century (often called bicycling's golden era), when cyclists on high-wheelers shared the roads with horsedrawn carriages, a 1898 issue of the Toronto Bicycle Club newsletter pointed out: "The fact is that bicyclists are out of their proper place and are trespassing when they use the sidewalk...As the bicycle has evidently come to stay, the sooner those using the machines know their position in reference to the use of sidewalks the better, not only for themselves but the public generally."

Signals

Use hand signals when turning or changing lanes. Extend your left forearm to indicate a left turn. For a right turn, either extend your right arm—the way this signal is usually done today—or extend your left forearm upward while the upper arm is straight—a leftover from the days when car drivers used hand signals. To indicate slowing down, point your left forearm down so that it is at right angles to your upper arm. Hand signals should be made at least 30 meters (100 feet) in advance of a turn.

Train Tracks

Be careful when approaching railway tracks. They can be very slippery. Cross them as close as possible to a perpendicular angle. Otherwise, the tracks can catch your front wheel, which will throw you onto the road.

Intersections

Most accidents between cars and bicycles occur at intersections, often because the bicycle is in the driver's blind spot.

Here's a common situation. You are beside a car that is in the right lane. You plan to ride straight ahead—but since you're beside the car, you cannot see if the driver is signaling to turn right or not. And the driver cannot see you between the car in the right lane and the sidewalk. The traffic light turns green, you proceed straight, but the car turns right, into your path.

Don't position yourself beside a car. Stay behind the car so you can see the signals of the car in front of you, and the driver behind can see you. Even if there are signal lights on the side of the car, the driver may neglect to signal or wait until the last second.

Making a left turn can sometimes be difficult. The safest way is to walk the bicycle across the pedestrian crosswalk, or ride through the intersection on the right, then turn the bike to the left and proceed through the intersection again.

Merges and Turn-offs

Be especially careful when you're on a highway and approaching a turn-off or a merge. Cars can turn into your path if you're going straight along the right side of the road. Look behind you and check for cars signaling that they're merging or turning off.

Parked Cars

When you're passing a row of parked cars look ahead into the cars to see if there's a driver or passenger who might open the car door into your path. To avoid this, cycle well out into the road away from parked cars. If the car is emitting exhaust it may be about to pull out onto the road.

Brakes

Most cyclists are aware that if you brake too hard on the front brake or use the front brake only—especially when going downhill—you'll go flying over the front handlebars. As a result there is sometimes a tendency to rely more on the rear brake.

On a bicycle equipped with front and rear hand brakes, the front brake does 80 percent of the braking. Using the back brake helps keep the bicycle under control. To stop effectively, you must use both brakes.

For better control when braking hard in a sudden stop, shift your weight back on the bicycle as you brake. This helps prevent you from being thrown forward.

Wet Roads

Rain makes roads slippery. The water also brings oil to the surface of the road, making things even more slippery. The rims of a bicycle's wheels get wet and the brakes work poorly on them.

When it rains, I usually stop at a restaurant or other sheltered place to sit it out. Not only can riding in the rain be more hazardous, the rain is cold and stings your face when you ride into it.

When you're riding in wet conditions, including right after a rain, ride slowly and look ahead so you can begin braking gently in advance. Dragging your brakes slightly will help remove water from your rims. Avoid those slippery oil slicks on the road.

Panniers

Baggage should be in panniers attached securely to your bicycle, not in a knapsack on your back. Keep the load as low as possible for better handling of the bike on the road. Loose panniers can slip into the spokes.

Rider Visibility

Make sure you can be seen. Wear bright, multicolored clothing that has some dark colors and some light colors. Red and yellow show up best. Your body is the largest object on your bike. Wearing clothing that will make you visible to motorists is more effective than attaching flags to your bike.

Available in most bicycle shops are the 2-meter (6-foot) bicycle flags. As they extend above the height of traffic and have brightly colored flags, they make you stand out on the highway and help motorists spot you.

Your bicycle should have reflectors fixed on the front and back, and on the spokes of both wheels. There should also be reflective tape on the bicycle frame. The reflectors should be large—at least 3.8 cm (1.5 inches) in diameter—and they should be visible for at least 90 meters (300 feet) at night. Pedals with built-in reflectors are a good safety device. If you ride at night, wear light-colored clothing that can be easily reflected in car headlights. Reflective safety vests are also an excellent idea.

Bicycle lights are not so much intended to light up the road ahead, which they do only minimally, as to make sure that drivers can see you on the road. A bicycle headlight should be visible from at least 150 meters (500 feet) at night.

There are two main types of bicycle lights: battery-powered and generator-driven. The generator-driven light has a wheel that revolves against the tire to produce current which powers the lights. They don't require batteries so you won't be caught with dead batteries and no light. However, a generator increases your pedaling resistance (although the newer models do so less than the older ones) and the light shines only when you are moving. As soon as you stop, the light goes out.

Leg lights that attach with a strap to your leg are very effective in attracting motorists' attention because the light beam goes up and down as you pedal.

Night riding is very different from daytime riding. At night, tired car drivers may not be able to see you, and their headlights can blind you for a few seconds. If you have to ride at night, choose a route on lighted roadways.

Helmets

Get the best helmet you can find and wear it. If you think helmets are an expensive accessory, consider how much your head is worth. In case of accident, a helmet could easily save your life. Most deaths from bicycle accidents are from head injuries.

Fortunately there are two standards for bicycle helmets: the American National Standards Institute (ANSI) Z90.4; and the more rigorous Snell Memorial Foundation standard. The standards a helmet has met are indicated on its packaging and on the helmet itself. Buy a helmet that has passed both standards. You have only one head, so buy the best helmet and add some reflective strips on both the front and back.

A cycling helmet that meets these standards has a hard, full cover shell that will distribute the effect of a blow to the head over as large an area as possible, shield the head from sharp objects, and provide an abrasion-resistant surface between your head and the road.

Helmet liners should be made of expanded polystyrene (similar to styrofoam) which will absorb a shock by crushing, and not bounce back at the head. The liner should be at least 1.2 cm (0.5 inch) thick, and if it crushes, stay crushed. Springy foam is added only for comfort and to ensure a snug fit. To keep the helmet on your head if you fall, it must have a good strap with a strong buckle D-ring fastener.

Note: never wear stereo headsets when cycling. You have to be able to hear cars and trucks approaching, pedestrians calling out, and emergency vehicles demanding the right of way.

Dogs

If a dog looks like it's going to run after you, the best thing to do is speed up. You can probably outrace it.

If you can't ride fast enough to get away, yell "Stop!" or "No!" loudly and shake your pump at the dog. This may make it turn around and go home. Another way is to talk soothingly to calm the dog. Or, try crossing to the other side of the road. This may be sufficient to remove your threat to the dog's territory.

Other techniques: use the chemical repellent carried by postmen; put lemon juice or diluted ammonia in a squeeze bottle or a water pistol; or just use your water bottle to squirt the dog, preferably in the eye area. A more peaceful way is to throw the dog some food and take off while the dog is distracted.

Trucks

Large trucks can be frightening for cyclists. When a truck is passing you, move as far as you can to the right. The suction that trucks create can knock you down if you are too close. Keep both hands on the handlebars and keep going as the truck passes. If you are worried about a truck getting too close, it may be best to pull off the road and stop to let the truck pass. Before moving back onto the road, wait until you see the entire truck in front of you. The truck may have two trailers.

The tours in this book generally follow roads with light traffic, but you may encounter heavy trucks, particularly logging trucks on the mountain roads of western Canada. If you're on a narrow road with little or no shoulder and you hear a logging truck or other heavy vehicle coming, the safest thing to do may be to get off the road completely and let the truck pass.

Health

The golden rule of cycle touring is: drink before you are thirsty and eat before you are hungry. Be careful to avoid sunstroke. Make sure you always carry fluids without sugar or caffeine to drink. Wear a shirt with a brightly colored back to reflect the sun.

Always be prepared for the worst weather that can be encountered in the area at that time of year. Carry clothing that will provide adequate warmth and dryness. Beware of hypothermia. Don't be afraid to stop and seek shelter if you begin to shiver, or if your body goes numb, or if you feel drowsy.

Keep in touch with your body. Stop when you get very tired. Your intellectual functions decrease when you're tired and your chances of having an accident are greater.

Bicycle Safety Check

Your safety and enjoyment depend on good working bicycle. Do a thorough check of your bicycle regularly. Examine the following components:

☐ *Brakes*: You should be able to apply your brakes with full force without the levers going more than halfway to the handlebars. Check the brake shoes to make sure they aren't worn, loose or rubbing against the wheel.

☐ *Cables*: Examine the brake and gear cables to make sure they aren't frayed where they attach to the brake or gear levers and to the brakes and derailleurs. If they are frayed, replace them now before they break. New brake cables stretch, so you have to adjust the brakes to take in that slack.

☐ *Gears*: Check the operation of both derailleurs. Keep the chain clean and oiled. Grease all bearings once a year.

☐ *Tires and Wheels*: Frequently check air pressure in both tires (the correct pressure is usually indicated on the tire) and look for cuts and wear. Make sure the wheels are tight in their mounts. Rims should be free from dents as this affects braking. Replace broken spokes. If the wheel wobbles it can be straightened—called trueing the wheel—by adjusting the spokes. If the wheel is badly dented, get a new one.

☐   *Looseness*: Many parts gradually become loose over time. Check your bike's pedals, cranks, and headset. Also check the nuts holding fenders, carrier racks, lights, water-bottle cages, horns, and other accessories. If anything is loose, tighten it.

Backcountry Bicycling

Riding all-terrain bikes through the backcountry involves some special rules to safeguard both the cyclist and the environment. Ride only on trails that have been designated for the use of all-terrain bikes.

Stay on the trails. Going off the path, especially in meadows, can damage vegetation and leave unsightly tire tracks. Don't ride on muddy trails. It will damage them. Don't litter.

An all-terrain bicycle can take you farther into the backcountry than you can walk out in a day. Be equipped to repair flats and mechanical problems, so you that can ride out. Carrying a tool kit, spare inner tube, patch kit, and pump is essential on all backcountry rides.

Don't startle hikers. Slow down and use a bell or call out to let them know you're coming. When cycling downhill or approaching blind corners, ride in anticipation of meeting hikers and horses.

When approaching a horse, get off the bicycle and if possible stand on the downhill side of the trail.

If you see wildlife on the trail, slow down and let it move off the trail before approaching and passing.

Bears

As cycling is a quiet means of transportation, cyclists have a better chance of seeing wildlife on a road or trail. But it also means they can surprise a bear, which may then feel threatened. Bears will generally leave you alone if they're aware that you're approaching. If you're traveling with the wind, the bear may be warned by your scent. But if you're riding into the wind, the bear may not get your scent and be unaware of your approach. Warn bears of your presence by riding in a group and talking, and carrying a bell or other noisemaker.

Watch for bear tracks and fresh bear droppings. Never approach a bear cub. A female bear will attack if she thinks her cub is in danger.

If you see a bear, make a wide detour or leave the area immediately. If you cannot detour or retreat, wait until the bear moves away from the path. Always leave the animal an escape route.

Cyclists as Drivers

Set an example to other drivers on how to share the road with cyclists.

When you plan to turn right and a cyclist wants to ride straight through the intersection, slow down and let the bicycle go, then make your turn. This is better than trying to get ahead and turning in front of the cyclist.

Before opening your car door after you've parked or when you are pulling out of a parking space, turn around and look for bicycles. Looking in the rear-view mirror isn't sufficient — there may be a bicycle in your blind spot.

If you see a cyclist riding toward an obstacle such as a pothole or sewer grate that the rider may have to swerve around, slow down or move over so the cyclist has more room.

Part Two: Where to Bicycle in Canada

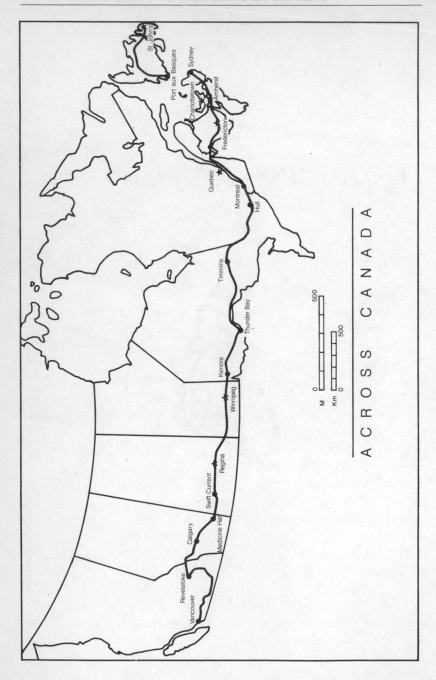

ACROSS CANADA

5 British Columbia

An immense diversity of spectacular scenery makes British Columbia an ideal bicycle touring destination. You can ride to wilderness Pacific coast beaches backed by rainforest, explore the picturesque and tranquil islands in the Strait of Georgia by ferry and by bike, cycle through northwestern British Columbia and board a ferry through the fjords of the Inside Passage, or ride from open ranchland in the interior to snow-capped mountains.

WEATHER: British Columbia has many different climates because of its location between the Pacific Ocean and the high mountain ranges. The warm Japanese current gives the coastal region a very moderate climate of mild, wet, and foggy winters and moderate dry summers. The west coast of Vancouver Island is the wettest part of Canada, with an average annual rainfall of 305 to 483 cm (120 to 190 inches). The Coast Mountains also receive a heavy rainfall from the moisture-laden winds from the Pacific. East of the Coast Mountains, the interior is dry. The higher air currents travel on to the lofty Selkirk Mountains, where it rains frequently. The Rocky Mountains are protected by the Selkirks and receive much less precipitation.

TOURIST INFORMATION: General tourist information, including a road map and an accommodations guide that lists campgrounds in provincial and national parks, as well as private campgrounds, is available from Tourism British Columbia, 1117 Wharf Street, Victoria, British Columbia V8W 2Z2. Telephone (604) 382-2127.

HOSTELS: Canadian Hostelling Association, Pacific Region, 3425 West Broadway, Vancouver, British Columbia V6R 2B4. Telephone (604) 736-2674.

AIRPORTS: The international airports at Vancouver and Victoria are served by Air Canada, Canadian Pacific Airlines, and other major airlines, with connections to smaller centers in British Columbia.

FERRIES: Ferry services from Horseshoe Bay and Tsawwassen in the Vancouver area to Vancouver Island and the Gulf Islands on the Sunshine Coast; from northern Vancouver Island to Prince Rupert; and from Prince Rupert to the Queen Charlotte Islands, are operated by British Columbia Ferry Corporation, 818 Broughton, Victoria, British Columbia V8W 1E4. Telephone: in Victoria, (604) 386-3431; in Vancouver, (604) 669-1211; in Nanaimo, (604) 753-1261.

Ferry service from Port Angeles, Washington State, to Victoria is operated by Black Ball Transport Inc., 430 Belleville Street, Victoria, British Columbia V8V 1W9. Telephone (604) 386-2202; in Port Angeles, (206) 457-4491. Service connecting Anacortes, Washington, to Sidney near Victoria is operated by: Washington State Ferries, Blaney Terminals Limited, Port Agents, 2499 Ocean Avenue, Sidney, British Columbia V8L 1T3. Telephone (604) 656-1531 or 381-1551; in Seattle, (206) 464-6400.

The inland ferries crossing rivers on the mainland are operated by the Ministry of Transportation and Highways Marine Services, 3D, 940 Blanshard Street, Victoria, British Columbia V8W 3E6. Telephone (604) 387-3053.

TRAINS: For information on VIA Rail in British Columbia, contact your local VIA Rail agent or call toll-free 1-800-665-8630. British Columbia Railway, which runs along the Sunshine Coast and through the interior to Prince George, can be contacted through: British Columbia Railway, 1311 West First Street, North Vancouver, British Columbia V6B 4X6. Telephone (604) 984-5246.

BUSES: Mainland British Columbia is served by Greyhound Lines, 150 Dunsmuir Street, Vancouver, British Columbia V6B 1W9. Telephone (604) 683-9277. Vancouver Island is served by Island Coach

Lines, 710 Douglas Street, Victoria, British Columbia V8W 2B3. Telephone (604) 385-4411.

CYCLING: Bicycling Association of British Columbia, 1200 Hornby Street, Vancouver, British Columbia V6Z 2E2. Telephone (604) 669-BIKE.

Gulf Islands

One of the west coast's most spectacular cycling areas, the Gulf Islands comprise approximately one hundred peaceful enchanting islands on the west side of the Strait of Georgia. In the distance are the snow-capped peaks on the mainland and Vancouver Island. Many islands are linked by ferry so you can explore them at your leisure. Beaches abound in marine life. Bring a local tide table and guidebook to explore the tidepools and mudflats at low tide.

The roads on the Gulf Islands are quiet, but they are narrow and tend to have some very steep (12 to 16 percent grade) hills. Traffic can be heavy near ferry sailing times. These islands can be a delight, but exercise caution at all times.

Provincial campgrounds are located on only three islands: Pender, Galiano, and Saltspring. Private campgrounds are also available. The number of campsites is limited and drinking water can be hard to find throughout the islands, so some advance planning is necessary. To ensure your cycling trip fits with the inter-island ferry schedule, don't plan on covering more than one island per day. Best bets are Pender Island and Saltspring Island, both with regular ferry service to Swartz Bay.

The best time for cycling is from May to mid-June, and late August to early October. July can be good, but tends to be rainy in most years. During July and August the roads have busy traffic. Winter cycling is best on the Gulf Islands and the Saanich Peninsula, but be prepared for rain. Following are the best tours of this very scenic region.

Saltspring Island and Vancouver Island
Saltspring Island is the largest Gulf Island and has about two days worth of touring. Saltspring also has ferry service direct to Vancouver

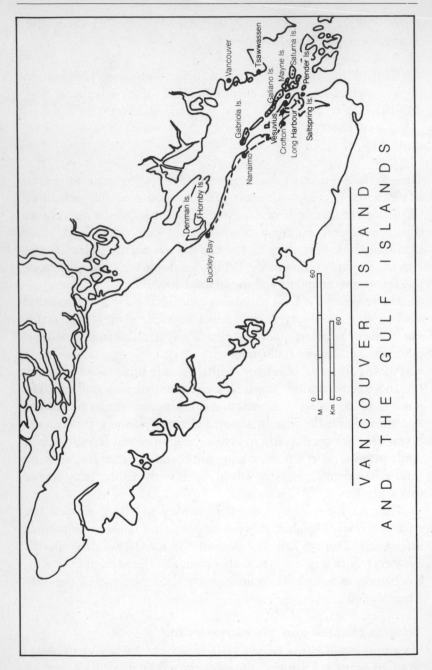

VANCOUVER ISLAND
AND THE GULF ISLANDS

Island from Vesuvius. This tour uses these ferries for a circuit tour visiting Saltspring Island and Vancouver Island.

LENGTH: 70 km (45 miles)

START: Long Harbour on Saltspring Island. Take the ferry from the Tsawwassen ferry terminal, south of Vancouver, or from Swartz Bay near Victoria to Fulford Harbour on Saltspring Island.

THE ROUTE: After disembarking from the ferry, wait for the car traffic to clear. Then explore this luscious green island. Along the road are farms and tall fir trees. The road on Saltspring Island is quite narrow, so ride well to the right. There is a long steep hill just south of Ganges and another long hill near Fulford Harbour. There is camping at Ruckle Provincial Park at Ruckle Point — where campsites overlook the strait and the ferry run to Vancouver, as well as at Mouat Provincial Park at Ganges.

When you're ready to leave Saltspring, follow the roads north to the ferry terminal at Vesuvius. Board the ferry and cruise over to Crofton on Vancouver Island. Crossing time is approximately 20 minutes.

To head toward Nanaimo, 39 km (24 miles) away, ride north on Highway 1A through Chemainus and Ladysmith, and then through the rolling hills and farm country around Yellow Point and Cedar on the Strait of Georgia. If it's a hot day, the Chemainus River is a good spot for a swim. From Ladysmith to Nanaimo, Highway 1A has a well-paved shoulder. At Nanaimo, the ferry takes you to Horseshoe Bay and the city of Vancouver.

Saturna Island, Pender Island, Galiano Island and Mayne Island

Explore one island per day. These Gulf Islands are accessible by ferries from Tsawwassen near Vancouver, Swartz Bay, near Victoria, or from Long Harbour on Saltspring Island. The islands are very scenic and quiet and have very little traffic to contend with. There are provincial parks with camping on Pender Island and Galiano Island. The roads are generally well-paved, but do not have paved shoulders.

Saturna Island

LENGTH: 34 km (21 miles)

START: Saturna Island ferry terminal

THE ROUTE: East Point Road is a very enjoyable ride with little traffic. It goes along the water and is bordered by tall trees. At East Point is a lighthouse and a good public beach. On a clear day you can see the outline of the Tsawwassen ferry terminal.

Pender Island

LENGTH: 42 km (26 miles)

START: Otter Bay ferry terminal on Pender Island

THE ROUTE: Explore the island's road past many scenic bays. Bedwell Harbour, Camp Bay, and Hope Bay are especially nice. The island has a very quiet lifestyle with many hobby farms.

Galiano Island

LENGTH: 73 km (45 miles)

START: Montague Harbour ferry terminal on Galiano Island

THE ROUTE: Montague Road and Porlier Pass Drive are the two main roads on the island. At the north end of island you'll see fishing boats in Porlier Pass. There is camping at Montague Harbour Provincial Park.

Mayne Island

LENGTH: 32 km (20 miles)

START: Village Bay ferry terminal on Mayne Island

THE ROUTE: Ride the island's quiet roads among picturesque farms. Many American miners stopped at Miner's Bay on their way to the

Cariboo gold rush, and a museum describes the area's history. Mayne Island was the first place apples were grown in British Columbia. Hotel accommodations are available.

Gabriola Island

LENGTH: 35 km (22 miles)

START: Gabriola Island ferry terminal, reached by ferry from Nanaimo. Crossing time is 20 minutes.

THE ROUTE: A highlight of this pleasant scenic island is the trip to sandstone formations at Orlebar Point. The South Road has many pleasant views of the water. There are numerous attractive farms on the island and a marina at Silva Bay. At the northwest corner of the island is Twin Beach. The island has no campgrounds, but does have lodges.

Denman Island and Hornby Island

Denman and Hornby Islands, south of Courtenay, are probably the easiest islands to tour. Moreover, road distances are short. Quadra Island near Campbell River can provide a pleasant afternoon, but most of the island's roads are unpaved.

LENGTH: 150 km (93 miles) return

START: Nanaimo, which can be reached by ferry from Horseshoe Bay near Vancouver

THE ROUTE: From Nanaimo head north on Highway 19 to Buckley Bay. The scenic highway is well-paved and has a wide paved shoulder. You have good views at Nanoose Bay, Parksville, Qualicum Beach, Qualicum Bay, Bowser, and Fanny Bay. The pleasant beaches along the highway are good stops. Campgrounds are available near Qualicum Bay and Fanny Bay.

Take the ferry from Buckley Bay to Denman Island. Crossing time is 10 minutes. From the Denman Island ferry terminal you have a steep climb. The Hornby Island terminal at the south end of

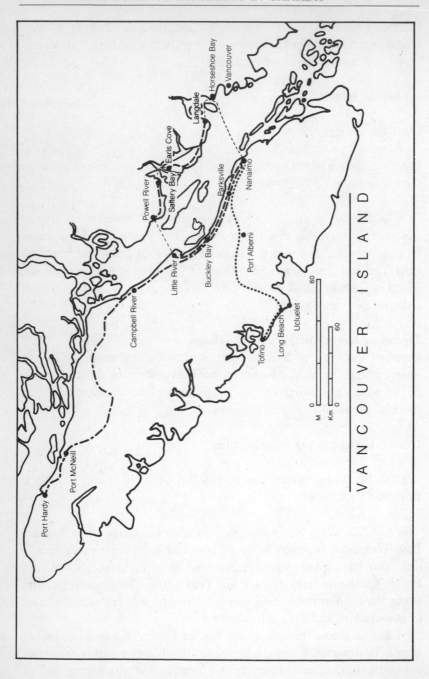

Denman Island is 11 km (7 miles) away. Fillongley Provincial Park with camping facilities is situated on the east side of the island.

When you're ready, take the ferry to Hornby Island. Again, crossing time is ten minutes. There are several campgrounds on the island.

At Helliwell Park are grassy cliffs dropping into the ocean. You can watch the birds, including eagles, and see whales during their migratory season. There are several bed-and-breakfasts available on both islands.

Vancouver Island

Sunshine Coast Loop

This challenging circuit goes north along the Strait of Georgia to the ferry at Little River. You then cross the strait to Westview and go south along the fjord-indented Sunshine Coast, which involves several ferry rides. You eventually reach Horseshoe Bay near Vancouver, where you can take the ferry back to Vancouver Island. If you choose to stay on the mainland, continue into the city of Vancouver.

This tour can be done in a clockwise or counter-clockwise direction. The complete loop takes three to four days. A seven-day trip could be arranged by adding several side trips to the route. Even though the coastal ride is called the Sunshine Coast, it can get some heavy rain.

LENGTH: 250 km (155 miles) loop

START: Nanaimo, reached by ferry from Horseshoe Bay north of Vancouver, or by road from Victoria

THE ROUTE: From Nanaimo, go north on Highway 19 along the Strait of Georgia for 124 km (77 miles) to Little River. Most of the highway is level and well-paved and has a wide, paved shoulder. At Parksville the shoulder is very rough. There is one long, very steep hill just before Comox. The route is scenic, with beautiful views of the Strait of Georgia and the Coastal Mountains. From Buckley Bay you could take a side trip to Denman and Hornby Islands. Take the time to enjoy the beaches at Parksville or Qualicum Beach. On this part of the route there are campgrounds near Qualicum Bay, Fanny Bay, and Courtenay, as well as numerous motels along the route.

At Courtenay turn off Highway 19, ride to Little River and take the ferry to Powell River/Westview. Crossing time is approximately one hour and twenty minutes.

Ride south from Powell River/Westview for 31 km (19 miles) to Saltery Bay along the Sunshine Coast. The highway is well-paved, but does not have paved shoulders. It's very hilly, especially near Saltery Bay, where there is a long hill. The view at the top is well worth the climb. Side trips can be taken by ferry from Powell River to Texada Island, or you can cycle north to Lund. There are good beaches at the Powell River and Saltery Bay campsites; another campground is located at Willingdon. Motels are located in Westview and Powell River.

From Saltery Bay take the ferry to Earls Cove. Crossing time is 50 minutes. From Earls Cove, you can take a 6-km (4-mile) side trip to Egmont, where you can hike 3 km (1.8 miles) to the Skookumchuck Narrows to view the tidal rapids.

Ride south on the scenic Sunshine Coast highway from Earls Cove to Langdale, a distance of 83 km (52 miles). The highway is well-paved and has a gravel shoulder. It's very hilly so make sure you have a low gear range. At Pender Harbour you have a splendid view of the rugged coastline and Earls Cove. Sechelt has a beautiful waterfront. The town of Gibsons is the setting for *The Beachcombers* television series. There is camping at Porpoise Bay just north of Sechelt and at Roberts Creek. Motels are available in Gibsons, Sechelt, and Pender Harbour.

Take the ferry from Langdale to Horseshoe Bay just north of Vancouver. Crossing time is 40 minutes. If you want to head back to this tour's starting point at Nanaimo, you can take the ferry from Horseshoe Bay to Nanaimo.

Long Beach: Pacific Rim National Park

Long Beach, part of Pacific Rim National Park, is 11 km (7 miles) of surf-swept sandy beaches and rocky headlands stretching along Vancouver Island's west coast between the tiny fishing villages of Ucluelet and Tofino. There are lots of good campsites. During the right season you can take a tour boat and watch Pacific gray whales diving offshore. Be prepared for rain.

The road across Vancouver Island, from Parksville through Port Alberni to Long Beach, is narrow, winding, and hilly. Between Port Alberni and Ucluelet there are 100 km (60 miles) of wilderness, so preparation is essential. Rain is guaranteed. Henderson Lake near Long Beach has an annual rainfall of 600 cm (236 inches).

A scenic alternative to the 150-km (93-mile) hilly road from Port Alberni to Ucluelet is to take the ferry *M.V. Lady Rose.*

LENGTH: 206 km (128 miles)

START: Nanaimo, reached by ferry from Horseshoe Bay north of Vancouver, or by road from Victoria

THE ROUTE: From Nanaimo go north on Highway 19 for 38 km (24 miles) to Parksville. Go west on Highway 4 for 47 km (29 miles) to Port Alberni. The road is well-paved, has a paved shoulder, and is fairly flat as far as Cameron Lake. At Coombs there is a farmers' market.

Cameron Lake is surrounded by towering trees. There are two picnic areas here and many nature trails. Cycling from Cameron Lake to Port Alberni, you climb over the Alberni Summit, also known as "the Hump." Port Alberni is a city with hotels, supermarkets, and good salmon fishing nearby.

To get to Long Beach from Port Alberni you have two options. The first is for you and your bicycle to board the foot-passenger ferry *M.V. Lady Rose* which departs from Port Alberni several times a week for Ucluelet, situated just 8 km (5 miles) south of Long Beach. The ferry ride cruises Alberni Inlet with good views of the rugged coastline and various inlets.

The second option is to cycle along Highway 4 for 91 km (56 miles) to Long Beach. The highway has spectacular scenery and is well-paved but has steep climbs and switchbacks. Sproat Lake Provincial Park is a nice spot to stop for a meal or overnight camping. You also pass Kennedy Lake, where there are campgrounds. There are no stores between Port Alberni and Long Beach so stock up on food supplies at Port Alberni and be prepared to camp overnight. Once you reach Long Beach you can find supplies and accommodation in the villages of Ucluelet or Tofino. Two campgrounds are also available.

MORE INFORMATION: The *M.V. Lady Rose* is operated by Alberni Marine Transportation Ltd., Box 188, Port Alberni, British Columbia V9Y 7M7. Telephone (604) 723-8213.

Park Superintendent, Pacific Rim National Park, Box 280, Ucluelet, British Columbia V0R 3A0. Telephone (604) 726-7721.

Nanaimo to Port Hardy

The northern stretch of Vancouver Island's Highway 19 (known as the Island Highway) takes you through a scenic and relatively remote part of the island. The Island Highway is the main, and in many stretches, the only north-south link on Vancouver Island. Port Hardy is the southern terminus for the ferry through the spectacular Inside Passage to Prince Rupert. From Prince Rupert, you can connect with ferries to the Queen Charlotte Islands, Alaska, and the Yukon, or you can cycle east on the Yellowhead Highway to Prince George and to Jasper.

LENGTH: 389 km (240 miles)

START: Nanaimo, reached by ferry from Horseshoe Bay north of Vancouver, or by road from Victoria

THE ROUTE: From Nanaimo, head north on Highway 19. Generally the highway is in good condition with a good shoulder, although at Parksville the shoulder is very rough. The road follows the scenic coast of the Strait of Georgia. There are numerous beaches, campgrounds, and motel accommodations. (Side trips to the Gulf Islands are described separately in this chapter.)

Campbell River has full facilities. From Campbell River, the Island Highway heads north for 250 km (155 miles) to Port Hardy. This lovely, remote stretch is generally a two-lane road with shoulder, and has little traffic. Roberts Lake, 40 km (25 miles) north, has a motel and campground. Sayward-Kelsey Bay, 70 km (43 miles) north of Campbell River, also has a motel and campground. From

Sayward to Port McNeill is a long 170 km (105 miles) ride through some beautiful country, including the Nimpkish Valley. There are few facilities en route. Expect to see deer and elk, and possibly brown bear and cougar.

Port McNeill has motels and a campground. From Port McNeill there is a ferry to Alert Bay, where the Kwakiutl Indian Museum is a worthwhile half-day trip.

Port Hardy, 41 km (25 miles) from Port McNeill, is at the end of the paved road. Most facilities can be found here.

Kamloops to Mount Robson

Kamloops, from the Indian word *kumcloops* meaning "meeting of the waters," lies at the confluence of the North and South Thompson Rivers, and the junction of the Trans Canada Highway and the Yellowhead Highway 5, about 430 km (267 miles) east of Vancouver. This three-day tour along Highway 5 traverses a variety of scenery as it winds north from the open dry grasslands and ranches around Kamloops, through the Cariboo Mountains and rugged Wells Gray Provincial Park, and on to the Monarch of the Canadian Rockies at Mount Robson Provincial Park, just east of Jasper National Park.

Mount Robson, the highest peak in the Canadian Rockies, towers 3,954 meters (12,972 feet) over the western entrance to Mount Robson Provincial Park. Bounded on the east by the Continental Divide, the park is 2,172 square km (839 square miles) of rugged snow-capped mountains, broad valleys, steep canyons, and glacier-fed lakes, rivers, and streams.

The route is relatively flat and has light traffic. There is one major climb just south of Blue River.

LENGTH: 330 km (205 miles)

START: Kamloops, served by VIA Rail

THE ROUTE: From Kamloops to Heffley Creek, a distance of 24 km (15 miles), Highway 5 has a poorly paved surface but wide shoulders. Exercise care on this road as it's used by heavy logging trucks which at times require all the paved surface. At Clearwater, 125 km

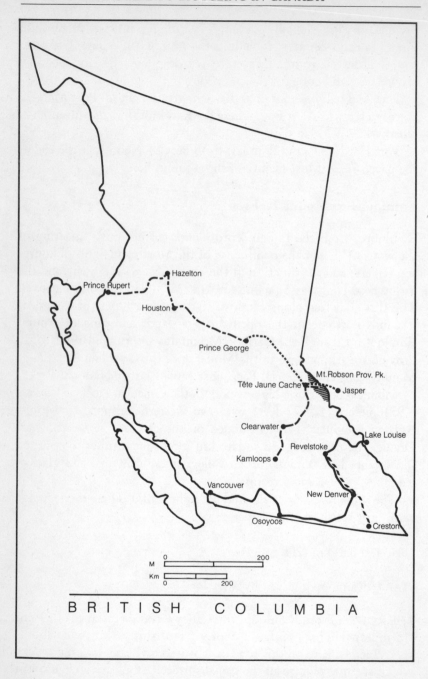

BRITISH COLUMBIA

(78 miles) from Kamloops, you can take a side trip to Wells Gray Provincial Park. A vast primitive area in the Cariboo Mountains, 5,200-square-km (2,008-square-mile) Wells Gray Park encompasses glaciers, alpine meadows carpeted with colorful flowers, numerous waterfalls—including 135-meter (450-foot) Helmcken Falls—extinct volcanoes, lava beds, and mineral springs. A network of 150 km (95 miles) of hiking trails takes you to the park's varied scenery.

There is also camping at North Thompson Provincial Park near Clearwater, and private campgrounds at Avola, 65 km (40 miles) from Clearwater, as well as at Blue River. Between Blue River and Valemount there are no facilities, no telephones, and few residences, so travel must be self-sufficient.

Continue on Highway 5 to Tete Jaune Cache, 148 km (92 miles) from Avola, and the junction with the Yellowhead Highway 16. From here head east to Mount Robson Park which has several campgrounds, and to Jasper at the northern end of the Icefields Parkway (described in the Alberta chapter).

MORE INFORMATION: District Superintendent, Mount Robson Provincial Park, Box 579, Valemount, British Columbia V0E 2Z0. Telephone (604) 566-4325.

District Superintendent, Wells Gray Provincial Park, Box 70, Clearwater, British Columbia V0E 1N0. Telephone (604) 674-9525.

Jasper to Prince George

This scenic route takes you on the Yellowhead Route from Jasper at the northern end of the Icefields Parkway (described in the Alberta chapter), past Mount Robson, the highest peak in the Canadian Rockies, and along isolated highways to Prince George at the geographic center of British Columbia. From Prince George you can continue to Prince Rupert which has ferries to Vancouver Island, the Queen Charlotte Islands, and Alaska.

The Yellowhead Route was named after an French-Iroquois guide whom the French voyageurs nicknamed *Tête Jaune*, "Yellowhead," because of his blond hair. Working for the Hudson's Bay Company, he crossed what became known as the Yellowhead Pass numerous times, and made a cache near what is now called Tête Jaune Cache.

Highway 16 is hilly, but it is well-paved and very scenic. Cycling season is April to October. Dress for the cooler mountain weather. Be prepared to see lots of wildlife.

LENGTH: 400 km (250 miles)

START: Jasper, Alberta, reached by VIA Rail

THE ROUTE: Jasper has camping facilities, hotel and motel accommodation, hiking trails, and stores in which you can stock up on food before heading out. Leaving Jasper, go west on the Yellowhead Highway 16, which has a wide shoulder. Go over the Yellowhead Pass, the gentlest of the five passes in the Canadian Rockies. You are now in British Columbia.

Mount Robson Provincial Park is 120 km (75 miles) from Jasper. Lofty and usually cloud-topped Mount Robson reaches 3,954 meters (12,972 feet), the highest peak in the Canadian Rockies. Here you will find campgrounds, a VIA Rail station, and motel accommodation. The hike along the Robson River through the Valley of a Thousand Falls to Berg Lake is popular.

After Tête Jaune junction, the highway has narrower shoulders. McBride, 200 km (125 miles) from Jasper, is surrounded by the snow-capped peaks of the Cariboo and Rocky Mountains. McBride has private campgrounds, motel and hotel accommodation, and VIA Rail service. Stock up on supplies here. There are no major towns between McBride and Prince George, 217 km (135 miles) to the west.

The isolated 128-km (80-mile) stretch of this tour, from McBride to Purden Lake Provincial Park, is on a good road with wide shoulders. Purden Lake Park is 72 km (45 miles) from Prince George.

The city of Prince George is situated at the geographical center of British Columbia, approximately 800 km (500 miles) from Vancouver, Prince Rupert, and Edmonton. The Rocky Mountains are located to the east and the Coast Mountains to the west.

Prince George to Prince Rupert

Prince George, at the geographic center of British Columbia, is at the junction of the Yellowhead Route and Highway 97, which runs north to the Yukon and south through the Cariboo Mountains to the Lower Mainland. Stock up on supplies in Prince George.

All the major towns en route are served by VIA Rail, in case you want to shorten your trip. At Prince Rupert you can board the ferry south to Vancouver Island or north to Alaska.

LENGTH: 733 km (455 miles)

START: Prince George, which can be reached by VIA Rail

THE ROUTE: Head west on Highway 16. At Bednesti Lake Resort, 48 km (30 miles) west of Prince George, there are camping facilities and motel accommodations.

Vanderhoof, 100 km (60 miles) west of Prince George, is a farming and logging center. Camping facilities, motel and hotel accommodation, and VIA Rail passenger service are available here. At the Nechako Bird Sanctuary you can see migratory birds including Canada geese, ducks, trumpeter swans, and seabirds, as well as great blue herons, bald eagles, cranes, and loons.

From Vanderhoof you can take a side trip north along Highway 27 for 64 km (40 miles) to the National Historic Park at Fort St. James, the oldest town in British Columbia. It's located on scenic Stuart Lake, with camping at nearby Paarens Beach Provincial Park, as well as hotel and motel accommodation.

Back on Highway 16, continue west to Fort Fraser, established in 1806 by explorer Simon Fraser for the Northwest Company. It became a Hudson's Bay Company post in 1821. Beaumont Provincial Park near Lejac, 16 km (10 miles) from Fraser Lake, has camping.

Fraser Lake, a lumber and mining town 60 km (37 miles) west of Vanderhoof, is on the shores of the attractive lake of the same name. Camping facilities, hotel and motel accommodations, and VIA Rail passenger service are available here. Hiking trails at nearby Mouse Mountain include a path across the extinct volcano and lava beds of Table Top Mountain.

Burns Lake and several smaller surrounding lakes are popular with anglers. There is camping at Ethel F. Wilson Memorial Park, 24 km (15 miles) north of Burns Lake.

Houston, 140 km (85 miles) from Fraser Lake, is also a logging and mining town. You can tour the local silver mine. Camping, hotel and motel accommodations, and VIA Rail passenger service are available. At Telkwa are a few small stores selling food. There is camping at Tyhee Lake Provincial Park.

Situated in the fertile Bulkley Valley, surrounded by mountains, rivers, and lakes, is Smithers, 71 km (44 miles) from Houston. It is a ranching, logging, and mining center. The Smithers Museum describes the area's history. Camping, hotel and motel accommodation, and VIA Rail service are available. At Driftwood Canyon Provincial Park you can see fossil beds, glacial deposits, and an exposed coal seam. There is also camping at Maclure Lake Park, 18 km (11 miles) east of Smithers. Another 7 km (4 miles) west, the Bulkley River cascades through a narrow gorge in spectacular Moricetown Canyon.

At Hazelton, 67 km (42 miles) north of Smithers, are camping facilities, hotel and motel accommodation, and VIA Rail service. Nearby at K'san Indian Craft Village, you can see traditional Pacific Northwest Coast Indian art produced by ancient methods, six communal houses decorated with carved interior poles, and five totem-pole villages, including a totem pole carved in 1850. There is a campground near the village.

From Hazelton west to Terrace, 142 km (88 miles), you ride along the banks of the Skeena River. You pass through meadows and small towns and settlements as you gradually descend to Kleanza Creek Provincial Park, which has camping facilities. The park has a trail to an ancient Tsimshian Indian village with totem poles, and a sluice box used to find gold in the river. *Kleanza* is the Gitskan Indian word for gold.

Terrace has camping facilities, hotel and motel accommodation, and VIA Rail service. The 153 km (95 miles) from Terrace to Prince Rupert continues along the scenic Skeena River. The road is relatively flat and has light traffic. There are few facilities along this section so carry sufficient supplies. Prudhomme Lake Provincial Park, 16 km (10 miles) east of Prince Rupert, has camping.

Prince Rupert is on Kalen Island. The largest natural ocean harbor on the Pacific Northwest coast, Prince Rupert is known for its heavy rainfall—although it tends to be lighter during the summer months. Here you can board ferries for Vancouver Island, the Queen Charlotte Islands, and Alaska. The town offers camping facilities, hotel and motel accommodations, and VIA Rail service.

MORE INFORMATION: The ferries from Prince Rupert to Vancouver Island and the Queen Charlotte Islands are operated by: the British Columbia Ferry Corporation, 818 Broughton, Victoria, British Columbia V8W 1E4. Telephone (604) 386-3431 in Victoria; (604) 669-1211 in Vancouver; or (604) 753-1261 in Nanaimo.

The ferry from Prince Rupert to Skagway, Alaska, with ports of call at Ketchikan, Wrangell, Petersburg, Sitka, Juneau, and Haines, is operated by: Alaska Marine Highway System, Pouch R, Juneau, Alaska 99811. Call toll-free in continental United States 1-800-544-2251; from other places (907) 465-3941; from the Prince Rupert Terminal (604) 627-1744. The trip is thirty-four to fifty-six hours long. Reservations are required.

The Kootenays: Revelstoke to Creston

Hot springs, ghost towns left over from the silver boom, fjord-like lakes crossed by free ferries, paddle-wheelers, spectacular mountain scenery, and fertile orchards are all found on this tour.

You pedal along a quiet highway through a valley between the Selkirk and Monashee ranges and along Upper Arrow Lake. Cross the lake on a free ferry and continue along the Slocan valley, the area of the silver boom, and then along Kootenay Lake to orchards near Creston. Roadside stands sell locally grown fruit.

Stock up on food in Revelstoke, as the tour goes through some remote territory and limited supplies are available en route. There are some climbs and you may encounter strong winds off Kootenay Lake.

LENGTH: 309 km (192 miles) one way

START: Revelstoke, served by VIA Rail

THE ROUTE: From Revelstoke, go south on Highway 23 along the shore of Upper Arrow Lake, a widening of the Columbia River which is the longest river flowing into the Pacific. After 50 km (31 miles) is Shelter Bay. Take the free ferry to Galena Bay, and continue south on Highway 23 for 49 km (30 miles) to Nakusp, nestled in the Selkirk Mountains. Nearby are the hot mineral waters of Nakusp Hot Springs.

To continue the tour, take Highway 6 southeast past Summit Lake, Rosebery Provincial Park, and Slocan Lake, which resembles a fjord. After 46 km (28 miles) is New Denver. This was the center of the silver boom in this valley in the nineteenth century. You can see artifacts of the era at the Silvery Slocan Museum.

Go left onto Highway 31A for 47 km (29 miles) to Kaslo. Along the way are ghost towns left from the silver rush. A few shacks remain at Retallack and Zincton. In Kaslo you can visit the museum on board the *S.S. Moyie*, the last of the paddle-wheelers that carried pioneers over the length of 120-km (75-mile) Kootenay Lake. From Kaslo, go south on Highway 31 for 36 km (22 miles) to Balfour. Along the way are the Ainsworth Hot Springs.

At Balfour take the free ferry across Kootenay Lake to Kootenay Bay, and head south on Highway 3A for 79 km (49 miles) to Creston. This part of the route is fairly level. There are several beaches on Kootenay Lake, and camping at Lockhart Beach Provincial Park. The Creston Valley's fertile green pastures are surrounded by dry hills. On the way into Creston are fruit stands selling locally grown apricots, apples, peaches, and plums.

Retrace your route to return to Revelstoke.

Across British Columbia

There are two highways from southwestern British Columbia to the Alberta boundary: Highway 1, which is the Trans Canada Highway, and the more southerly Highway 3. This route combines the best of each and traverses a variety of British Columbia's spectacular terrain.

From Vancouver you ride through the lower Fraser River Valley on Highway 7 to Hope. From Hope eastward to Rock Creek, this tour follows Highway 3 through the Cascade Mountains of Manning Provincial Park and the Okanagan Valley's orchards and vineyards.

At Osoyoos you cycle through a small desert. At Castlegar you turn north on quiet highways through the Kootenay Mountains and past fjord-like lakes, hot springs, and ghost towns.

Reaching the Trans Canada Highway at Revelstoke, the tour turns east and goes through the massive, snow-capped Columbia Mountains and then climbs along the Kicking Horse River through the Rockies to Kicking Horse Pass and the Alberta boundary.

LENGTH: 1082 km (672 miles)

START: Vancouver

THE ROUTE: From Vancouver, take Highway 7A east past Burnaby Mountain Park to Port Moody. Continue east on Highway 7 along the Fraser River Valley for 145 km (90 miles) to Hope. Traffic can be heavy along Highway 7, but it has wide shoulders. Bicycles are prohibited on Highway 1 (the Trans Canada Highway) between Vancouver and Chilliwack. Highway 1 often runs parallel to Highway 7.

At Hope, stock up on food. Follow the signposting for cyclists here as some routes are prohibited to cyclists. Take Highway 3—the scenic Hope-Princeton Highway, which has a wide shoulder—through the Cascade Mountains of Manning Provincial Park for 66 km (41 miles) to the village of Manning Park. The park has a selection of campgrounds. The route follows the Old Dewdney Trail, an old stagecoach road of the 1890s, which was also used during the Kootenay Gold Rush.

Continue on Highway 3 for another 66 km (41 miles) along the Sumallo and Skagit Rivers. Ride over the 1,340-meter (4,400-foot) Allison Pass and pedal to Princeton, at the junction of five rivers that flow into Similkameen River. Another 38 km (24 miles) brings you to Stemwinder Provincial Park, which offers camping.

You enter the Okanagan Valley region in the province's sunny and dry interior. The Okanagan is known for its orchards and vineyards. Roadside stands sell locally grown cherries, apples, apricots, peaches, plums, pears, and grapes.

Descend on Highway 3 along the Similkameen River for 36 km (20 miles) to Keremeos, a fruit-growing center. Ride Highway 3 along the Similkameen River for 64 km (40 miles). The ride involves a 396-meter (1,300-foot) climb over 3 km (2 miles) to Richter Pass, followed by a 9-km (5-mile) descent to Osoyoos, in a small desert of cactus, sagebrush, and horned lizards.

From Osoyoos, Highway 3 ascends Anarchist Mountain. At the summit, 21 km (13 miles) from Osoyoos, you have spectacular views of Mount Baldy to the north and the United States to the south. Descend from the mountain and ride through rolling country to Rock Creek, 31 km (19 miles) farther. In this area Highway 3 parallels the United States border.

Ride through the towns of Midway and Greenwood to Grand Forks, a distance of 75 km (47 miles) from Rock Creek. Continue on Highway 3 for 96 km (60 miles) over 1,535-meter (5,036-foot) Bonanza Pass to Castlegar, a Doukhobor village. Stock up on food for the ride through the Kootenay Mountains, as there are limited supplies available en route.

Take Highway 3A north for 20 km (12 miles) to Crescent Valley. Then ride Highway 6 north for 79 km (49 miles), past farms along the Slocan River, through the village of Slocan, and then along the shores of glittering Slocan Lake (which resembles a fjord) to New Denver. This area experienced a silver rush during the nineteenth century and you can see reminders of the era in the abandoned silver mines and ghost towns, and in the artifacts in the Silvery Slocan Museum.

Continue riding on Highway 6 for 46 km (28 miles) along Slocan Lake and past Summit Lake, taking the remote stretch of highway to Nakusp. Nearby are the hot mineral waters of Nakusp Hot Springs. Go north on Highway 23 for 49 km (30 miles) along the shore of Upper Arrow Lake, a widening of the Columbia River. At Galena Bay take the free ferry across Upper Arrow Lake to Shelter Bay. Continue north on Highway 23 along Upper Arrow Lake for 50 km (31 miles) to Revelstoke, an important railway center where food supplies can be replenished and other services are available.

Leaving Revelstoke, follow Highway 1 (the Trans Canada Highway) east for 21 km (13 miles). You enter Mount Revelstoke National Park, which covers 260 square km (100 square miles) of the massive, snow-capped mountains and narrow valleys of the Columbia Mountains. There are no campgrounds in the park.

After 15 km (9 miles) on Highway 1, you leave Mount Revelstoke Park. Continue for 12 km (7 miles) to Glacier National Park, covering 1,350 square km (521 square miles) of the jagged Purcell and Selkirk Mountain ranges, capped with sparkling glaciers. Glacier Park has a selection of campgrounds.

Ride Highway 1 in Glacier National Park to the summit of 1,330-meter (4,364-foot) Rogers Pass through the Selkirk Mountains. From the pass is a view of the Illecillewaet Glacier, Lookout Mountain, Glacier Crest, Feuz Peak, Asulkan Pass, and Michel Peak.

This part of the route is mountainous, with a good number of climbs. When you pass through tunnels and avalanche snowsheds, put on your lights and wear a reflective safety vest.

It's a 45-km (28-mile) ride on Highway 1 through Glacier Park. Once you're past the park's eastern boundary, it's another 56 km (35 miles) to Golden, a major center where you can buy supplies.

Highway 1 climbs steeply for 20 km (12 miles) overlooking the Kicking Horse River through the Rockies. The highway is narrow and used by logging trucks. If there are a lot of trucks, take a break, stop, and enjoy the spectacular views.

You enter 1,313-square-km (507-square mile) Yoho National Park, 25 km (15 miles) east of Golden. The Emerald Lake turn-off, 27 km (17 miles) east of the Yoho Park gate, leads 8 km (5 miles) to Emerald Lake at the base of the President Range.

The railroad town of Field is 2.5 km (1.6 miles) past the Emerald Lake turn-off. Another 4 km (2.5 miles) is the turn-off for the Yoho Valley. This worthwhile side trip leads 13 km (8 miles) to 384-meter (1,259-foot) Takakkaw Falls, the highest falls in Canada.

Highway 1 climbs steeply up Kicking Horse Pass. Be sure to stop at the viewpoint of the Spiral Tunnels, where trains spiral through two mountains to climb or descend the pass. The summit of Kicking Horse Pass is 16 km (10 miles) east of Field. Kicking Horse Pass is part of the Continental Divide and is the provincial boundary. Cycle into Alberta and Banff National Park, and descend along Highway 1 to Lake Louise.

Guidebooks

Bicycling Vancouver Island and the Gulf Islands, by Simon Priest. Available from: Douglas and McIntyre, 1615 Venables Street, Vancouver, British Columbia V5L 2H1. Price $12.95 (For mail orders, add postage of $1 plus 50 cents per book.)

Bicycling Southwestern British Columbia and the Sunshine Coast, by Simon Priest. Available from: Douglas and McIntyre. Price $9.95.

The British Columbia Bicycling Guide, by Teri Lydiard. Available from: Gordon Soules Book Publishers Ltd., 1352B Marine Drive, West Vancouver, British Columbia V7T 1B5. Price $7.95.

The Canadian Rockies Bicycling Guide, by Gail Helgason and John Dodd. Available from: Lone Pine Publishing, 414, 10357 - 109 Street, Edmonton, Alberta T5J 1N3. Price $8.95.

The Greater Vancouver Bicycling Guide, by Maggie Burtinshaw. Available from: Gordon Soules Book Publishers Ltd. Price $9.95.

6 Alberta

Alberta's majestic Rocky Mountain scenery provides some of North America's most spectacular tours. It attracts many cyclists every year. The Icefields Parkway, which winds through magnificent alpine scenery of glaciers, turquoise lakes, and meadows carpeted with flowers, is the best known of these tours. Less well known but offering equally breathtaking mountain scenery are tours through Kananaskis Country along Canada's highest paved road, and a loop route known as the "Golden Triangle" that crosses the Great Divide twice.

The Rocky Mountains constitute only a part of Alberta's 660,933 square km (255,200 square miles). To the east are the foothills and the Alberta Plateau; the third prairie level is in the south, and there is forest, lake, and river country in the north. These areas offer scenic touring as well. Around Drumheller are the fascinating Badlands, famous for dinosaur skeletons and unusual geological formations.

ROADS: Most of the roads in Alberta have wide, paved shoulders. The Trans Canada Highway from Calgary to the British Columbia border has a lot of traffic. Where possible, try to use the recommended alternatives described in this chapter.

WEATHER: Alberta receives the most sunshine in Canada; in Banff the July average is 255 hours. Summers are hot and winters are cold, since the Rocky Mountains block the moderating influence of the

Pacific Ocean. Snow is usually gone from along the road by the beginning of May.

TOURIST INFORMATION: General tourist information, including a road map and accommodation guide, is available from: Travel Alberta, 15th Floor, 10025 Jasper Avenue, Edmonton, Alberta T5J 3Z3. Call toll-free in Alberta, 1-800-222-6501; elsewhere in Canada and the United States, 1-800-661-8888.

HOSTELS: Information on hostels in Alberta can be obtained from the Southern Alberta Hostelling Association, 1414 Kensington Road NW, Calgary, Alberta T2N 3P9. Telephone (403) 283-5551.

AIRPORTS: Calgary and Edmonton airports are served by major airlines and have connections to smaller centers.

TRAINS: The routes through Edmonton to Jasper, and through Calgary to Banff, have baggage cars that will carry bikes. It's possible to transport your bike from Edmonton to Calgary, but bring the bike in two days ahead. For information on VIA Rail service, call toll-free within Alberta, 1-800-665-8630.

BUSES: Greyhound bus lines will carry boxed bicycles. During high season they may not be able to transport your bike on the same day as you are traveling, so bring in your bike a day or two in advance. Red Arrow bus service between Calgary and Edmonton accepts bikes unboxed.

BICYCLING: Alberta Bicycling Association, 1234 - 18th Street NW, Calgary, Alberta T2N 2G7. Telephone (403) 289-7061.

Banff and Jasper National Parks: The Columbia Icefields Parkway

Snow-capped peaks, glaciers, turquoise lakes, and waterfalls line this highway through the grandeur of the Rocky Mountains. Spectacular mountain scenery and verdant green valleys, plus a wide paved shoulder have made this four- to six-day tour between the towns of Banff and Jasper one of Alberta's most popular routes.

Traversing Banff and Jasper Parks, the Icefields Parkway skirts the chain of icefields lying along the Continental Divide, the source of many rivers draining into the Pacific Ocean, the Arctic Ocean, and the Atlantic Ocean via Hudson Bay. Moose, deer, elk, bear, goat, sheep, and many other species of wildlife can often be seen from the road.

Within an easy day's ride are campsites offering washrooms with cold running water, as well as cooking shelters, free firewood, and interpretive programs. The Canadian Hostelling Association operates a network of hostels along the route. If you want to use the hostels, plan to arrive early in the day or make reservations in advance. Stock up on supplies in Banff or Jasper, as only limited supplies are available along the route.

The route has numerous small hills and two major passes. Near the Bow Summit, the Icefields Parkway climbs to its highest point at 2,069 meters (6,786 feet). At 2,029 meters (6,658 feet), Sunwapta Pass is the boundary between Banff and Jasper parks, just south of the Columbia Icefields.

LENGTH: 290 km (180 miles)

START: Banff or Jasper. Both are served by VIA Rail. The route here is described from Banff north to Jasper.

THE ROUTE: From Banff take Highway 1 (the Trans Canada Highway) for 5.6 km (3.5 miles) along the base of Mount Norquay past the Vermilion Lakes viewpoints. (An underpass is being built from Vermilion Lake Drive to bypass this very busy section of Highway 1.) Turn off the Trans Canada Highway and cycle the quieter Bow Valley Parkway along the Bow River. The road is relatively level.

At Johnston's Canyon is a 5.8-km (3.6-mile) nature trail leading past waterfalls to the colorful Ink Pots pools. The Banff-Windermere Parkway, which goes through Kootenay National Park in British Columbia, joins the Bow Valley Parkway at Castle Junction. The Bow Valley Parkway ends at the Trans Canada Highway 2 km (1.2

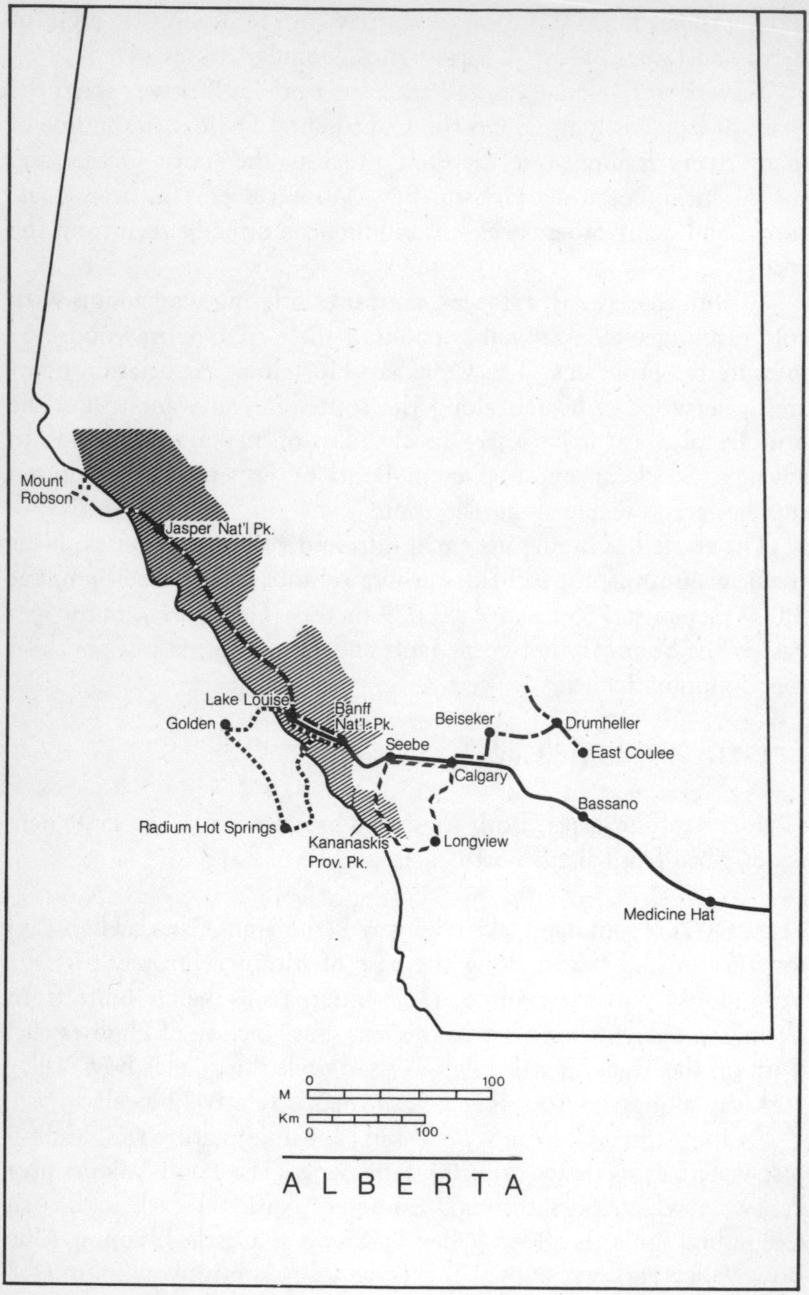

Mount Robson

Jasper Nat'l Pk.

Lake Louise

Golden

Banff Nat'l Pk.

Beiseker

Drumheller

Seebe

East Coulee

Calgary

Radium Hot Springs

Kananaskis Prov. Pk.

Longview

Bassano

Medicine Hat

M

0   100

Km

0   100

ALBERTA

miles) south of Lake Louise. Located 55 km (34 miles) from Banff, the Lake Louise area offers camping, hotels (including the Chateau Lake Louise), motels, and hostels.

From Lake Louise, go north for 3 km (2 miles) on the Trans Canada Highway to the Icefields Parkway (Highway 93). Over the next 40 km (25 miles), you gradually climb 500 meters (1,640 feet) toward Bow Pass, the route's highest point. Along the way you skirt green Herbert Lake, and pass the viewpoint overlooking Hector Lake. Mosquito Creek campground and hostel is 27 km (16 miles) north of Lake Louise. At the Bow Lake viewpoint, the turquoise waters reflect the surrounding glaciers and limestone cliffs.

The last 4 km (2.5 miles) to the summit of 2,069-meter (6,787-foot) Bow Pass climbs steeply. During the summer, the meadows here are covered with wildflowers. Near the pass is a viewpoint overlooking blue Peyto Lake. It's generally downhill from here to the Saskatchewan River Crossing, 36 km (22 miles) away.

You pass viewpoints overlooking Snowbird Glacier, Barbette Glacier, and the Waterfowl Lakes where moose can be seen. The Waterfowl Lakes campground, 17 km (10.5 miles) north of the Bow Pass, offers a 4-km (2.5-mile) hiking trail leading to Cirque and Chephren Lakes. The Mistaya Canyon trail, 14 km (9 miles) north of the Waterfowl Lakes campground, is a 0.3-km (0.2-mile) trail to the gorge of the Mistaya Canyon.

After crossing the North Saskatchewan River, 5 km (3 miles) farther, you climb to a viewpoint overlooking the Howse Valley, which fur trader David Thompson traversed in 1807. At the junction with Highway 11 (the David Thompson Highway) is accommodation, a restaurant, and a store where limited supplies are available.

Continue north on the Icefields Parkway along the North Saskatchewan River to Rampart Creek campground and hostel, a distance of 90 km (56 miles) from Lake Louise.

From Rampart Creek, the parkway ascends gradually along the North Saskatchewan River through Graveyard Flats and past the Cirrus Mountain campground and the Weeping Wall viewpoint. The parkway switchbacks 425 meters (1,400 feet) over 11 km (7 miles) up the "Big Hill." As you climb, look back at the spectacular view of the valley.

Parker's Ridge Trail, 29 km (18 miles) north of Rampart Creek, is a 3-km (1.8-mile) round-trip walk leading above the tree line to an alpine meadow carpeted with wildflowers and shrubs. Along the path is a view of the Saskatchewan Glacier, part of the Columbia Icefield and the source of the North Saskatchewan River.

Approximately 1 km (0.6 mile) farther on the road is the Hilda Creek Youth Hostel, a 30-km (19-mile) ride north of the Rampart Creek Hostel.

The parkway ascends to the summit of 2,035-meter (6,676-foot) Sunwapta Pass, the watershed of the North Saskatchewan and Athabasca rivers, and the boundary with Jasper National Park. Descend past the Wilcox Creek campground to the Columbia Icefield and the Athabasca Glacier, 8 km (5 miles) north of the Hilda Creek Hostel.

The largest icefield in the Rockies, the Columbia Icefield covers 325 square km (125 square miles). From here water flows to three oceans. The Athabasca River flows north to the Mackenzie River and the Arctic Ocean; the North Saskatchewan River flows east to Hudson Bay; and the Columbia River flows west to the Pacific. At the icefield is a chalet and an information booth. Snowmobile tours of the lower portion of the Athabasca Glacier are available here.

After visiting the Columbia Icefield, continue north on the parkway and ascend to Sunwapta Canyon viewpoint. Over the next 4 km (2.5 miles) the road drops 300 meters (1,000 feet) to the floor of the Sunwapta Valley. You pass the Tangle Falls viewpoint (where you may see sheep), the Stutfield Glacier viewpoint, and Stanley Falls on the way to the Beauty Creek Hostel. It's 25 km (16 miles) from the Hilda Creek Hostel to the Beauty Creek Hostel, and another 87 km (54 miles) to Jasper.

From Beauty Creek, the road goes past Jonas Creek campground to the Sunwapta Falls turn-off, 31 km (19 miles) from Beauty Creek. Take the turn-off and walk to the falls.

Continuing north on the Icefields Parkway you pass Honeymoon Lake campground, a viewpoint of the Athabasca Valley, and a mineral lick where mountain goats and bighorn sheep can be seen. Situated 24 km (15 miles) north of the Sunwapta Falls turn-off, Athabasca Falls drops into a narrow canyon, and is one of the most powerful falls in the Canadian Rockies.

At Athabasca Falls you can continue to Jasper via Highway 93, which is flat and downhill, or take the quieter, but narrower and hillier, Highway 93A along the west side of the Athabasca River. Route 93A rejoins Highway 93 7.5 km (4.6 miles) south of the Jasper townsite. From Athabasca Falls it's about 30 km (19 miles), via either route, to the Jasper townsite.

MORE INFORMATION: Park Superintendent, Banff National Park, Box 900, Banff, Alberta T0L 0C0. Telephone (403) 762-3324.

Park Superintendent, Jasper National Park, Box 10, Jasper, Alberta T0E 1E0. Telephone (403) 852-4401.

Banff-Radium Hot Springs-Golden Loop

This spectacular loop tour, known as the "Golden Triangle," crosses the Continental Divide twice and takes you through mountain scenery of peaks, forests, and waterfalls. It is a four-day trip through Banff and Kootenay National Parks, along the Columbia River, and through Yoho National Park back to Banff.

The roads through the national parks are in good condition and have wide, paved shoulders. The parts of this route outside the parks have narrower shoulders. Limited accommodation on parts of the route requires that you plan ahead.

LENGTH: 341 km (212 miles) loop

START: Banff, which can be reached by VIA Rail

THE ROUTE: From Banff ride the Bow Valley Parkway for 28 km (17 miles) to Castle Mountain Junction, where there is a hostel. Go west on the wide-shouldered Banff-Windermere Highway (also known as the Banff-Radium Highway). The route winds past Vermilion Pass Fire viewpoint and the Vista Lake viewpoint and climbs to 1,640-meter (5380-foot) Vermilion Pass at the Continental Divide. This is the boundary of Banff and Kootenay National Parks, and lies between the provinces of Alberta and British Columbia. At the summit of the pass is the Fireweed Trail through an area burned in July 1968 in a forest fire started by lightning. The forest is now regenerating.

At Vermilion Pass is the watershed for waters flowing west via the Columbia River to the Pacific; and waters going east into the

Bow River, the Saskatchewan River, and the Nelson River to Hudson Bay.

Continue cycling on the Banff-Windermere Highway. The Marble Canyon Campground, 7 km (4.5 miles) from Vermilion Pass, offers camping. Nearby is a 2-km (1.2-mile) nature trail along the rim of Marble Canyon. The Paint Pots nature trail, 2.5 km (1.5 miles) farther, leads through ocher-colored meadows to three Paint Pot pools. The Indians used the colors for body paint.

At the Mount Assiniboine viewpoint, 21 km (13 miles) from the Paint Pots, is a view of the 3,618-meter (11,870-foot) pyramid-shaped mountain known as the "Matterhorn of the Rockies." The Simpson Valley viewpoint, 7 km (4 miles) farther, has a monument to George Simpson, a governor of the Hudson's Bay Company who explored the area searching for a more southerly route for fur traders crossing the Rockies. Just 1 km (0.6 mile) past the monument is an animal lick, where moose, elk, and deer lick the mud for salt and minerals. Continue up the short climb to Hector Gorge viewpoint overlooking the Vermilion River. You can get food at Kootenay Crossing, just south of Hector Gorge. You then descend to the McLeod Meadows campground, 60 km (37 miles) from the Marble Canyon Campground.

From McLeod Meadows, you start climbing toward Sinclair Pass. Along the way you will pass the scenic pull-off, offering a view of the Mitchell Range and the Vermilion Range, and the Kootenay Valley viewpoint with a view of the Banff-Windermere Parkway. The Cobb Lake trail leads 2.7 km (1.6 miles) to a small lake. There is a small picnic area and shelter at Olive Lake near the top of the pass.

From the summit of 1,486-meter (4,875-foot) Sinclair Pass, you descend along tumbling Sinclair Creek, which drops 50 meters per km (250 feet per mile) through the narrow canyon, and passes red cliffs known as the Iron Gates.

Ride 25 km (16 miles) from McLeod Meadow campground to Radium Hot Springs. Take a dip in the natural hot springs at the Aquacourt. Water temperature ranges from 35 to 47°C (95 to 116°F). There is also a swimming pool nearby.

Descend through the narrow gap at Sinclair Canyon and then exit from Kootenay National Park to the town of Radium. Radium has many motels and hotels, stores, and restaurants. Stock up on supplies here for the trip to Golden. Although there are several campgrounds, only the Redstreak campground allows tents. A walking trail leads there from the Aquacourt, eliminating the steep hill on the road to Redstreak.

From Radium, take Highway 95 north through the scenic Columbia River Valley in the Rocky Mountain Trench. To the west are the Purcell and Bugaboo ranges of the Columbia Mountains. It's 105 km (65 miles) from Radium Hot Springs to Golden. The road's shoulder is narrower here than through the parks; however, there is much less traffic.

This section has limited accommodation. Edgewater, 10 km (6 miles) north of Radium Hot Springs, has an inn, a store, and campground. At Spur Valley, 9 km (5.5 miles) north of Edgewater, is a campground and motel. At Taliesin, 52 km (32 miles) north of Edgewater, is a guest house. Otherwise, find a secluded spot and camp out. There are stores at Brisco, Spillimacheen, and Harrogate.

Golden has complete services and all types of accommodations. There is a municipal campground near the curling rink. Turn east on Highway 1 (the Trans Canada Highway). The road climbs intermittently for 20 km (12 miles) and overlooks the Kicking Horse River. Watch out for the sharp turn onto the bridge across the river. The Trans Canada Highway here is narrow and busy. If traffic gets hectic, and even if it doesn't, take a break and enjoy the spectacular views.

You enter Yoho National Park 25 km (15 miles) east of Golden. Numerous viewpoints along the road offer views of the Kicking Horse Valley and the President Range. You pass the 2.4-km (1.5-mile) Wapta Falls trail where the Kicking Horse River plummets over a wide ledge; the 3.5-km (2.2-mile) Mount Hunter trail to a ridge with a panoramic view; and the 1-km (0.6-mile) Avalanche nature trail to the toe of an avalanche slope. The Emerald Lake turn-off, 27 km (17 miles) east of the Yoho Park west gate, leads 8 km (5 miles) to the Natural Bridge and Emerald Lake, at the base of the President Range. Emerald Lake is a highlight of Yoho Park.

Continue on Highway 1 past the railroad town of Field, 2.5 km (1.6 miles) past the Emerald Lake turn-off. Approximately 4 km (2.5 miles) past Field is the turn-off for the Yoho Valley. This challenging and worthwhile side trip leads 13 km (8 miles) to 384-meter

(1,259-foot) Takakkaw Falls, the highest falls in Canada. A hostel, campgrounds, and a store are located nearby.

The Trans Canada Highway climbs up Kicking Horse Pass. Along the way you have a view of the Spiral Tunnels, built in 1909, where the railway spirals through two mountains to reduce the grade. The road is very busy here.

At the summit of Kicking Horse Pass, which is on the Continental Divide, 16 km (10 miles) from Field, you are back in Alberta and Banff National Park. Descend on Highway 1 to Lake Louise. At Castle Mountain Junction, 28 km (17 miles) past Lake Louise, ride the Bow Valley Parkway back to Banff.

Day tours in Banff National Park
Banff Park has a number of scenic routes suitable for day outings from Banff and Lake Louise. Some suggested routes starting in Banff townsite are:

• Mount Norquay Drive, 6 km (4 miles), which climbs to a viewpoint 300 meters (1,000 feet) above the Bow Valley. Branching off Mount Norquay Drive is the tour on Vermilion Lakes Drive to the picturesque Vermilion Lakes. It is 5 km (3 miles) each way.

• The 25-km (15-mile) Lake Minnewanka loop, which takes you along the lower slopes of Cascade Mountain and climbs steadily to Lake Minnewanka, Banff Park's largest lake. Along the way are the trailheads of the 4-km (2.5-mile) Bankhead Trail and the Stewart Canyon and Aylmer viewpoints.

• The 14-km (9-mile) climb up Moraine Lake Road from Lake Louise to the Valley of the Ten Peaks. It's a steep ascent, but leads to spectacular scenery.

For other day tours, do part of the multi-day routes. For example, ride the Bow Valley Parkway from Banff to Lake Louise, head up part of the Icefields Parkway, and return (as described in the Icefield Parkways tour). Or cycle from Lake Louise to Emerald Lake in Yoho Park (described in the Banff-Radium Hot Springs-Golden Loop Tour).

Backcountry Bicycling in Banff National Park

Banff Park has 330 km (205 miles) of trails designated for all-terrain bicycling. They range from short trails near Banff and Lake Louise townsites, which are suitable for day tours, to longer trails that can be combined for overnight or longer tours. In the immediate vicinity of Banff and Lake Louise townsites are 50 km (31 miles) of trails for use by all-terrain cyclists.

All-terrain cyclists are not permitted to ride off the trails and should not disturb wildlife. If you're camping overnight in the backcountry, get a park use permit. Topographical maps are available at the park office in Banff. For detailed descriptions of the routes, consult the trail guides listed at the end of this chapter. Generally, cyclists are restricted to fire roads.

- The 3.7-km (2.3-mile) Sundance Trail goes from the Cave and Basin to Sundance Canyon Trailhead.

- Healy Creek Road goes 4.8 km (3 miles) from Sundance Trail junction to Sunshine Road.

- The route along Brewster Creek goes 48 km (30 miles) from Healy Creek Road to Bryant Creek via Allenby Pass.

- From the Banff Springs Hotel, the Spray Fireroad is a 38.8-km (24-mile) route to the Spray Reservoir.

- The Goat Creek Trail goes 8.4 km (5.2 miles) from the Spray Fireroad to the park boundary and Canmore road.

- The 15.8-km (9.8-mile) Bryant Creek route goes from the trail center to Assiniboine Pass with a 2-km (1.2-mile) side trail to Marvel Lake.

- The Redearth Trail is 25.1 km (15.5 miles) of all-terrain biking from a parking lot on Highway 1 to Egypt Lake via Pharoah Creek and a 4.2-km (2.6-mile) side trail to Shadow Lake.

- The 36.3-km (22.5-mile) Lake Minnewanka Trail goes from the lake to Devil's Gap.

- The Cascade Fireroad is a 9-km (5.6-mile) route from Upper Bankhead parking lot to Stoney Creek.

- The Elk Lake Cascade loop is a 38.7-km (24-mile) round trip from the Norquay parking lot over Elk Summit to Stoney Creek and the Cascade Fireroad.

- The 14.3-km (8.8-mile) Skoki route goes from Temple Road parking lot via Deception Pass to Skoki.

- The Rundle Riverside Trail goes 8.3 km (5.1 miles) from the far end of the golf course to the park boundary.

- The Johnston Lake Loop Trail is 11.7 km (7.2 miles) long.

Jasper to Mount Robson

Lofty Mount Robson is the highest peak in the Canadian Rockies. The one- to two-day cycling tour from Jasper to Mount Robson Provincial Park is relatively easy. Along the way are rugged snow-capped peaks, lakes, rivers, and wildflowers. Mount Robson is usually cloud-topped. If the weather is good you may catch a glimpse of the peak.

LENGTH: 83 km (51 miles) each way

START: Jasper townsite, served by VIA Rail

THE ROUTE: Leave Jasper on Highway 16, the Yellowhead Highway, which has a wide, paved shoulder. The road has no difficult climbs as you ascend to Yellowhead Pass, 25 km (15 miles) west of Jasper.

At 1,131 meters (3,710 feet), Yellowhead Pass is one of the lowest passes in the Continental Divide. This is the watershed dividing waters that go east via the Miette, Athabasca, and Mackenzie Rivers to the Arctic Ocean; and the waters that go west into the Fraser River to the Pacific. The divide is also the boundary between Jasper National Park and Mount Robson Provincial Park, and between Alberta and British Columbia.

Highway 16 skirts the shores of Yellowhead Lake, the Fraser River, and Moose Lake. You then descend to the Mount Robson viewpoint. Here you will find campgrounds and the trailhead of a 22-km (14-mile) hike up through the Valley of a Thousand Falls. It leads to Berg Lake, from which Mount Robson rises 2,400 meters (7,872 feet).

From Mount Robson, you can continue into British Columbia. From Tête Jaune Cache you can tour on Highway 5 to Kamloops, or on Highway 16 to Prince George and Prince Rupert (both tours are described in the British Columbia chapter).

MORE INFORMATION: Park Superintendent, Jasper National Park, Box 10, Jasper, Alberta T0E 1E0. Telephone (403) 852-4401.

Park Superintendent, Mount Robson Provincial Park, Box 579, Valemount, British Columbia V0E 2Z0. Telephone (604) 566-4325.

Day Tours in Jasper National Park
For a pleasant short outing, ride the level 10-km (6-mile) route past Beauvert Lake, Jasper Park Lodge, and Annette Lake to Edith Lake. There are beaches on Annette and Edith Lakes.

One of the most scenic routes in Jasper Park, the Maligne Lake Road, 44 km (27 miles) each way, is a challenging day-long cycling tour. Beginning at the junction 4 km (2.5 miles) east on Highway 16, the road climbs steeply for most of its route to Maligne Lake. The highest elevation is over 600 meters (2,000 feet).

Some of Maligne Lake Road's highlights make good objectives for a shorter tour. Maligne Canyon, 6 km (4 miles) from Highway 16, is a spectacular gorge through the limestone rock. Medicine Lake, 15 km (9 miles) farther, is 6 km (4 miles) long.

From Jasper you can head south on the Icefields Parkway to thundering Athabasca Falls, 30 km (20 miles) away. Make it a loop tour by cycling Highway 93A one way and Highway 93 the other. (See the Icefields Parkway Tour description.)

Backcountry Bicycling in Jasper National Park
Jasper National Park allows all-terrain bicycles on much of its 1,000-km (600-mile) network of trails, which wind through the mountains. Cyclists should stay on the trail and not disturb wildlife. Overnight camping requires a camp use permit.

The trails where all-terrain bicycling is not permitted are the Skyline Trail, Tonquin Trail, Lake Annette Trail, Maligne Canyon Trail from the first to the sixth bridge, and Mount Edith Cavell day-use trails.

A popular route is the 2.3-km (1.4-mile) Valley of the Five Lakes Trail, which begins on the Icefields Parkway 10 km (6 miles) south of Jasper and goes to five picturesque, turquoise lakes.

Topographic maps are available at the park headquarters. For trail details consult the trail guides listed at the end of this chapter.

Kananaskis Country

Kananaskis Country is a magnificent mountain recreation area along the eastern border of Banff National Park, only 100 km (60 miles) west of Calgary. Within its 4,000 square km (1,600 square miles) of wilderness are seventeen peaks over 3,000 meters (10,000 feet), including 3,400-meter (11,300-foot) Mount Joffre, and the most southerly glacier in Alberta's Rocky Mountains. You will also encounter alpine meadows and blue lakes. Sheep, wapiti, moose, weasel, coyote, hares, pikas (also called rock rabbits though they resemble guinea pigs), marmots, warblers, chickadees, spruce grouse, and Canada jays are among the animals and birds that can be seen here.

Kananaskis Country encompasses Bragg Creek, Bow Valley, and Peter Lougheed Provincial Parks. The latter park is the heart of Kananaskis Country.

Kananaskis Trail to Highwood Pass to Calgary

This very scenic route takes you through the Kananaskis Valley, with spectacular mountain vistas of several ranges of snow-covered peaks and the Continental Divide to the west.

Highway 40, known as the Kananaskis Trail, is a well-graded highway with a wide, paved shoulder for cyclists. There are many picnic areas and campgrounds in scenic surroundings. You can ride to Peter Lougheed Provincial Park and use it as a base to explore the area, including the park's system of paved off-road bicycle trails. Return via the same route. Or you can do a loop by continuing south on Highway 40 over 2,227-meter (7,306-foot) Highwood Pass, Canada's highest paved road, and turning east through the foothills to Longview and then north through ranchland to Calgary.

The road over Highwood Pass, 68 km (42 miles) south of the Trans Canada Highway, is usually open to cars from June 15 to November 30, but can be used by cyclists during the off-season as well. If you're cycling over Highwood Pass, carry all your food.

LENGTH: 50 km (31 miles) one way to Peter Lougheed Park; 210 km (130 miles) for the whole loop.

START: Seebe, at the junction of Highway 40 and the Trans Canada Highway, 61 km (38 miles) west of Calgary, and 47 km (29 miles) east of Banff, the nearest VIA Rail stops.

THE ROUTE: Head south on Highway 40. The Barrier Lake Information Center is 6 km (4 miles) south of the Trans Canada Highway. The road is level as you pass man-made Barrier Lake and dam, and the University of Calgary's 6,070-hectare (15,000-acre) Kananaskis Forest Experimental Station. Here there are 2.3 km (1.4 miles) of interpretive trails on forest management, and a lookout tower.

Continue south past O'Shaughnessy Falls, a man-made waterfall 14 km (9 miles) south of Seebe. Follow the fast-flowing Kananaskis River past Wasootch Creek and the Mount Lorette Ponds, which are stocked with trout and are popular for fishing.

Ribbon Creek, 23 km (14 miles) south of Seebe, is a recreation area offering a youth hostel, 60 km (37 miles) of hiking trails, and a paved cycling path. The Evan Thomas bicycle trail leads 8 km (5 miles) over a flat route parallel to Highway 40 to Wedge Pond where it links with Highway 40.

The Kananaskis Golf Course is 3.5 km (2 miles) farther along Highway 40. You pass the Mount Kidd Recreational Vehicle Park, the Eau Claire campground, and the Fortress Mountain ski area. You can buy groceries at the Fortress Mountain turn-off. Enter Peter Lougheed Provincial Park 18 km (11 miles) after the golf course.

Take the turn-off for the Kananaskis Visitor Center, 6 km (3.7 miles) past the park entrance. The road leads to the Upper and Lower Kananaskis Lakes and several campgrounds — including the Interlakes campground, which is for tents only. This is the area to use as a base to explore the bicycle paths and the surrounding area, including Highwood Pass. Return to the Trans Canada via the same route.

To continue on the loop route, ride south on Highway 40. The 17-km (10-mile) road climbs gradually at first, and then steeply. It passes through subalpine meadows and spectacular mountain scenery to the summit of Highwood Pass, Canada's highest paved road.

At Elbow Pass Junction is a picnic area that is a good resting spot 2 km (1.2 miles) before Highwood Pass. Nearby is the 0.4-km (0.2-mile) Rock Glacier interpretive trail. At the summit of Highwood Pass is subalpine Highwood Meadows with two interpretive trails: the 1-km (0.6-mile) Highwood Meadows Trail and the 5-km (3-mile) Ptarmigan Cirque Trail.

After exploring the meadows, continue south on Highway 40. Descend gradually. After 1.6 km (1 mile) you pass the Peter Lougheed Park boundary, although you're still in Kananaskis Country. As you descend along the Highwood River you gradually emerge from the mountains to the foothills and ranching country.

You pass a good selection of picnic areas here. One of them is Trout Ponds which, as its name suggests, offers well-stocked ponds for fishing. There is also good fishing at many of the picnic areas on the Highwood River.

Turn east at Highwood Junction, 37 km (23 miles) from Highwood Pass, onto Secondary Road 541. At Highwood Junction is a store for food and limited supplies. Ride road 541 — leaving Kananaskis Country — to Longview, 43 km (26 miles) from Highwood Junction.

To head to Calgary, ride north on Highway 22 (which has narrow shoulders) and then west on Highway 22X. It is 66 km (41 miles) to the city.

To head back to Highway 1 (the Trans Canada Highway), or quieter Highway 1A, both of which go west to Banff or east to Calgary, continue north on Highway 22. Go through Bragg Creek to Highway 1, a distance of 90 km (56 miles). Or go another 13 km (8 miles) on Highway 22 to Highway 1A, just west of Cochrane. From here it's approximately 50 km (30 miles) west to this tour's starting point at Highway 40. The route along Highway 1A is part of the Across Alberta Tour (described separately in this chapter).

Bicycle Paths in Kananaskis Country
Within Peter Lougheed Provincial Park are 70 km (43 miles) of paved bicycle paths that take you through forests and along the shores of lakes. The paths are wide and well-marked.

- The 5-km (3-mile) Lodgepole Trail goes from the Kananaskis Visitor Center to the Elkwood campground and picnic area. From Elkwood the 9.4-km (5.8-mile) Wheeler Trail is a loop to the Boulton campground parking lot and offers scenic views.

- The 5-km (3-mile) Lakeside Trail from Boulton to Elk Pass parking lot has several steep hills approaching Upper Kananaskis Lake. These three trails connect to form a 20-km (12-mile) path from the Visitor Center to Elk Pass.

- In the Ribbon Creek area, the 8-km (5-mile) Evan Thomas Trail goes from the Ribbon Creek parking area and parallels Highway 40 to the Kananaskis Golf Course, then continues to Eau Claire and Wedge Pond.

- In the Eau Claire recreational area, located 6 km (4 miles) off Wedge Pond on Highway 40, there is a 1.5-km (1-mile) paved loop.

Backcountry Bicycling in Kananaskis Country
Kananaskis Country offers a variety of backcountry routes for all-terrain bicycling. Popular day-tours include the 19-km (12-mile) Skogan Pass Trail from Dead Man's Flat to Ribbon Creek; the 7-km (4.4-mile) Moose Mountain Fire Road from Elbow Falls Trail; and the 14.5-km (9-mile) Plateau Mountain traverse from Wilkinson Summit to Livingstone River (return by the Forestry Trunk Road 940).

On the 10-km (6-mile) Carnarvon Lake Trail, you can ride your all-terrain bikes along the stretch of trail which happens to be a logging road, lock the bike to a tree, and scramble up the headwall.

A popular two-day trip is a circuit along parts of the Sheep River Trail, Forget-Me-Not Ridge, and the Big Elbow Trail.

For trips of two to five days, explore trails in the extensive network of logging and exploration roads in the West Highwood, East Highwood, Upper Oldman, Livingstone, West Elbow, and West Sheep areas.

Topographic maps are available at the park headquarters. For trail details, consult the trail guides listed at the end of this chapter.

MORE INFORMATION: Kananaskis Country, 1011 Glenmore Trail SW, Suite 412, Calgary, Alberta T2V 4R6. Telephone (403) 297-3362.

Drumheller Dinosaurs and Badlands: Calgary to Drumheller

The Alberta Badlands near Drumheller are known for the rich deposits of dinosaur skeletons and fossils that have been found there. Mushroom-shaped hoodoos, eroded from hills, give the arid surroundings of Red Deer Valley an eerie atmosphere. You can also explore remains of pioneering settlements and mines.

This tour goes from Calgary to Drumheller and then guides you to the area's attractions. During the summer the Red Deer Valley can be very warm, so always carry sufficient water. The area can also experience strong winds from the west.

LENGTH: 138 km (85 miles) each way

START: Calgary, served by VIA Rail, bus lines and an international airport

THE ROUTE: Go east on Highway 1 (the Trans Canada Highway), for approximately 20 km (12 miles) to the junction with Highway 9. Cycle north on Highway 9 through prairie farmland and the town of Irricana to Beiseker, 45 km (28 miles) from the Trans Canada Highway. At Beiseker, Highway 9 turns east for 44 km (27 miles) to Drumheller. There are municipal campgrounds at Irricana and Beiseker.

You descend 120 meters (394 feet) from the prairie level into the Red Deer Valley and the town of Drumheller. Use Drumheller as a base to explore the area. A good selection of accommodations and campgrounds are available. Nearby Midland Provincial Park is a day-use park and does not have camping.

The Drumheller Dinosaur Museum at 385 First Street East, has exhibits on the prehistoric life and geological phenomena in this area known as the "Valley of the Dinosaurs."

Just 6 km (3.7 miles) west of Drumheller on a route called the "Dinosaur Trail," is Midland Provincial Park, in the midst of the Badlands. Interpretive trails explore the geological formations, and hiking trails go through an old mine site and the surrounding Badlands. Here also is the Tyrrell Museum of Palaeontology, featuring a variety of fossils that trace the evolution of life, and an extensive display of dinosaurs. The interactive displays use computers and videos.

Take Highway 10 southeast of Drumheller toward East Coulee. The Rosedale Swinging Bridge, 8.5 km (5 miles) from Drumheller, leads to trails through the old mining area. The bridge was built by the men of the Old Star Mine. At 18 km (11 miles) you can see hoodoos, formations that are the result of years of wind and water erosion. There are picnic facilities here. East Coulee, 20 km (12 miles) southeast of Drumheller on Highway 10, was an important coal mining camp.

Another worthwhile route to explore from Drumheller is Secondary Highway 837 along the Red Deer River to the free Bleriot Ferry. Built in 1913, it's the last cable ferry operating on the Red Deer River. Ride the ferry and cycle back to Drumheller on Highway 838. You pass Horsethief Canyon Viewpoint overlooking variations of sedimentary strata in the canyon. Paths lead down to petrified oyster beds.

To return to Calgary, retrace your route back from Drumheller. Or take Route 10 to the junction with Route 56 and cycle south to Deadhorse Lake. Turn west at Hussar and follow Route 561 to Highway 1 (the Trans Canada Highway), which goes through Strathmore and back to Calgary.

Across Alberta

Crossing Alberta from west to east takes you from the heights of Kicking Horse Pass on the British Columbia border and through the Rocky Mountain grandeur of Banff National Park. From Banff you descend through the Rocky Mountain Foothills, flat ranchland, and prairie wheatfields to Saskatchewan.

The route described below goes from west to east and, if you have a choice, that direction is recommended. Strong winds often come down off the mountains, helping cyclists riding east, and adding wind resistance for those cycling west. There is generally a good selection of campgrounds and accommodations throughout Alberta.

LENGTH: 471 km (293 miles)

START: Lake Louise, Alberta, just east of the Kicking Horse Pass on the British Columbia border, is served by VIA Rail.

THE ROUTE: From Lake Louise, follow the Bow Valley Parkway (which has less traffic than the Trans Canada Highway) to Banff (this road is part of the Icefields Parkway tour).

From Banff, take Highway 1 (the Trans Canada Highway). Near Canmore, just outside the Banff National Park gates, turn onto Highway 1A which winds along the north side of the Bow River. It, too, is quieter than the Trans Canada Highway, but it is narrow and may be busy around Ghost Lake. The part of the route between Banff and Calgary has only a few campgrounds, so if you're camping, plan your route in advance. Bow Valley Provincial Park, 25 km (15 miles) east of Canmore, has camping.

The turn-off for Seebe, approximately 47 km (29 miles) east of Banff, leads to Highway 40, known as the Kananaskis Trail. (This tour is described separately in this chapter.)

Continuing east on Highway 1A, you cycle along scenic Ghost Lake as you gradually traverse the Rocky Mountain Foothills to the prairie. Ride through Cochrane, 50 km (31 miles), east of the Exshaw turn-off for Seebe. Ride Highway 1A to Calgary, 38 km (24 miles) farther.

From Calgary, take Highway 1 (the Trans Canada Highway), east through Strathmore, Bassano, Brooks, and Medicine Hat to the Saskatchewan border.

Guidebooks

A Cyclist's Guidebook to the Canadian Rockies, by Larry Barnes, details the Columbia Icefields Parkway route. Available from: Rocky Mountain Cycle Tours, Box 1978, Canmore, Alberta T0L 0M0. Price $6.95 ($7.50 postpaid).

Backcountry Biking in the Canadian Rockies, by Gerhardt Lepp. Available from: Rocky Mountain Books, 106 Wimbledon Crescent SW, Calgary, Alberta T3C 3J1. Price $11.95.

The Canadian Rockies Bicycling Guide, by Gail Helgason and John Dodd. Available from: Lone Pine Publishing, 414, 10357-109 Street, Edmonton, Alberta T5J 1N3. Price $8.95.

The Canadian Rockies Trail Guide, by Brian Patton and Bart Robinson. Available from: Summerthought Ltd., Box 1420, Banff, Alberta T0L 0C0. Price $14.95 (for mail orders add $3.00).

The Complete Guide to Kananaskis Country, by Norma Ramage and Jim Wilson. Available from: Lone Pine Publishing. Price $8.95.

Kananaskis Country Trail Guide, by Gillean Daffern. Available from: Rocky Mountain Books. Price $12.50.

Parkways of the Canadian Rockies, by Brian Patton. Available from: Summerthought Ltd. Price $14.95 (for mail orders add $3.50).

7 *Saskatchewan*

There's far more to Saskatchewan than its stereotyped image of tree-less prairie, traversed on your way across Canada. Saskatchewan has exciting tours for cyclists. Discover glacier-carved valleys, lakes, forests, wildlife, and important historic sites.

Cutting across Saskatchewan are valleys with lakes and forests which are preserved in provincial parks. Northern Saskatchewan is covered by coniferous forest and has many lakes and rivers. Bicycle tours explore the diverse scenery in Saskatchewan's national and provincial parks and their surrounding areas. You can use the parks as a base from which to tour. The small towns, many of them containing museums depicting the area's pioneer days, let you discover more about Saskatchewan.

Many of the parks are within bicycling distance of a town or city served by a train that will transport your bike. For cyclists on their way across Canada, a suggested route across Saskatchewan is also given.

ROADS: Most of Saskatchewan's highways have wide paved shoulders, which make cycling safe and enjoyable.

WEATHER: Saskatchewan has a continental climate with short hot summers and long cold winters. During the summer the average temperature varies from 10°C (50°F) at sunrise to 24°C (75°F) in the afternoon. Average annual precipitation is 28 to 51 cm (11 to 20 inches), with half occurring during June, July, and August.

TOURIST INFORMATION: For general tourist information, including a map and a Saskatchewan Accommodation and Campground Guide, contact Tourism Saskatchewan, 2103-11th Avenue, Regina, Saskatchewan S4P 3V7. Call toll-free, in Saskatchewan, 1-800-667-7538, elsewhere in Canada and the United States, 1-800-667-7191.

HOSTELS: Hostels in Saskatchewan are operated by the Saskatchewan Hostelling Association, Saskatchewan Sport and Recreation Center, 2205 Victoria Avenue, Regina, Saskatchewan S4P 0S4. Telephone (306) 522-3651.

AIRPORTS: Major airports are located at Regina, Saskatoon, and Prince Albert.

TRAINS: For information on VIA Rail train service, call the local VIA Rail agent. In Saskatchewan call toll-free, 1-800-665-8630.

BUSES: Saskatchewan Transportation Company bus lines, 2041 Hamilton Street, Regina, Saskatchewan S7P 2E2. Telephone (306) 787-3360.

BICYCLING: Saskatchewan Cycling Association, 2205 Victoria Avenue, Regina, Saskatchewan S4P 0S4. Telephone (306) 522-3651.

Moose Jaw to Buffalo Pound Provincial Park Loop

The southern part of the province is the flat featureless prairie that most people picture as Saskatchewan. The flatness is broken by the deep Qu'Appelle Valley, reaching 120 meters (400 feet) below the level of the prairie. Here you can enjoy prairie wildflowers, many varieties of trees, lush meadows, and sparkling waters.

The glacier-carved Qu'Appelle Valley crosses two-thirds of Saskatchewan and includes Buffalo Pound Provincial Park, 30 km (19 miles) north of Moose Jaw. The park's name recalls the days when Indians drove buffalo here to be slaughtered. Today, at the Bison Range, you can see a herd of bison in their natural prairie habitat. At Nicolle Flats, another of the park's features, is a marshlands nature

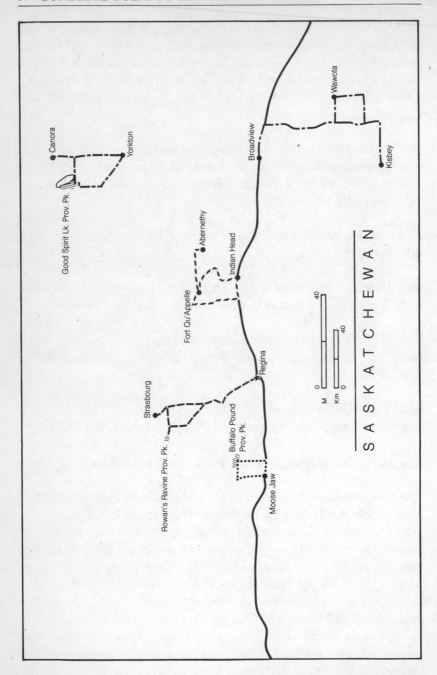

walk where many species of birds can be seen. After exploring the park, you can use it as a base to explore the neighboring countryside.

In Moose Jaw, attractions include the Moose Jaw Museum, the Moose Jaw Wild Animal Park, and Bushell Park at the Canadian Forces Base which is the home of the Saskatchewan Air Show. Camping facilities are located in southeast Moose Jaw. The river here bends in the shape of a moose's jaw, hence the name of the town.

LENGTH: 60 km (37 miles) round trip

START: Moose Jaw, which is served by VIA Rail

THE ROUTE: Head north for 18 km (11 miles) on Highway 2, which has a wide, paved shoulder. Just outside Moose Jaw, the road climbs up from Moose Jaw Creek. Go east on Highway 202 across flat, open fields for 11 km (7 miles) to Buffalo Pound Provincial Park.

To return to Moose Jaw, ride south on Highway 301 for 23 km (14 miles) over flat terrain, and then go down the Moose Jaw Valley to Highway 1 (the Trans Canada Highway), which has wide, paved shoulders. Go west on Highway 1 for 5 km (3 miles) to Moose Jaw.

MORE INFORMATION: Park Superintendent, Buffalo Pound Provincial Park, 110 Ominica Street West, Moose Jaw, Saskatchewan S6H 6V2. Telephone (306) 693-2678.

Regina to Rowan's Ravine Provincial Park Loop

Situated on the east shore of Last Mountain Lake in the Qu'Appelle basin, Rowan's Ravine Park is known for its beach. Accessible by Highway 220 from Bulyea, the park is 76 km (47 miles) north of Regina. Close by is North America's oldest bird sanctuary.

LENGTH: 178 km (110 miles)

START: Regina, the provincial capital of Saskatchewan, is served by VIA Rail and an airport.

THE ROUTE: From Regina, take Highway 11 for 26 km (16 miles) to Lumsden. Take Highway 99 for 8 km (5 miles) to Craven, on the floor of the Qu'Appelle Valley. Go left onto Highway 20, which has wide, paved shoulders. The valley floor is mostly grazing land with some marshy areas. The Qu'Appelle River meanders through the valley, framed by the rolling hills.

The road climbs out of the valley for some 3 km (1.8 miles), with a picnic site about halfway up. At the top of the valley is a spectacular view of the Qu'Appelle Valley basin. Continue north on Highway 20 to the junction with Highway 322, 5 km (3 miles) from Craven. Here is Last Mountain House Historic Park, where reconstructed buildings show life in a fur-trading outpost of the 1870s.

From Silton take Route 322 for 24 km (15 miles) to Highway 220. About 1 km (0.6 miles) out of Silton is Saskatchewan Beach Regional Park. The terrain is mostly gently rolling hills, but there are several steep rises. The road surface is rough pavement with a narrow but rideable shoulder. Go left on Highway 220 and ride 8 km (5 miles) to Rowan's Ravine Provincial Park.

From the park go east on Highway 220. It is roughly paved, but has a shoulder. Ride through the gently rolling terrain for 23 km (14 miles) to Bulyea, at the junction with Highway 20. Turn north for 13 km (8 miles) along a paved shoulder through farm country to Strasbourg. A campground is situated here. The local museum, in the old Canadian Pacific Railway station, displays Indian and pioneer artifacts.

To return to Regina, go south for 45 km (28 miles) on Highway 20 through Bulyea to Craven. Turn right on Highway 99 and ride 8 km (5 miles) to Lumsden, and then turn left on Highway 11 for 26 km (16 miles) to Regina.

MORE INFORMATION: Park Superintendent, Rowan's Ravine Provincial Park, Box 370, Strasbourg, Saskatchewan S0G 4V0. Telephone (306) 725-4423.

Indian Head to Echo Valley and Katepwa Provincial Parks Loop

Echo Valley and Katepwa Provincial Parks are cradled in the scenic glacier-etched Qu'Appelle Valley. Echo Valley Park covers 6.5 square km (2.5 square miles) along the shorelines of Echo and Pasqua Lakes.

It is located approximately 50 km (31 miles) north along Highway 56 out of the town of Indian Head. Katepwa Park covers 8 hectares (20 acres) along Katepwa Lake. These tours wind along the hilly and winding lake edge roads from Indian Head to Echo Valley Park with a sidetrip to Motherwell National Historic Park.

LENGTH: 184 km (114 miles)

START: Indian Head, which is served by VIA Rail

THE ROUTE: In Indian Head, opposite the local information center, is a gravel road leading 2 km (1.2 miles) to a tree nursery featuring nature trails, a picnic area, and a campground.

Leave Indian Head by going north on Highway 56, which has gravel shoulders 1.5 meters (5 feet) wide. You ride through tree-dotted farmland for 16 km (10 miles) and then descend into the Qu'Appelle Valley. The slope down to the valley floor is a 6 percent grade and about 1 km (0.6 mile) long. Katepwa Provincial Park, on the valley floor, is 26 km (16 miles) from Indian Head, and has campgrounds, beaches, and most services.

Continuing along Highway 56, 10 km (6 miles) from Katepwa Beach is Lebret. Another 6 km (3.7 miles) along the lake-edge highway is Fort Qu'Appelle, the site of a Hudson's Bay Company trading post built in 1864. Here are stores, a museum, and a nearby campground.

When leaving Fort Qu'Appelle, take Broadway Street west along B-Say-Tah Road to Echo Valley Provincial Park, which has camping facilities and is a good place to set up a camp from which you can explore the area on the following tour.

From Echo Valley Park take an interesting 88-km (55-mile) return side trip to the Motherwell Homestead National Historic Park. Go north from the Echo Valley Park entrance for 1 km (0.6 mile). Then go east on hilly and winding Highway 56 to Fort San 6.4 km (3.9 miles) away. A sanitorium from 1913 to 1972, Fort San is now a convention center and home of the Summer School of Arts. From Fort San, continue east on Highway 56 for about 4 km (2 miles). At the junction take Highway 10, which has paved 2-meter (6-foot) wide shoulders. Follow it east toward Balcarres, 16 km (10 miles) away. After 1 km (0.6 mile) you approach a steep hill. Balcarres has many services.

Continue east on Highway 10 for 8 km (5 miles), then turn south on Highway 22, which has gravel shoulders. Ride through low rolling hills for 6 km (3.7 miles) to Abernethy. Here there are retail stores, but no hotel accommodation or camping facilities.

From Abernethy take the gravel road straight south for about 3 km (1.6 miles) to Motherwell Homestead National Historic Park. Here is the gracious, Italianate-style stone house of William Motherwell, a farmer and politician who worked for the cause of the western farmer. Return to Echo Valley Provincial Park by retracing your route.

From Echo Valley Park take Highway 210 south. It has gravel shoulders 1 meter (3 feet) wide, and climbs the steep edge of the valley to the flat prairie. After about 12 km (7 miles), turn left onto Highway 10 and go 2 km (1.2 miles). Then turn south on Highway 35, and ride 19 km (12 miles) to the town of Qu'Appelle. Picnic and camping facilities are available here.

When leaving Qu'Appelle, take Highway 1 (the Trans Canada Highway), which has paved, 1.5-meter (5-foot) wide shoulders. Go east for 14 km (9 miles) through rolling prairie to Indian Head.

MORE INFORMATION: Park Superintendent, Echo Valley and Katepwa Provincial Parks, Box 790, Fort Qu'Appelle, Saskatchewan S0G 1S0. Telephone (306) 332-5615.

Superintendent, Motherwell Homestead National Historic Park, Abernethy, Saskatchewan S0A 0A0. Telephone (306) 333-2116 or 662-2645.

Broadview to Moose Mountain Provincial Park

Covering 388 square km (150 square miles) in the southeastern plains region of Saskatchewan, Moose Mountain Provincial Park is a thick forest of white birch and aspen on an elevated plateau contrasting with the surrounding grassland region. The park's knob-and-kettle terrain has a topographic relief of 90 to 120 meters (300 to 400 feet) and there are more than 1,200 small lakes in the depressions. Many of the lakes offer good fishing. Kenosee Lake and its beaches are the focal point of the park.

This tour goes from Broadview 80 km (50 miles) to Moose Mountain Park. Then, using the park as a base, it follows two other tours: a 68-km (42-mile) loop to Cannington Manor Historic Park, and a 52-km (32-mile) ride to Arcola.

LENGTH: 250 km (155 miles)

START: Broadview, served by VIA Rail station, is 80 km (50 miles) north of the park.

THE ROUTE: From Broadview, ride east on Highway 1 (the Trans Canada Highway) for 21 km (13 miles) to Whitewood. Go south on Highway 9, which has wide, paved shoulders, for 58 km (36 miles) to Moose Mountain Park.

Using the park as a base, you can ride a 68-km (42-mile) loop to Cannington Manor Historic Park. Ride northwards on Highway 9 for 8 km (5 miles) through a wooded area. Go east on Highway 48 through farmland toward Wawota. Along Highway 48 are several vacation farms offering horseback riding and meals at short notice.

From Wawota, go south on Grid Road 603 for 11.5 km (7 miles). The road is gravel and tricky to ride if you don't have an all-terrain bike. At the end of Grid Road 603, turn west, go for 1.6 km (1 mile), and then turn north for 1 km (0.6 mile) to Cannington Manor Historic Park. Cannington Manor, established in 1882, was a college where wealthy English families sent their troublesome children.

From Cannington Manor, take the same gravel road south for 1 km (0.6 mile) and then head west for 5 km (3 miles). At the intersection, take the road heading north. After approximately 10 km (6 miles), take the Christopher Trail, which is lightly graveled and easy riding. At Highway 9 turn north. The Moose Mountain Park entrance is about 200 meters (650 feet) farther on.

Another trip from Moose Mountain Park is the 52-km (32-mile) one-way trip to Arcola. From the park, go south along the flat, tree-lined Highway 9 for 22 km (14 miles) to Carlyle. Named for Scottish author Thomas Carlyle, the town has a Rusty Relic Museum in the old Canadian National Railway station.

Go west for 16 km (10 miles) on Highway 13 (it has a paved shoulder), through flat countryside with few trees, to Arcola. The feature film based on W.O. Mitchell's novel *Who Has Seen the Wind?* was filmed at Arcola. The Arcola Museum features pioneer artifacts.

From Arcola take Highway 13 west for 13 km (8 miles) toward Kisbey. A picnic area and campground is located 4 km (2.4 miles) before you get to the town. The main attraction in Kisbey is its museum. Return to Moose Mountain Provincial Park by the same route.

To return from Moose Mountain Park to Broadview, retrace your route north on Highway 9 for 58 km (36 miles) to Whitewood, and then go west for 21 km (13 miles) on Highway 1 to Broadview.

MORE INFORMATION: Park Superintendent, Moose Mountain Provincial Park, Box 100, Carlyle, Saskatchewan S0C 0R0. Telephone (306) 577-2131.

Yorkton, Good Spirit Lake Provincial Park, and the Donut Run

Good Spirit Lake Provincial Park, covering 20 square km (7.8 square miles) in southeastern Saskatchewan, has sandy beaches, sand dunes, and nature trails. You can use the park as a base to explore the surrounding area. In Yorkton is the Western Development Museum and the Godfrey Dean Cultural Centre, as well as accommodations and campgrounds.

LENGTH: 129 km (80 miles)

START: Yorkton. The nearest VIA Rail station is in Melville, 43 km (26 miles) on Highway 10 southwest of Yorkton.

THE ROUTE: Farmland with some thickets characterizes this two-day trip. From Yorkton take Highway 16, which has a shoulder, for 26 km (16 miles) through flat terrain to Springside. Along the way you pass the Canadian Forces Base, 14 km (9 miles) from Yorkton.

Go north on Highway 47 to Highway 229, a flat road that has no shoulder and a rough edge, for approximately 7 km (4 miles) to Good Spirit Lake Provincial Park.

From the park, go east on Highway 229 for 16 km (10 miles) to Highway 9. Turn north on Highway 9 and head for Canora 16 km (10 miles) away. The road has a wide, paved shoulder, and runs through flat fields and grazing land. At the White Sand River is a pleasant picnic area.

At the entrance to Canora is the Lesia Welcoming Statue to offer you bread and salt, a traditional form of Ukrainian greeting. The town of Canora is home to bakeries known for their donuts, hence the name of this tour. A campground is located nearby. To return to Yorkton, ride south on Highway 9 for 50 km (31 miles).

MORE INFORMATION: Park Superintendent, Good Spirit Lake Provincial Park, 2A Provincial Building, Yorkton, Saskatchewan S3N 2Y4. Telephone (306) 792-2110.

Swift Current to Saskatchewan Landing Provincial Park

Saskatchewan Landing Provincial Park is one of three provincial parks on Lake Diefenbaker. The center of this 57-square-km (22-square-mile) park is at the west end of the lake, in a steeply sloped and wooded valley marking the intersection between the South Saskatchewan River and Lake Diefenbaker. The lake has sandy beaches and is popular for boating.

This tour goes from the city of Swift Current to the park. Attractions in Swift Current include the Prairie Wildlife Center and Wright Historical Museum.

LENGTH: 100 km (60 miles) round trip

START: Swift Current, served by VIA Rail, is 50 km (31 miles) south of the park.

THE ROUTE: From Swift Current go north on Highway 4 for 50 km (31 miles) to Saskatchewan Landing Park. Highway 4 has a paved 1-meter (3-foot) wide shoulder. Gently rolling fields and a few trees line the road. You then descend the valley's slope. Return by the same route.

Prince Albert Nat'l Pk.

Prince Albert

Fort Carlton Historic Pk.

Batoche

Rosthern

Benito

Pelly

Duck Mtn. Prov. Pk.

Kamsack

Saskatchewan
Landing
Prov. Pk.

Regina

Swift Current

Moose Jaw

Broadview

M 0 100

Km 0 100

S A S K A T C H E W A N

Kamsack to Duck Mountain Provincial Park Loop

This 240-square-km (93-square-mile) park lies on the Duck Mountain Upland of the Manitoba Escarpment, the edge between the Manitoba Plain (the first prairie steppe) and the Saskatchewan Plain (the second prairie steppe). Duck Mountain Park is the southernmost park in Saskatchewan's forest and lake belt and is adjacent to the Manitoba border. At the heart of the park is Madge Lake with beautiful beaches and good fishing.

This route is a loop from Kamsack through Duck Mountain Park, north through Manitoba, west through Pelly, and south to Kamsack.

LENGTH: 137 km (85 miles)

START: Kamsack, approximately 30 km (19 miles) from the park's Madge Lake, is served by VIA Rail's Winnipeg-Churchill route.

THE ROUTE: From Kamsack, go east on Highway 5 for 8 km (5 miles) to Highway 57. The trees give way to fields but the long low hills remain. The shoulders on this stretch of highway are 1.2 meters (4 feet) wide and paved. Go northeast on Highway 57, over long low hills on a tree-lined route for 19 km (12 miles) to Madge Lake in Duck Mountain Provincial Park. The shoulders of the road are paved but narrow.

From Duck Mountain Park, ride northeast on Highway 57 for 4 km (2.4 miles) to Highway 83 just over the Manitoba border. Go north on Highway 83, which has gravel shoulders, for 29 km (18 miles). You will travel through rolling tree-covered hills, to Benito. If you wish, you can go into Benito where there are restaurants and a hotel, or you can save the 6-km (3.7-mile) round trip and turn onto Highway 49 outside the town. This highway has wide gravel shoulders for the 2 km (1.2 miles) to the Saskatchewan border. Once you're back in Saskatchewan, the shoulders are paved and wide.

The 26-km (16-mile) trip into Pelly is through rolling hills covered with grain fields. In Pelly there is a campground, a hotel, and the Fort Pelly-Livingstone Museum featuring Indian artifacts and local history. Nearby are the sites of Fort Pelly, a trading post built by the Hudson's Bay Company in 1824, and Fort Livingstone, built in 1874 as a post for the North-West Mounted Police and used in 1877 for the first session of the North-West Territorial Council.

Take Highway 8 south for 32 km (20 miles) to Kamsack. The road is through rolling hill country dotted with homesteads. In Kamsack there is a campground and hotels if you wish to stay overnight.

For an interesting side trip from Kamsack, continue west on Highway 5 through fairly flat farmland. The road has paved, 1.2-meter (4-foot) wide shoulders that are rough in spots. Cycle 13 km (8 miles) to Veregin, the site of the National Doukhobor Heritage Village and Museum. Here an early-1900s Doukhobor village has been recreated, and the story of their immigration to Canada and their struggle to remain a people is documented. Retrace your route to return to Kamsack.

MORE INFORMATION: Park Superintendent, Duck Mountain Provincial Park, Box 39, Kamsack, Saskatchewan S0A 1S0. Telephone (306) 542-3482.

Prince Albert to Prince Albert National Park

The rugged country of the Canadian Shield is the setting for this cycling tour. Prince Albert National Park, situated 200 km (120 miles) north of the city of Saskatoon, is in the transition zone between the northern forest (which covers half the park) and aspen parkland and prairie grasslands. The park's roads lead to lakes and points of interest.

The park can be reached by Saskatchewan Transportation Company bus, which will take boxed bicycles on a space-available basis. This means that you shouldn't depend on their taking your bicycle in high season.

LENGTH: 184 km (114 miles)

START: The city of Prince Albert, which can be reached by Saskatchewan Transportation Company bus.

THE ROUTE: Go north on Highway 2 for 77 km (49 miles) to Highway 264. Turn left at Highway 264 and ride 13 km (8 miles) to the Waskesiu Lake townsite in Prince Albert National Park.

Explore the park. When you're ready to head back, go south on Highway 263 to the park's south gate, 41 km (25 miles) from Waskesiu Lake. Continue on shoulder-less Highway 263 past Emma Lake, where there are seven beaches. Just 2 km (1.2 miles) after you go through the hamlet of Christopher Lake is Highway 2. Go south on Highway 2 for 40 km (25 miles) to the city of Prince Albert.

Day Touring and Backcountry Bicycling in Prince Albert Park
The Narrows Tour, which is 25 km (15 miles) each way, goes from the beach at Waskesiu Lake. Go south along Lake View Drive, following Highway 263 for 5 km (3 miles). Turn left where the road is signposted for the Narrows Campground. The Narrows Road is fairly hilly and rough in places, but the scenery makes up for it. Along the way are Paignton and Tree Beard's nature trails and the South Bay and Trippe's beaches. At the end of the trip is the Narrows Campground. Return along the same route.

Prince Albert National Park has a 250-km (155-mile) network of backcountry trails that take cyclists with all-terrain bicycles into the seldom-visited southwestern area of the park. The trails range from graveled roadways to overgrown pathways. The 13-km (8-mile) Elk Trail, formerly used for hauling freight from Prince Albert to La Ronge, traverses rolling hills with grades that may require you to push your bike. The 5-km (3-mile) Westside Boundary Road, a gravel roadway through the Sturgeon River Valley and Fox/Rabbit Creek Basins (there is camping at Nesslin Lake), combined with the 44-km (27-mile) Fifty-Seven Trail is a good overnight circuit. Guides to some of the backcountry trails, as well as topographic maps, are available. Contact the park office for more information.

MORE INFORMATION: Park Superintendent, Prince Albert National Park, Box 100, Waskesiu Lake, Saskatchewan S0J 2Y0. Telephone (306) 663-5322.

The Battle Tour

In 1885 the Métis of the North-West Territories (as the provinces of Saskatchewan and Alberta were then known) proclaimed their own government at Batoche under the leadership of Louis Riel and Gabriel Dumont. An armed rebellion ensued. These tours in the South Saskatchewan River Valley and Prince Albert areas explore the historic sites of the Riel Rebellion, including three of the main battle sites.

LENGTH: 227 km (141 miles)

START: Prince Albert, served by an airport and Saskatchewan Transportation Company bus lines.

THE ROUTE: Prince Albert's attractions include the Heritage Museum, Lund's Wildlife Museum, and the former home of Prime Minister John Diefenbaker.

Take Highway 2 south from Prince Albert for 32 km (20 miles), passing through hilly countryside, to St. Louis on the South Saskatchewan River. Here are picnic sites. Continue south on Highway 2 for 16 km (10 miles) to Highway 225. Go west on Highway 225 for 27 km (17 miles) into Batoche, established by the Métis in the 1870s.

Batoche was the heart of the rebellion. It was the site of the final battle between the Métis and the North-West Field Force who reasserted government sovereignty. Here you can see the NWFF encampment, bulwarks, and foxholes, as well as a museum.

Leave Batoche by Highway 225 and travel south for 10 km (6 miles) to Highway 312. A 30-km (18-mile) return side trip for cyclists with all-terrain bikes, or for those who don't mind riding gravel, is to go south at the junction to Fish Creek. Here you will see an abandoned church; the encampment site of General Middleton after the Battle of Fish Creek (which is reached by riding over a dirt road through the valley of Fish Creek); and the site of the Battle of Fish Creek, marked only by a cairn, where the Métis surprised the NWFF.

Go west on Highway 312 for 15 km (9 miles), across the South Saskatchewan River into Rosthern. Here there are campgrounds as well as the Rosthern Cultural Museum, which depicts the history of the local Mennonites and other ethnic communities. From Rosthern go north on Highway 11 for 18 km (11 miles) to Duck Lake.

Just outside Duck Lake is a cairn marking the site of the first battle of the rebellion. In town, the Duck Lake Historical Museum presents the history of the rebellion, and includes an old North-West Mounted Police jail on its grounds. Three km (1.8 miles) south of town is the replica of Duck Lake as it was in 1895.

From Duck Lake, it's a 26-km (16-mile) side trip each way on lightly traveled Highway 212 (which has no shoulder) to Fort Carlton Historic Park. At Fort Carlton is a replica of the fort when it was a Hudson's Bay post and North-West Mounted Police station. Take the road leaving the fort to the cairn marking the signing of the treaty.

Upon leaving Duck Lake and reaching the junction of Highway 11 and Highway 212, you can take another side trip. Go north on Highway 11 and take the next right onto a dirt road to the Shrine of Our Lady of Lourdes and a prehistoric buffalo kill site. This road should be attempted only on an all-terrain bike. Retrace your route back to Highway 11. From Duck Lake continue north on Highway 11 for 55 km (34 miles) to Highway 2, and then go 7 km (4 miles) to Prince Albert.

Across Saskatchewan

If you're going across Saskatchewan, Highway 1 (the Trans Canada Highway) is the most popular route with cyclists. Paved shoulders 3 to 3.6 meters (10 to 12 feet) wide extend along the entire route through the province. The cities and towns along the way can supply your needs. Numerous campgrounds and a good variety of accommodations are available. Take the time to explore some of the tours described separately in this chapter, several of which are accessible from the Trans Canada Highway.

LENGTH: 654 km (406 miles) from the Alberta boundary to the Manitoba boundary

START: The route is described here going east, starting at the Trans Canada Highway at the Alberta-Saskatchewan boundary. VIA Rail serves the major centers along the Trans Canada Highway.

THE ROUTE: From the Alberta boundary, go east on the Trans Canada Highway through the agricultural land around Maple Creek and past the Great Sand Hills near Gull Lake.

Around Swift Current are some of Saskatchewan's oil and gas wells. From Swift Current you can explore the tour to Saskatchewan Landing Provincial Park. On the way to Moose Jaw you descend the Missouri Coteau, the long narrow escarpment that extends from south-central Saskatchewan into northeastern Alberta and separates the Saskatchewan Plain and the Alberta Plateau. At Moose Jaw you can take the tour to Buffalo Pound Provincial Park.

Regina, Saskatchewan's provincial capital, had its beginnings as a tiny settlement near what was known as Pile of Bones Creek. It was later named in honor of Queen Victoria. In the heart of this modern city is Wascana Lake, encompassed in a 930-hectare (2,300-acre) park. Here also are the Legislative Buildings, the Saskatchewan Museum of Natural History, the Wild Bird Sanctuary, and the Diefenbaker Homestead. From Regina you can link with the tour to Rowan's Ravine Provincial Park.

Leaving Regina, ride east on the Trans Canada Highway to Indian Head, named after the westerly peak of a range of hills southeast of the community. Here you can take a side tour on the Echo Valley and Katepwa Provincial Parks Tour.

Continue east on the Trans Canada Highway. At Broadview you can join with the Moose Mountain Provincial Park Tour. The last center before the Manitoba border is Moosomin, a Cree Indian word meaning "mooseberry," or high bush cranberry.

8 Manitoba

Manitoba offers cyclists much more than its settled image of flat wheatfields might suggest. You can tour in the rugged forests and beside the clear lakes of the Precambrian Shield, which covers the eastern and northern part of the province. Or you can ride through the wooded hills and valleys of the Manitoba Escarpment, a highland plateau rising above the surrounding prairie along the western edge of the Manitoba Plain. Cycling on the prairie of southern Manitoba also makes for enjoyable touring.

The tours in this chapter explore the variety that Manitoba offers: white sand beaches, wilderness, rivers once traveled by fur traders, and pioneering towns. Many towns offer historical museums with displays describing the area's pioneer past. A number of the tours start from Winnipeg, Manitoba's largest city, which is served by an international airport, VIA Rail, and Greyhound and Grey Goose bus lines.

ROADS: Except for the Trans Canada Highway, which does have a paved shoulder, most of the province's other roads do not have paved shoulders.

WEATHER: Manitoba has the most temperate climate of the three prairie provinces. Summer temperatures range from 10°C (50°F) at night to about 24°C (75°F) during the day. Average annual precipitation across the province varies from 41 to 53 cm (16 to 21 inches), and most falls during the summer.

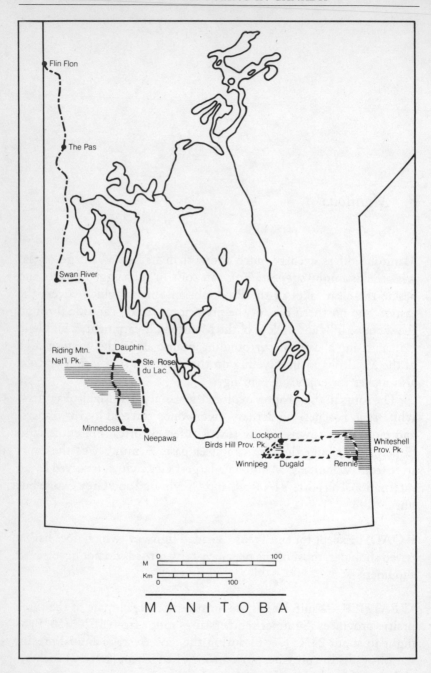

MANITOBA

TOURIST INFORMATION: For general tourist information, including a road map and vacation guide describing campgrounds, hotels, motels, and bed-and-breakfasts, contact: Travel Manitoba, 155 Carlton Street, 7th Floor, Winnipeg, Manitoba R3C 3I18. Call toll-free 1-800-665-0040.

HOSTELS: Manitoba Hostelling Association, 1700 Ellice Avenue, Winnipeg, Manitoba R3H 0B1. Telephone (204) 786-5641. The association operates hostels in Winnipeg and Brandon, as well as a farm hostel near Glenboro, 160 km (100 miles) west of Winnipeg.

AIRPORTS: Winnipeg International Airport is served by major airlines, and offers connections to smaller centers.

TRAINS: For information on VIA Rail service, call in Winnipeg, (204) 949-1830; from elsewhere in Manitoba, call toll-free 1-800-282-8070.

BUSES: Manitoba is served by two bus lines: Greyhound Bus Lines, 487 Portage Avenue, Winnipeg, Manitoba R3B 2E3. Telephone (204) 775-8301. Grey Goose Bus Lines, 301 Burnell Street, Winnipeg, Manitoba R3G 2A6. Telephone (204) 786-8891.

BICYCLING: Manitoba Cycling Association, 1700 Ellice Avenue, Winnipeg, Manitoba R3H 0Z2. Telephone (204) 786-5641.

Riding Mountain National Park Loop

Rising dramatically above the flat Manitoba prairie, Riding Mountain National Park is 2,978 square km (1,150 square miles) of forest wilderness contrasting with the surrounding wheatfields. The park, 265 km (165 miles) northwest of Winnipeg, is on the Manitoba Escarpment, a rolling highland plateau that rises 450 meters (1,500 meters) above the prairie, and forms the edge between the Manitoba Plain, the first prairie steppe, and the Saskatchewan Plain, which is the second prairie steppe.

Within the park is 750-meter (2,460-foot) Riding Mountain, Manitoba's third highest point. Black bear, wapiti, moose, and white-tailed deer are among the larger mammals in the park. Beaver can be seen in almost every pond. Northern pike, walleye, whitefish, lake trout, and brook trout can be taken from the park's lakes. Riding Mountain Park's 320-km (200-mile) network consists of seventeen day-use trails and fourteen overnight trails.

This three- to five-day tour takes you on a loop through Riding Mountain Park and along the edge of the Manitoba Escarpment. Campgrounds and accommodations are available at the park, as well as along the route outside the park.

LENGTH: 273 km (170 miles)

START: Neepawa, Manitoba, which is along the Across Manitoba Tour. Towns on this tour that can be reached by VIA Rail are McCreary and Ochre River. Dauphin, 10 km (6 miles) from the northwestern-most point of this tour, is also served by VIA Rail.

THE ROUTE: In Neepawa is a historical plaque marking the Saskatchewan Trail, once a major route for settlers traveling west. From Neepawa go west, climbing the Manitoba Escarpment for 35 km (22 miles) on Highway 16 — the Yellowhead Highway. At Minnedosa turn north on Highway 10, past a campground, and through Erickson, 26 km (16 miles) north of Highway 16. Another 18 km (11 miles) brings you to Wasagaming, the entrance to Riding Mountain National Park.

When you're ready to leave Riding Mountain Park, ride north on Highway 10 to Highway 5, 60 km (37 miles) north of Wasagaming. From this junction you can go 10 km (6 miles) north to Dauphin and link with the Northern Parks Tour (described separately in this chapter).

Continuing on the loop tour, turn east on Highway 5 before you get to Dauphin. You leave the Manitoba Escarpment near Ochre River and travel to Ste. Rose du Lac, 40 km (25 miles) away. Stay on Highway 5 as it turns south to McCreary, 32 km (20 miles) south of Ste. Rose du Lac. For the next 60 km (37 miles), you go through or near several small towns before riding into Neepawa, this tour's starting point.

MORE INFORMATION: Park Superintendent, Riding Mountain National Park, Wasagaming, Manitoba R0J 2H0. Telephone (204) 848-2811.

Northern Parks Tour

This six- to eight-day tour takes you north through or near provincial parks and forests on the Manitoba Escarpment, and through northern Manitoba wilderness from Dauphin to Flin Flon. The terrain is generally level and the summer evenings are long. There are few services between towns. Be sure to stock up at the major towns en route. From Cranberry Portage or The Pas you can take the VIA Rail train to return south to Dauphin or Winnipeg.

Duck Mountain Provincial Park's broad valleys are dominated by 831-meter (2,727-foot) Mount Baldy, Manitoba's highest point. Great blue herons, double-crested cormorants, pelicans, and great horned owls, as well as elk and mule deer, can be seen.

In 2,089-square-km (807-square-mile) Porcupine Provincial Forest, an unpaved road leads to the base of 823-meter (2,700-foot) Hart Mountain, Manitoba's second highest point. The clear blue lake is the main feature of the 595-square-km (230-square-mile) Clearwater Lake Provincial Park. It is known for its large lake trout and northern pike. Grass River Provincial Park, 2,288 square km (230 square miles) in area, encompasses the 130-km (80-mile) Grass River canoe route.

Flin Flon, the tour's end, acquired its unusual name in 1915 when prospectors found a copy of the novel *The Sunless City* on a portage near the Churchill River. The town's name is an abbreviation for Professor Josiah Flintabbetey Flonatin, the novel's hero, who discovers a city of gold in the center of the earth.

LENGTH: 544 km (338 miles) one way

START: Dauphin, Manitoba, which is served by VIA Rail's Winnipeg-to-Churchill service. This tour can be a continuation of the Riding Mountain National Park Tour (described separately in this chapter).

THE ROUTE: From Dauphin, the site of the Ukrainian Folk Arts Center, go west on Highway 5 for 16 km (10 miles) and then go north on Highway 10 toward Ashville, where there is a game farm featuring lions, tigers, and monkeys. There is a campground to the north of Ashville, on the way to Ethelbert, 60 km (37 miles) from

Dauphin. The turn-off for Duck Mountain Provincial Park is 18 km (11 miles) north of Ethelbert. It's a 29-km (18-mile) side trip on unpaved roads to the center of the park.

At Minitonas, 97 km (60 miles) from Ethelbert, is another game farm. The farm can only be toured in horse-drawn wagons or on horseback. Swan River, 16 km (10 miles) farther, is the largest community in the area. Stock up on food here. There are also two museums of local history.

Approximately 40 km (23 miles) north of Swan River, and just north of Birch River, Route 365 leads off Highway 10 into Porcupine Provincial Forest. The lakes and rivers contain northern pike, walleye, rainbow trout, whitefish, lake trout, perch, and goldeye. There are several campgrounds in the area.

North of Mafeking, you leave the Manitoba Escarpment and ride near the shores of Dawson Bay and Overflowing Bay of Lake Winnipegosis. The next 155 km (96 miles) of Highway 10 to The Pas is isolated, passing through the small settlements of Overflowing River, Westray, and Freshford. Be sure you have sufficient food supplies. There are campgrounds along the route.

The Pas is a major center in northern Manitoba offering accommodation, campgrounds, and other services. Here is the Little Northern Museum featuring natural history specimens, local history, and native artifacts. A cairn honors Henry Kelsey, the Hudson's Bay Company fur trader and explorer, who traveled inland from York Factory to the Saskatchewan River via The Pas.

Clearwater Lake Provincial Park is 19 km (12 miles) north of The Pas on Highway 10. You can see through the waters of the lake to a depth of 11 meters (35 feet). Caves, created by the water's constant motion on the dolomite cliffs, can be seen along the lake's southern shore. Trophy-sized lake trout, northern pike, and whitefish inhabit the waters. Accommodation and campgrounds are available in the park.

Grass River Provincial Park, 74 km (46 miles) north of The Pas, is a wilderness of lakes and evergreen forest straddling the Precambrian Shield country and limestone flatbeds. The park is home to woodland caribou, timber wolves, and bald eagles. The river system is ideal for canoeing and more than 150 lakes have northern pike, trout, walleye, and whitefish. Campgrounds are available.

Continuing on Highway 10, cycle to Simonhouse, where Route 391 branches off toward Grass River Provincial Park. Continue on to Flin Flon, 67 km (42 miles) northwest of the park entrance. In Flin Flon is a statue designed by cartoonist Al Capp, representing Josiah Flintabbetey Flonatin, the hero of the novel from which the town took its name. To return, ride south on Highway 10 for 54 km (33 miles) to Cranberry Portage and board the VIA Rail train, which goes to The Pas. There you can catch another train south to Dauphin and Winnipeg.

Winnipeg to Birds Hill Provincial Park

The closest provincial park to Winnipeg, Birds Hill Park is an enjoyable destination for a day tour or an overnight camping trip. Birds Hill Park covers 31 square km (12 square miles) of hills, ridges, and valleys formed as a result of sediment deposits from ancient glacial lakes and rivers. A large population of white-tailed deer inhabit the forest. Within the park are hiking trails, campgrounds, and a 32-hectare (80-acre) man-made lake. The park's 7.2-km (4.5-mile) Pine Ridge Bicycle Trail winds through pine groves and aspen stands and circles the lake.

LENGTH: 25 km (15 miles) one way

START: Winnipeg

THE ROUTE: Ride east on Dugald Road which is Route 115 in Winnipeg and becomes Highway 15 near the Red River Floodway. Go east on Highway 15 to Route 206 near the town of Dugald. Turn left and ride north straight to the park. Once you're there, explore the Pine Ridge Bicycle Trail.

Whiteshell Provincial Park Loop

See the transition from flat prairie to Precambrian Shield forest and lake. Cycle to Whiteshell Park, Manitoba's oldest and largest provincial park: 2,734 square km (1,056 square miles) of thick Precambrian Shield forest dotted with more than 200 lakes. Streams contain northern pike, perch, small-mouth bass, walleye, and lake trout. Wildlife that can be observed includes moose, fox, coyote, lynx, deer, black bear, beaver, bald eagle, turkey, vultures, spruce grouse, and ruffed grouse.

Whiteshell Park is popular for canoeing and hiking. The 60-km (37-mile) Mantario Hiking Trail, 16-km (10-mile) Hunt Lake Hiking Trail, and several short interpretive trails explore the forest.

Accommodation and campgrounds are available in Whiteshell Park. If it takes you more than one day to get to the park, accommodations are available in the towns along the route. Whiteshell Park is situated along the Ontario boundary. The route from Winnipeg to the park is part of the Across Manitoba tour.

LENGTH: 113 (70 miles) one way from Winnipeg to Whiteshell Park; 273 km (170 miles) loop tour

START: Winnipeg

THE ROUTE: From Winnipeg, cycle east on Route 15 along flat terrain through Dugald (the site of Canada's only costume museum), Anola, Vivian, and Ste. Rita to Agassiz Provincial Forest, which has picnic sites but does not offer camping. At Elma, 75 km (46 miles) from Winnipeg, turn north on Highway 11 for 8 km (5 miles), and then go east on Highway 44 over rolling country. At Rennie, 30 km (19 miles) farther, you enter Whiteshell Provincial Park. You have traveled approximately 113 km (70 miles) from Winnipeg.

Explore Whiteshell Park on routes 307 and 309. When you're ready to leave, take Route 307 north and west through the park past Seven Sisters Falls to Highway 11. It's 79 km (49 miles) along Route 307 from Rennie northwest through Whiteshell Park to Highway 11. Go south for 5 km (3 miles) to Highway 44, and then west on Highway 44 for 63 km (39 miles), through Beausejour and Garson, to Lockport on the Red River. Lockport has a number of historic buildings dating back to the Red River settlement of the mid-nineteenth century. Take Route 204 back into Winnipeg.

MORE INFORMATION: Whiteshell Provincial Park, Park Headquarters, Rennie, Manitoba R0E 1R0. Telephone (204) 369-5232.

Lake Winnipeg Beaches Loop

Here's a good tour for the warm days of summer. Grand Beach is known for its white beaches and shifting sand dunes that reach 8 meters (29.5 feet) in height. Behind the dunes is a lagoon that is home to orioles, finches, pelicans, and cranes. Grand Beach Provincial Park, 34 square km (13 square miles) in area, also features interpretive nature trails and campgrounds. From Victoria Beach you can explore the white sands and see the bank swallows of Elk Island Heritage Park.

LENGTH: 282 km (175 miles)

START: Winnipeg

THE ROUTE: From Winnipeg take Henderson Highway—Route 42 within the city, and Route 204 outside the city— along the banks of the Red River. Along the way you pass through Lockport. Situated 30 km (19 miles) north of Winnipeg is Lower Fort Garry National Historic Park, a stone Hudson's Bay Company fur-trading post dating from the 1830s.

Continue on Route 204, and at East Selkirk get on Highway 59. Approximately 42 km (26 miles) farther, turn off onto unpaved Route 500 along the shore of Lake Winnipeg. At Route 12 turn left to Grand Beach Provincial Park, which has camping.

From Grand Beach Park, go 6 km (4 miles) east along Route 12 to Route 59 (which can be very busy in summer), and go north along Route 59 for 23 km (14 miles) to Victoria Beach. From here, depending on how high the water is, you can walk, wade, or boat to Elk Island Heritage Park. It is separated from the mainland by a narrow strait.

To continue the loop tour, go south from Victoria Beach for 10 km (6 miles) to Highway 11. Ride Highway 11 alongside Traverse Bay and the Winnipeg River, a former fur trade route of the voyageurs between Lake Superior and Lake Athabasca. Ride along Highway 11 to Great Falls, 50 km (31 miles) away, and Lac du Bonnet, 20 km (12 miles) farther. Another 26 km (16 miles) from Lac du Bonnet brings you to Highway 44. From here you can link with the Whiteshell Provincial Park Tour, or go 19 km (12 miles)

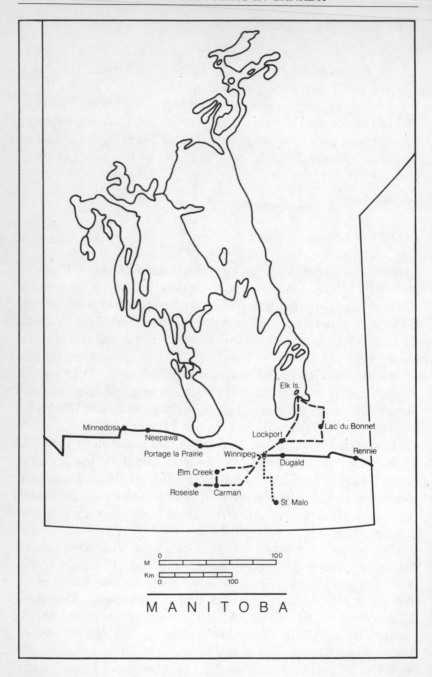

MANITOBA

southeast along Highway 44 and connect with the Across Manitoba
Tour (both tours are described separately in this chapter).

To complete the loop tour, go west on Highway 44 for 63 km
(39 miles) to Lockport, and take Route 204 back into Winnipeg.

Winnipeg to St. Malo

Here's an easy two-day tour over flat terrain. St. Malo Recreation
Park offers camping, a beach, fishing, and three short trails. Also in
St. Malo is Le Pionnier Museum, where the pioneer life of the early
settlers is depicted.

LENGTH: 75 km (47 miles) one way

START: Winnipeg

THE ROUTE: Go south from Winnipeg on Route 200 through St.
Adolphe to Route 311. Go east on Route 311 through Niverville to
Highway 59. Then go south on Highway 59 through St. Pierre-
Jolys where you can see La Place des Colons Park and Museum, a
replica of a pioneer log cabin depicting a French-Canadian pioneer
home. Continue to La Rochelle. A few kilometers farther, take the
turn-off for St. Malo. Return by the same route.

Winnipeg to Stephenfield Provincial Recreation Park Loop

A pleasant, easy two-day tour from Winnipeg. Camp at Stephenfield
Park which, in addition to campgrounds, offers fishing and a beach.

LENGTH: 188 km (117 miles)

START: Winnipeg

THE ROUTE: From Winnipeg, take Highway 2 for 53 km (33 miles)
to Elm Creek. Go south on Highway 13 for 19 km (12 miles) to
Carman. At Carman is Dufferin Historical Museum, with displays
depicting pioneer life, and Friendship Field, home of restored Second
World War aircraft.

Go west on Route 245 for approximately 16 km (10 miles) to Stephenfield Provincial Recreation Park near Roseisle. After exploring the park, head back east on Route 245 to Carman. At Carman, continue east on Highway 3 for 64 km (40 miles) back to Winnipeg.

Across Manitoba

This route takes you off the more heavily traveled Trans Canada Highway and onto less traveled routes that connect with some of the tours in this chapter. This route is about 60 km (38 miles) longer than taking the Trans Canada Highway the whole way across Manitoba, but it's more scenic.

LENGTH: 550 km (340 miles)

START: The Saskatchewan-Manitoba border on the Trans Canada Highway. The nearest VIA Rail stops are at Virden, Manitoba, 22 km (14 miles) east of the boundary, and Moosomin, Saskatchewan, 41 km (25 miles) west.

THE ROUTE: Starting from the border, go east for 35 km (22 miles) on the Trans Canada Highway to Highway 83. Go north for 27 km (17 miles) on Highway 83, and then east for 82 km (51 miles) on Route 24. At Highway 10, go north for 16 km (10 miles), almost to Minnedosa. Then continue east on Highway 16, the Yellowhead Highway, through Neepawa and Gladstone to Highway 1 (the Trans Canada Highway), just west of Portage la Prairie, 123 km (76 miles) farther.

Go east on Highway 1 and take Highway 1A through Portage la Prairie. Then ride Highway 26 for 62 km (38 miles) through Poplar Point to the Trans Canada Highway just west of Winnipeg. Take the Trans Canada Highway into Winnipeg.

From Winnipeg, take Highway 15 east 75 km (47 miles) through Agassiz Provincial Forest, and then go 8 km (5 miles) north on Highway 11 to Highway 44. Cycle 62 km (38 miles) east on Highway 44 through Whiteshell Provincial Park, where you link with the Trans Canada Highway. From here you can continue east on the Trans Canada Highway into Ontario.

9 Ontario

Ride these tours and discover that there is a lot more to Ontario than six-lane expressways and endless suburban development. These tours take you on picturesque country roads with minimal traffic, through farmlands, orchards, and charming Victorian villages that have retained an unhurried pace. You can explore nature trails and bird sanctuaries, or ride along historic canals, lakeshores, sand beaches, and limestone cliffs. Absent on many routes is the commercialism often found in other scenic areas. During autumn, nature puts on a spectacular display of colors.

Most of these routes involve a series of connecting county roads. The directions may appear a bit confusing to read, but once you're on your bike the routes are not difficult to follow.

ROADS: Ontario's best cycling is on the county roads through rural Ontario. Bicycles are not allowed on controlled-access highways in Ontario, such as the 400 series (Highway 401, etc.), the Queen Elizabeth Way, Toronto's Don Valley Parkway and Gardiner Expressway, and Ottawa's Queensway. All of the routes in this chapter are well-marked on the provincial road maps. If you would like more detailed maps of the individual counties or districts, they are available from: Ministry of Transportation and Communications, Information Management Office, Map Unit, East Building, 1201 Wilson Avenue, Downsview, Ontario M3M 1J8. Telephone (416) 248-3476.

WEATHER: During June, July, and August, days are usually warm, though nights can be cool, particularly in northern Ontario. During fall (from mid-September to mid-November) and spring (from mid-March through April), medium-weight clothing is required.

TOURIST INFORMATION: For general tourist information, including a road map and guides to accommodation and provincial parks and campgrounds, contact Ontario Travel, Queen's Park, Toronto, Ontario M7A 2E5. Telephone (416) 965-4008 or toll-free, 1-800-268-3735.

HOSTELS: For eastern Ontario, contact: Canadian Hostelling Association, Ontario East, 18 Byward Market, Ottawa, Ontario K1N 7A1. Telephone (613) 235-2595. For information on hostelling in southwestern Ontario, contact: Great Lakes Hostelling Association, 223 Church Street, Toronto, Ontario M5B 1Z1. Telephone (416) 368-1848.

AIRPORTS: Toronto's Pearson International Airport is the province's largest airport. It is served by numerous airlines with connections to airports in other cities including Ottawa, Hamilton, Thunder Bay, and Sault Ste. Marie.

TRAINS: For information on VIA Rail services in Ontario, contact: in Toronto, (416) 366-8411; in Ottawa, (613) 238-8289; in Hamilton, (416) 522-7533; in Kingston, (613) 544-5600; in London, (519) 672-5722; in Windsor, (519) 256-5511. Elsewhere in area code 416, call toll-free 1-800-268-9511; in area codes 519 and 613, call toll-free 1-800-268-9520; in area code 705, call toll-free 1-800-268-9520; in area code 807, call toll-free 1-800-665-8630.

BUSES: Voyageur Bus Lines requires that bicycles be dismantled and boxed. They are charged at the bus parcel rate for an 11-kg (25-pound) parcel.

BICYCLING: Ontario Cycling Association, 1220 Sheppard Avenue East, Willowdale, Ontario M2K 2X1. Telephone (416) 495-4141.

Lake Simcoe and Huronia Highlands Loop

Huronia is a popular recreation area directly north of Toronto. It encompasses rural communities like Cookstown, includes the shores of Georgian Bay, and extends east to the shores of Lake Simcoe. The region is named for the Huron Indian tribe which first settled in this area. As early as 1610, Étienne Brûlé visited the Huron Indians here.

This three- to four-day loop tour goes through Cookstown, along the beaches on Lake Simcoe, then turns west to beaches on Georgian Bay and returns through Cookstown to Toronto. Or, from Orillia, you can go east along Lake Simcoe and south to Toronto. The terrain starts out flat but becomes hilly north of Orillia.

LENGTH: 300 km (186 miles)

START: Toronto, Ontario's largest city. Orillia and Barrie are the towns along the loop that are also served by VIA Rail.

THE ROUTE: From Toronto, go north on Weston Road (County Road 56) to Highway 9. Go left on Highway 9 for a short distance and then right on Rupke Road. Go right on Canal Road along the Holland Canal. At County Road 54 go left to Cookstown, 50 km (31 miles) from Toronto.

From Cookstown go east on Highway 89, which has some traffic. Go left on County Road 53 northward, then right onto Highway 27. You will travel down a steep hill into Barrie to Blake Street (Highway 11 north). Situated on Lake Simcoe's Kempenfelt Bay, Barrie is a major center in the area. It's a 22-km (14-mile) ride from Cookstown to Barrie.

Ride through Barrie to Shanty Bay Road (County Road 20) along the Lake Simcoe shoreline. At the T-junction, go right over tracks and left onto gravel. At the next T-junction keep right, onto pavement. Follow along the lake edge past Eight Mile Point Road to Highway 12. Turn right into Orillia, a ride of 35 km (22 miles) from Barrie. There is a youth hostel at Borland Street, and camping at Mara Provincial Park. Situated on the narrows between Lake Couchiching and Lake Simcoe, Orillia is a major link in the Trent-

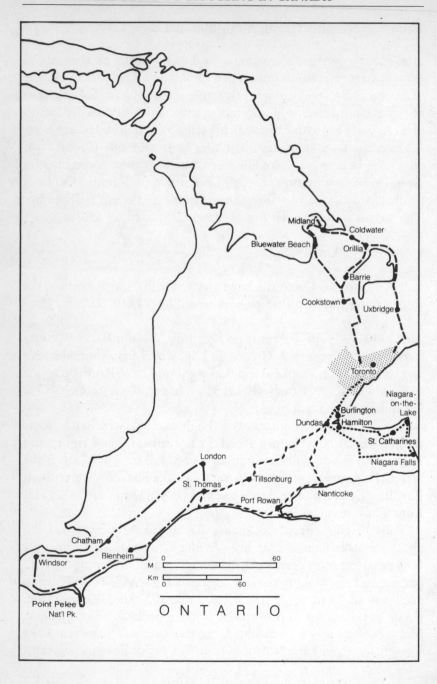

Midland
Coldwater
Bluewater Beach
Orillia
Barrie
Cookstown
Uxbridge
Toronto
Niagara-on-the-Lake
Burlington
Dundas
Hamilton
St. Catharines
Niagara Falls
London
St. Thomas
Tillsonburg
Port Rowan
Nanticoke
Chatham
Blenheim
Windsor
Point Pelee
Nat'l Pk.

M   0   60
Km 0   60

ONTARIO

Severn Canal System. Among its attractions is the house of Stephen Leacock, built in 1929 on the lakeshore.

From Orillia, you have the option of going east around Lake Simcoe and south to Toronto. To follow this 125-km (75-mile) option go east on Highway 12, past the turn-offs for Mara Provincial Park and McRae Point Provincial Park. At Brechin, turn right on County Road 47, which joins with County Road 23. Ride County Road 23 south and go right on County Road 82. Then turn left onto County Road 1 through Uxbridge, and onto County Road 21. Go right on County Road 21 to Coppin's Corners, left on County Road 1, and right again on Concession Road 4 to County Road 27. Go left on County Road 27, then right on Concession Road 3, and right again on Pickering Town Line. Turn left onto Steeles Avenue, the boundary of Metropolitan Toronto, just north of the Metro Toronto Zoo.

To continue from Orillia on the Huronia Loop Tour, take Highway 12 for 18 km (11 miles) past the turn-off for Bass Lake Provincial Park and through Prices Corner and Warminster. Just past the turn-off for Coldwater, turn left onto County Road 23 through a forest. Turn right at County Road 58, which rejoins Highway 12. You can visit the reconstructed seventeenth-century Jesuit mission Ste. Marie Among the Hurons, the Martyrs' Shrine, and the Wye Marsh Wildlife Centre on your way to Midland, 20 km (12 miles) from Coldwater. Turn right for downtown. At the waterfront turn left, then right, along the water's edge.

Take the third crossroad, which leads into Penetanguishene, 6 km (4 miles) farther. Here is the restored Historic Naval and Military Establishment built after the War of 1812. You can either stay in Penetanguishene or follow County Road 26 to camp at Awenda Provincial Park. The park has a view of Giant's Tomb Island in Georgian Bay.

Take County Road 26 from Penetanguishene 12 km (7 miles) to Lafontaine, and turn left past Lafontaine onto what becomes the Lakeshore Road. Follow this road past several beaches. After Bluewater Beach, a ride of 20 km (12 miles) from Lafontaine, take County Road 29 southward. Turn right onto County Road 22 at the T-junction, and then left onto Highway 26 east. At Minesing, go right onto County Road 28, then right again on County Road 40.

Cross Highway 90 and continue south on County Road 58. Go left on Highway 89 to Cookstown, 64 km (40 miles) from Bluewater Beach. Retrace your route from Cookstown back to Toronto, 50 km (31 miles) farther.

Niagara Escarpment and Orchards

This tour explores part of the Niagara Escarpment. On the way are orchards and vineyards. Niagara wineries offer wine tours and samples. Niagara-on-the-Lake is one of the best-preserved nineteenth-century towns in North America, and is the home of the Shaw Festival. You ride the Niagara Parkway past gardens and nature trails and along the Niagara River to Niagara Falls, Canada's most popular tourist destination.

LENGTH: 350 km (125 miles)

START: Toronto. If you want to begin outside Toronto, you can take the VIA Rail train to Hamilton and pick up the tour from there.

THE ROUTE: From Toronto, go west on Dundas Street. Turn right onto Burnhamthorpe Road. Follow Burnhamthorpe out through Mississauga. At first the road may have some traffic, but past Erin Mills the route is flat and has little traffic. Go left on Fourth Line and then right on Highway 5. Go right on Tremaine Road (County Road 22). Ride over the tracks, then turn left onto No. 2 Sideroad. At the T-junction turn left, and then right, and follow No. 1 Sideroad into Waterdown, 65 km (40 miles) from Toronto.

In Waterdown turn left at Main Street, which runs into Snake Road. Ride down the escarpment to Plains Road (Highway 2) in Burlington and turn left. Turn right at Lasalle Park Road and then left on North Shore Road East, which eventually rejoins Highway 2. Turn right onto Lakeshore, and then left at Beach Boulevard on the spit facing the steel mills of Hamilton. If you're camping, head to the Confederation Park campground near Highway 20 and the Queen Elizabeth Way.

Follow Highway 20 south through Stoney Creek, 11 km (7 miles) from Waterdown. Here you will find the Historic Battlefield House and Monument, a 1759 settler's home that is now a museum devoted to the Battle of Stoney Creek, fought during the War of 1812.

Climb Highway 20 up the escarpment to Ridge Road. Turn left and follow this panoramic road along the top of the escarpment. Ridge Road ends at R.R.14, south of Grimsby. Turn right on R.R.14, and then left onto Fly Road (R.R.73). Ride through Campden to R.R.24. Turn right and then left into the Ball's Falls Conservation Area, 43 km (27 miles) from Stoney Creek. The Ball's Falls Conservation Area, which has camping, includes an old mill site on Sixteen Mile Creek.

Go north on R.R.24. Then turn right onto R.R.81 and take it into St. Catharines, where it becomes St. Paul Street. St. Catharines, 15 km (9 miles) from the Ball's Falls Conservation Area, is in the heart of the wine country and Niagara fruit belt. You can see ships go through the locks on the nearby Welland Canal.

From St. Catharines, take County Road 87 for 15 km (9 miles) along the lakeshore to Niagara-on-the-Lake, situated on Lake Ontario at the mouth of the Niagara River. Along the way are wineries which offer tours and tasting. Niagara-on-the-Lake has many well-preserved nineteenth-century neoclassical and Georgian homes. It is the home of the annual Shaw Festival and Fort George National Historic Park.

Leaving Niagara-on-the-Lake, ride south along the Niagara Parkway. At Queenston is the Brock Monument overlooking the site of the Battle of Queenston Heights, an important victory for the British during the War of 1812.

Continue south past the floral clock to Niagara Falls, Canada's most popular tourist destination. It's a 20-km (12-mile) ride from Niagara-on-the-Lake. After you've seen thundering Niagara Falls, there are many attractions here. There is a wide range of accommodation—a hostel, hotels, bed-and-breakfasts, and campgrounds—in the Niagara area.

Continue on the Niagara Parkway south to Chippawa. Turn right onto Lyons Road which becomes R.R.47. Turn left onto R.R.84 and then right onto R.R.27 into Welland, 25 km (15 miles) from Niagara Falls. Ships from all over the world cruise the Welland Canal through the center of the city.

Turn right onto Prince Charles, and then left at Thorold Road.

Turn right onto South Pelham Road and go north to Fonthill. Turn left onto Highway 20 and then left onto R.R.63 through Fenwick, into the flat plains of Wellandport.

Follow R.R.63 along Oswego Creek to Canborough. Turn right onto R.R.2 through Caistorville. Turn left onto R.R.622 and go through Binbrook. Stay on R.R.622 as it becomes R.R.22 and then Carluke Road. Follow it to R.R.222 and go north on R.R.222 and then Highway 52, to Copetown. Go right here onto R.R.399 into the town of Dundas. Dundas is in a valley surrounded by the escarpment, a ride of 100 km (62 miles) from Welland.

Turn left at King Street and then right onto Old York Road to Highway 6. A quick right and then left will take you to Snake Road. Turn left on Snake Road and follow it to Waterdown, 10 km (6 miles) from Dundas. Camping and accommodation are available at Waterdown.

Return the 65 km (40 miles) to Toronto by the same way you left on the first part of the tour. Ride up Snake Road to Main Street. Turn right onto Parkside Drive, which becomes No. 1 Sideroad. At the T-junction, turn left and then right. At the next T-junction at Tremaine Road, turn right and go to Highway 5. Turn left onto Highway 5, then left onto Fourth Line. Turn right onto Burnham-thorpe Road, and follow it to Dundas Street and into Toronto.

Lake Erie Edge and Tillsonburg Tobacco Plains

Ride on quiet highways and country roads along the scenic shoreline of Lake Erie, passing through small port towns. You cycle the Talbot Trail, a route followed by pioneers settling the area.

Then, turning inland, you go through Ontario's tobacco country. In the town of Tillsonburg are the largest auction exchanges in the tobacco belt. Many vegetables are also grown in this area.

LENGTH: 335 km (210 miles)

START: Dundas, served by VIA Rail. If you want to ride to Dundas from Toronto, see the first part of the Niagara Escarpment and Orchards Tour, described separately in this chapter.

THE ROUTE: From Dundas take Old Dundas Road to Wilson Street (Highway 2). Go right on Wilson Street into Ancaster, a ride of 14 km (9 miles) from Dundas. From Ancaster continue on Wilson Street, go south on Fiddlers Green Road, and turn right on R.R. 222. Past Carluke, go left onto R.R.22. At Highway 54, turn right and go through Middleport. Go left at the Pauline Johnson Homestead and cross the Grand River to Ohsweken. The Six Nations Indian Reserve here is the last tract of land grant given to Indians in the late 1700s.

Continue south and turn left on R.R. 20 and then right onto R.R. 55. Ride through Springvale. Cross Highway 6 and Highway 3 to R.R. 3 and the Talbot Trail. Turn right onto the Talbot Trail and ride into Nanticoke. Just past Nanticoke, turn left and follow the shore of Lake Erie to the picturesque town of Port Dover, a distance of 75 km (47 miles) from Ancaster. Turn left down to the harbor. Go up the main street and turn left to Hay Creek Conservation Area. At Hay Creek Conservation Area, turn left and go through Port Ryerse.

You are now on the Talbot Trail. Continue along the shore road, past Turkey Point Provincial Park, to Port Rowan, 30 km (19 miles) from Port Dover. At Port Rowan you can take R.R.42 north to Backus Mill, a restored mill dating back to the early 1800s that is still producing flour by water power. Follow R.R.42 back to Port Rowan. There is camping at Long Point Provincial Park: take Highway 59 south to the Long Point Peninsula which juts into Lake Erie.

Leaving Port Rowan, continue on R.R. 42 through Port Burwell, a distance of 30 km (19 miles) from Port Rowan, to Highway 73, which leads to Port Bruce. Go right onto County Road 24 to County Road 22. Turn right on County Road 22 and ride into St. Thomas, 50 km (31 miles) from Port Burwell. The road becomes Fairview Avenue and eventually Burwell Road. Turn right on South Edgeware Road, and then left onto Centennial Avenue (County Road 30) going north.

Turn right onto County Road 52 and head through Springfield. Turn left at County Road 49, and then right onto County Road 48. The road jogs to the right and becomes County Road 20. Go through Brownsville and Tillsonburg, 44 km (27 miles) from St.

Thomas. At County Road 13, turn left through Springford and a Mennonite farming area.

Turn right onto County Road 18 and go through Norwich. The road becomes County Road 3 on the other side of Norwich, and County Road 4 between Scotland and Oakland. Turn left at Oakland onto County Road 24 (not Highway 24). North of Mount Pleasant, turn right onto County Road 18. Follow County Road 18 around Brantford onto Highway 54. At Highway 2, turn right. Go on here a short distance, then turn left onto Jerseyville Road (County Road 17). Follow it into Ancaster, a 90-km (56-mile) ride from Tillsonburg, and retrace your route to Dundas, this tour's starting point.

Lake Erie and the Thames Valley: London to Windsor Loop

This tour can be combined with the preceding Lake Erie Edge and Tillsonburg Tobacco Plains Tour. Highlights of this tour include the Lake Erie beaches, and peaceful towns with charming Victorian architecture. At Point Pelee National Park, over 300 bird species have been observed. On the return route, you ride through the farmland along the Thames River.

LENGTH: 480 km (300 miles)

START: London, a major center in southwestern Ontario, is served by VIA Rail.

THE ROUTE: London is situated on the Thames River and many of the street names are the same as those of its British namesake. From London, go south on Wellington Road, which becomes County Road 36 after crossing over Highway 401. Continue south on County Road 36 to Glanworth. Turn right onto County Road 35, and then left onto County Road 25 to St. Thomas, a distance of 30 km (18 miles) from London. St. Thomas has a wealth of Victorian architecture. Take County Road 16, known as the Talbot Trail, through Fingal to the shore of Lake Erie. Ride along the shore of Lake Erie. County Road 16 ends at a T-junction. Turn right and then left onto Highway 3. At Morpeth, 75 km (47 miles) from St. Thomas, you can turn off and take Route 17 to Rondeau Provincial Park. The park offers camping.

Continue on Highway 3 through Blenheim and along the shore of Lake Erie. At Wheatley, 65 km (40 miles) from Morpeth, is Wheatley Provincial Park which offers camping.

On the way to Leamington are tomato fields as far as the eye can see. At Leamington, 13 km (8 miles) from Wheatley, is the access via Route 33 to Point Pelee National Park: a sandspit reaching 10 km (6 miles) into Lake Erie. The 1,619-hectare (4,000-acre) park is Canada's southernmost point, on the same latitude as northern California, and is well-known for its birdwatching. A boardwalk winds through the marshes, and a 4.5-km (2.8-mile) bicycle trail parallels the road leading to the park's sand beaches. There are no campgrounds in the park.

From Leamington, continue west on Highway 18 to Route 9. Turn right on Route 9 for 25 km (15 miles) into Windsor. The southernmost city in Canada, Windsor is an important industrial center and is heavily involved with the automobile industry based in Detroit across the river.

Route 9 becomes Howard Avenue. Take Howard Avenue through Windsor to Wyandotte Street. Turn right on Wyandotte Street, then left on Walker Street to Riverside Drive along the Detroit River. Turn right on Riverside Drive. At Puce, ride along Highway 2. Past Belle River, turn off Highway 2 onto County Road 2 along the shore of Lake St. Clair.

Stay on County Road 2. Past Jeannettes Creek, it becomes County Road 36. Ride County Road 36 along the south side of the Thames River into Chatham, 80 km (50 miles) from Windsor. Like its namesake in England, the town is situated near the mouth of the Thames River. Before the American Civil War, Chatham was a northern terminus of the "Underground Railroad," a secret route which brought slaves from the southern states north to freedom.

In Chatham take Highway 40 south to County Road 18. Turn left onto County Road 18 and take it to Highway 21. Turn left onto Highway 21 to Thamesville, 28 km (17 miles) from Chatham, and then right onto Highway 2. Turn left onto County Road 22, and then right onto County Road 14. Ride County Road 14 into London, 80 km (50 miles) from Thamesville.

Grand River Valley Tour

The historic valley of the Grand River is an area of woodlots and rolling hills. At Elora Gorge the Grand River flows swiftly through a 22-meter (70-foot) deep gorge.

Brantford, this tour's starting point, was named for Indian Chief Joseph Brant, who led the Six Nations Indians from their lands in upper New York State to this site on the Grand River. Brantford is also known as the place where Alexander Graham Bell invented the telephone.

On this route you go past Cambridge's stately stone buildings and through Kitchener, which is known for its annual Oktoberfest celebrations. Kitchener is in Amish and Mennonite farm country, and has had a farmers' market since 1830, where a wide range of produce is sold by vendors, many of them Mennonites. At West Montrose is Ontario's last covered bridge.

LENGTH: 225 km (140 miles)

START: Brantford, served by VIA Rail

THE ROUTE: Take Highway 2 (called Brant Avenue, and later Paris Road) out of Brantford. Turn right onto Golf Road, and when it ends turn left onto Highway 5. Turn right at the edge of Paris onto County Road 53 (Green Lane). Go right again onto the East River Road (County Road 14) through to Glen Morris, then left onto County Road 28 across the Grand River. Turn right and follow along the West River Road, which offers scenic views of the river valley.

Follow this road into Cambridge, where it becomes Glenmorris Street. Go right on Cedar Street, and then turn left onto Blair Road (which becomes County Road 42). Follow Blair Road out of Cambridge to Fountain Street. Turn left onto Fountain Street and ride over Highway 401 and into the village of Doon.

.The road becomes Huron Road Boulevard. Turn right onto Manitou Drive, which becomes Courtland Avenue. Follow this road into Kitchener, a ride of 40 km (25 miles) from Brantford. Turn right onto Ottawa Street, then left onto Weber Street. Follow Weber Street through Waterloo. Turn right on Northfield Drive

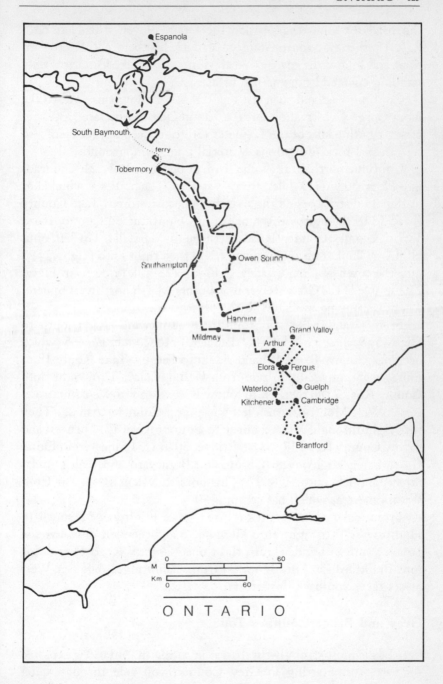

Espanola

South Baymouth.

ferry

Tobermory

Southampton

Owen Sound

Hanover

Mildmay

Grand Valley

Arthur

Elora   Fergus

Waterloo   Guelph

Kitchener   Cambridge

Brantford

M 0   60

Km 0   60

O N T A R I O

and head for Conestogo beside the Grand River. Turn left onto R.R.17, then right onto County Road 22. Just before R.R.86, turn right and follow the road to West Montrose, where Ontario's only standing covered bridge is still in use.

Continue east and turn left on R.R.23. Follow this road to the Elora Gorge Conservation Area, a picturesque 134-hectare (330-acre) park on both banks of the 22-meter (70-foot) deep gorge. Here also are unusual rock formations, waterfalls and campgrounds.

Continue north on the same road. It becomes R.R.21, and leads into Elora, 30 km (19 miles) from Waterloo. The houses and buildings of the old district beside the river have been restored. Take County Road 18 to the nearby town of Fergus. Continue on County Road 18 (it becomes County Road 3) through Marsville. Go left onto Highway 25, left onto Highway 9, and then right onto Highway 25 into the town of Grand Valley, a 40-km (25-mile) ride from Elora. The source of the Grand River is at Luther Marsh northwest of here. There is camping available nearby.

From Grand Valley the tour turns southward. Ride south to Highway 9. Take a quick right, then left, onto County Road 5 (which becomes County Road 19) and ride into Fergus. Take Route 18 to Elora, a 35-km (22-mile) ride from Grand Valley. Turn right onto County Road 7 and then left to follow River Road to West Montrose.

At West Montrose, turn left and go up County Road 23. Then turn right through Winterbourne to County Road 17. Turn left and follow County Road 17 to Cambridge, 50 km (31 miles) from Elora. Go right on Highway 8 (Coronation Boulevard and then Dundas Street) and left onto R.R.97. This goes to Valens Reservoir Conservation Area, which has camping.

From Valens Conservation Area, take Highway 52 south to Highway 5. Turn right onto Highway 5 and then left onto Lynden Road. South of Lynden, turn right onto County Road 11 and ride into Brantford, 50 km (31 miles) from Cambridge. A left at West Street takes you back downtown.

Grey and Bruce Counties Tour

One of the most strongly rural areas in southern Ontario is explored on this tour. Starting in Grey County, you ride through quiet villages and along roads through rolling hills to the Bruce Peninsula, which divides Lake Huron and Georgian Bay. On the Bruce Peninsula you take a road that winds beneath the limestone cliffs of the Niagara Escarpment, along the shore of Georgian Bay.

You can see caves and rock pillars called flowerpots. Along the edge of the escarpment is the Bruce Trail. At Tobermory there is scuba diving at Fathom Five Underwater Provincial Park. Riding south you go along Lake Huron's sandy beaches.

LENGTH: 500 km (310 miles)

START: Guelph, served by VIA Rail

THE ROUTE: From Guelph, take Norfolk Street (which becomes Highway 6) to County Road 7. Ride County Road 7 to County Road 12, turn right and ride into Arthur, a distance of 40 km (25 miles) from Guelph.

From Arthur, go north on Highway 6, then turn right at a large church onto the Conn Road (County Road 14). Follow this flat road to Conn. Turn right onto Highway 89, and then left onto County Road 14, and ride past swampy lakes with few farms. At Highway 4, turn left and follow the rolling hills into Durham, a 70-km (44-mile) ride from Arthur. There is great swimming here, plus overnight camping.

Follow Highway 4 for 19 km (12 miles) west of Durham to Hanover. Go north on County Road 10 (signed to Elmwood) which has some cottage traffic. Turn right onto County Road 25 and then left onto County Road 3. It is gravel at first and then pavement.

Go north on County Road 3 and turn right on County Road 4 to Desboro. The road bends north and then east. Turn left at the second road past the big bend north of Desboro. Follow County Road 5 into Owen Sound, a 60-km (37-mile) ride from Hanover. Owen Sound is a port town on Georgian Bay, surrounded by the limestone cliffs of the Niagara Escarpment.

Take the Balmy Beach Road (County Road 1) up the scenic shore of the peninsula along the clear waters of Georgian Bay. Follow County Road 1 through Kemble and onto some gravel. (Route 26 through Big Bay along the shore is a bad gravel road and not recommended for cycling.)

At Highway 6 turn right and go into Wiarton, an old-world town on Colpoys Bay at the base of the Bruce Peninsula. It's a 40-km (25-mile) ride from Owen Sound to Wiarton. Go north from Wiarton on Highway 6. Go right on County Road 9 through Lion's Head, situated on a sheltered harbor. At the T-junction go left on County Road 9A to Highway 6, and then go right on Highway 6. Along the way is the turn-off for Cyprus Lake Provincial Park, which offers camping. Follow Highway 6 to Tobermory, a 75-km (47-mile) ride from Wiarton.

At Tobermory, at the tip of the peninsula, is Fathom Five Underwater Provincial Park offering scuba diving among wrecks in the waters of Georgian Bay. Flowerpot Island, part of Georgian Bay Islands National Park, abounds in caves and walking trails. It is the terminus for the ferry *M.S.S. Chi-Cheemaun* (Ojibway for "the big canoe") to South Baymouth on Manitoulin Island. (A tour of Manitoulin Island is described separately in this chapter.)

From Tobermory, head south on Highway 6 and take the turn-off for Pike Bay. Follow this road along the shore of Lake Huron, through Howdenvale and Red Bay. You connect with County Road 21. Follow County Road 21 through Sauble Falls and Sauble Beach to Southampton, a 100-km (62-mile) ride from Tobermory. Turn right onto Highway 21. When you're out of town, turn left onto County Road 3. Take this road through Paisley and the rolling hills past the Saugeen Bluffs Conservation Area. Continue south on County Road 3, and turn right on Highway 4. Go left onto County Road 12 and through Formosa, the site of the old Formosa Springs Brewery.

Continue south on County Road 12, and turn left onto County Road 24 to Mildmay, a 70-km (44-mile) trip from Southampton. Go north on Highway 9 and then turn right onto County Road 16 to Neustadt. This is the birthplace of Prime Minister John Diefenbaker.

Turn right onto County Road 10 to Clifford. Go left onto County Road 2 to Highway 89. This area is Old Order Mennonite country. You might see a few horse-drawn buggies. Go left and follow Highway 89 to County Road 6. Turn right onto County Road 6 and follow this scenic road to Highway 9. Turn left onto Highway 9 and follow it into Arthur, 75 km (47 miles) from Mildmay. From Arthur, retrace the 40-km (25-mile) route to Guelph, this tour's starting point.

MORE INFORMATION: A map-brochure on cycling in Grey and Bruce counties is available from: Grey Bruce Tourist Association, R.R.5, Owen Sound, Ontario N4K 5N7. Telephone (519) 371-2071 or 1-800-265-3127.

The Tobermory-South Baymouth ferry is operated by Ontario Northland Marine Services, 1155 First Avenue West, Owen Sound, Ontario N4K 4K8. Telephone (519) 376-6601.

Manitoulin Island Loop

The world's largest freshwater-surrounded island, Manitoulin Island has sand beaches along its picturesque shoreline, numerous lakes and bays, and quiet towns and villages. Only 80 km (50 miles) long and ranging from 5 to 75 km (3 to 47 miles) in width, the island has more than twenty inland lakes. Along the island's north shore are cliffs ringing fjord-like bays. High on the cliffs are hiking trails and picnic sites. On the south side are flat plains. At one time an Indian stronghold, Manitoulin Island today has six Indian reserves.

LENGTH: 132 km (82 miles)

START: South Baymouth, reached by ferry from Tobermory

THE ROUTE: From South Baymouth, ride along Highway 6 for 13 km (8 miles) to the junction with Route 542. Go left on Route 542 through Sandfield to Mindemoya, 26 km (16 miles) farther.

Go north from Mindemoya for 12 km (7.4 miles) to West Bay, an Indian reserve. Turn right and ride Route 540 for 30 km (18 miles) along the base of the escarpment to Little Current. From Little Current you can go north for 53 km (33 miles) on Highway 6, across the white La Cloche Mountains which rise from Georgian Bay. Passing through the town of Espanola to Highway 17, you can link up with the Across Ontario Tour, described separately in this chapter.

To continue the loop tour of Manitoulin Island, ride south from Little Current on Highway 6 for 64 km (40 miles) to South Baymouth, this tour's starting point.

Prince Edward County: Quinte's Isle

Sand dunes and villages untouched by time characterize this rural peninsula on Lake Ontario, just south of Belleville. Prince Edward County—within easy reach by train or car from Toronto, Ottawa, and Montreal—is a popular tourist area for a weekend, or for a longer tour.

The spectacular sand dunes of Sandbanks Provincial Park, and the wide beaches washed by the waves of Lake Ontario, are reminiscent of an ocean setting. Prince Edward County's beaches are within an easy day's ride of Belleville.

Settled by the United Empire Loyalists after the American Revolution, the county has retained its unhurried pace and charming nineteenth-century homes. It lacks the commercialism found in other areas of such natural beauty.

LENGTH: 40 km (64 miles) each way

START: Belleville, which can be reached by VIA Rail.

THE ROUTE: Ride through Belleville and cross the bridge to Prince Edward County. Follow Highway 14, which begins at the bridge, for 28 km (17 miles) to Bloomfield. Then take County Road 12 for 10 km (6 miles) to Sandbanks Provincial Park. The 3-km (1.8-mile) sandbar at the park juts into Wellington Bay, almost touching the other side at the town of Wellington.

Explore Sandbanks Park and then use it as a base to explore the county's narrow, tree-lined country roads. You pedal past cornfields, cow barns, and orchards. In addition to Sandbanks Park there are two day-use parks well worth visiting. North Beach Provincial Park, similar to Sandbanks, has a 1.2-km (0.7-mile) bay-mouth sandbar sheltering North Bay from Lake Ontario. Take Highway 33 west for 25 km (15 miles) from Bloomfield through Wellington to North Beach Park.

On the other side of the county is Lake on the Mountain Provincial Park. It borders a small lake, a stone's throw from the edge of the Prince Edward Escarpment which rises nearly 62 meters (204 feet)

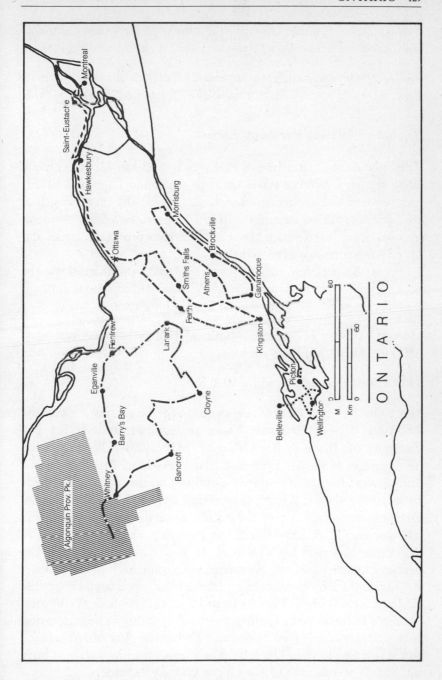

over the Bay of Quinte. Go east on Highway 33 for 18 km (11 miles) from Bloomfield through Picton to Lake on the Mountain Park.

MORE INFORMATION: Park Superintendent, Sandbanks Provincial Park, R.R.1, Picton, Ontario K0K 2T0. Telephone (613) 393-3314.

Thousand Islands Parkway Loop

The famous Thousand Islands Parkway is a 35-km (22-mile) route along the St. Lawrence River through the scenic Thousand Islands area between Gananoque and Brockville. Beside the entire length of the parkway is a new (completed in 1987), paved, two-lane, 1.8-meter (6-foot) wide bicycle path. En route are two provincial parks and St. Lawrence Islands National Park.

From the parkway bicycle path, this tour continues along the St. Lawrence River to Upper Canada Village. It then returns through a rural area of forests and lakes to form a loop tour.

LENGTH: 35 km (22 miles); Thousand Islands Bikeway one way, 220 km (135 miles) loop

START: Gananoque, served by VIA Rail

THE ROUTE: From Gananoque, cycle on the bicycle path along the Thousand Islands Parkway. There are campgrounds at Ivy Lea Campsite and Brown's Bay Campsite. Mallorytown Landing is the headquarters of the St. Lawrence Islands National Park. There is a campground here, and primitive campsites on thirteen of the park's twenty-two islands, which are accessible only by boat. Commercial water taxis operate between the mainland and the park's islands. The parkway ends at Brockville, a 35-km (22-mile) ride from Gananoque. Brockville is served by VIA Rail. If you want to cycle just the parkway bicycle path, you can retrace your route back to Gananoque.

To ride the loop route, continue along Highway 2 from Brockville. At Prescott, 20 km (12 miles) from Brockville, is Fort Wellington National Historic Park. The first British fort at this strategic location on the St. Lawrence River was built during the War of 1812. It fell to ruins after the war. The second fort now standing here was built in 1838-39 in response to the Upper Canada Rebellion.

Near Morrisburg is Upper Canada Village, a recreated nineteenth-century pioneer village including a millstone, sawmill, blacksmith shop, and general store, and corduroy roads. You can spend a whole day exploring the extensive site. It's a 45-km (28-mile) ride from Prescott to Upper Canada Village.

From Upper Canada Village, go north on Route 8 and turn left onto Route 18. At Route 1 turn right, then turn left onto Route 21. Turn right on Route 15 to North Augusta, and then go left on Route 28 to Highway 29. Take Highway 29 west to Athens, an 85-km (53-mile) ride from Upper Canada Village. Then take Route 40. Along the way is Charleston Lake Provincial Park, which offers camping and hiking trails.

Go left on Route 2 and then left onto Route 3 at Lyndhurst. Ride through Outlet and Lansdowne to the Thousand Island Parkway just east of Gananoque, a 45-km (28-mile) trip from Athens and this tour's starting point.

MORE INFORMATION: The St. Lawrence Parks Commission, Box 740, Morrisburg, Ontario K0C 1X0. Telephone (613) 543-2951.

Park Superintendent, St. Lawrence Islands National Park, Box 469, R.R.3, Mallorytown Landing, Ontario K0E 1R0. Telephone (613) 923-5261.

Algonquin Provincial Park Loop

The land of lakes, rivers, hills and forests east of Algonquin Provincial Park is explored on this hilly circuit tour. This picturesque region is on the Frontenac Axis, a southern extension of the rocky Precambrian Shield. In this transition zone between the northern and southern forests, flora and fauna of both forest types are found together.

At Bon Echo Provincial Park you can hear your echo on Mazinaw Rock, a 114-meter (275-foot) cliff that drops to Lake Mazinaw. Indian pictographs can be seen at canoe level.

Algonquin is Ontario's oldest provincial park, as well as one of its best-known. Its wilderness offers camping, canoeing, and hiking, and there are exhibits about the park's pioneer logging past.

LENGTH: 460 km (285 miles)

START: Renfrew, situated 130 km (80 miles) west of Ottawa and 320 km (200 miles) northeast of Toronto, is the only town on this loop served by VIA Rail.

THE ROUTE: From Renfrew, go east on County Road 6 and turn right on County Road 2 for 15 km (9 miles) to Burnstown. Go right onto hilly County Road 508 for 16 km (10 miles) to Calabogie. This is a ski area. Turn left onto Secondary Highway 511 and ride 54 km (34 miles) to Lanark, and then go right on County Road 12 for 25 km (16 miles) to Elphin. Go right on County Road 36 for 5 km (3 miles) to Snow Road Station.

Go right on Secondary Highway 509 through Ompah, Plevna, and Fernleigh, where the road becomes Secondary Highway 506. Ride Secondary Highway 506 to Highway 41, a ride of 65 km (40 miles) from Snow Road Station. Turn right at Highway 41 through Cloyne.

Along the way is the entrance to Bon Echo Provincial Park, which offers camping, canoeing, and hiking. The scenic highlight of this 66-square-km (25-square-mile) park is Mazinaw Rock, a 114-meter (275-foot) cliff that drops to Mazinaw Lake. The name Bon Echo refers to the rock's acoustic properties. Scattered along the rock at canoe level are scores of Indian pictographs.

Turn left onto Highway 28 at Denbigh, situated 45 km (28 miles) from Cloyne. Continue for 60 km (38 miles) on the hilly road through McArthur Mills and Hermon to Bancroft, the major center for the Hastings Highlands area. The region offers swimming, canoeing, and fishing and is a well-known center for rock collectors. Stock up on food supplies at Bancroft as there are few facilities between here and Barry's Bay (or Whitney, if you're taking a side trip into Algonquin Park). From Bancroft take Highway 62 north to Maynooth, then take Highway 127 and turn right onto Secondary Highway 523. It connects with Highway 60, a ride of 60 km (38 miles) from Bancroft.

If you want to take a side trip to Algonquin Provincial Park, continue for 39 km (24 miles) on Highway 127 from Maynooth, to Highway 60 near Whitney. Turn left and ride into the park. Located on the southern edge of the Precambrian Shield, Algonquin Park is 7,600 square km (2,925 square miles) of rounded hills, rocky ridges, spruce bogs, fast-flowing rivers, and thousands of lakes, ponds, and streams. You can camp, canoe, and hike. The park's museum and a pioneer logging exhibit are worth a visit. To leave the park, ride east on Highway 60 and rejoin this loop tour just past Madawaska.

Continuing the loop tour, go east on Highway 60 through the lumber town of Barry's Bay, 28 km (17 miles) from the junction with Secondary Highway 523. At Barry's Bay you can arrange river rafting trips. Take Highway 62 for 18 km (11 miles). Just east of Combermere, take Secondary Highway 515 and turn left onto the county road through Rockingham. At the T-junction go left. At the next T-junction go right, and ride the hilly county road east to Secondary Highway 512. Follow Secondary Highway 512 to Foymount, 25 km (15 miles) from Highway 62.

Just past Foymount, go left along Secondary Highway 512 for 25 km (15 miles) to Eganville, which is in a deep valley bisected by the Bonnechere River. You can visit the nearby Bonnechere Caves in summer. Cross Highway 41 and follow the county road along the Bonnechere River to Secondary Highway 513. Go left on Secondary Highway 513. It soon becomes County Road 22. Turn right on County Road 5 to Highway 132. Turn left and ride into Renfrew, 35 km (22 miles) from Eganville and this tour's starting point.

Rideau River Loop

The scenic Rideau Canal system linking Kingston and Ottawa was built after the War of 1812 to ensure that British gunboats could travel from Ottawa to Kingston on Lake Ontario without the threat of attack from American shore batteries along the St. Lawrence River. Built from 1826 to 1832, the Rideau system spans 200 km (125 miles) including forty-nine locks and 19 km (12 miles) of excavated channels. The canal was never used in a war, but it became an artery for immigration and commerce. Today it is popular with recreational boaters.

The country crossed by the Rideau waterway includes beautiful lakes, forests, rocky granite hills, and rolling farmland. This loop tour takes you on backroads through the scenic attractions from Kingston to Ottawa.

Kingston, strategically located at the point where Lake Ontario flows into the St. Lawrence River, is at the southern end of the Rideau Canal. The city has an impressive concentration of nineteenth-century buildings, including Old Fort Henry, which was one of Canada's mightiest fortresses, and Bellevue House, once the home of Sir John A. Macdonald, Canada's first prime minister.

Ottawa, the capital of Canada, is situated at the junction of the Rideau River and the Ottawa River. It has many attractions worth visiting, including the Parliament Buildings, which house Canada's government, and a variety of museums.

LENGTH: 340 km (210 miles)

START: Kingston or Ottawa, both served by VIA Rail

THE ROUTE: From Kingston, take County Road 11 north through Sunbury, Battersea and Jones Falls to Highway 15. Go north on Highway 15. At Crosby, take County Road 14 and turn right onto County Road 21. Along the way is Murphys Point Provincial Park, which offers camping. Go right onto County Road 1, and then left onto County Road 18 to Port Elmsley.

Turn right on Highway 43 for Smiths Falls, a 100-km (62-mile) ride from Kingston. At one time Smiths Falls was an important trading center and railway junction. For boats traveling the Rideau Canal, this is the halfway point.

Take County Road 4 out of Smiths Falls. After crossing County Road 3, it becomes County Road 6. Continue on County Road 6 through North Gower and across the Rideau River. Turn left onto County Road 19 along the Rideau River into Ottawa, where this route becomes River Road. It's 75 km (47 miles) to Ottawa from Smiths Falls. The capital city has many attractions, including its scenic network of bicycle paths along the Rideau Canal and the Rideau River.

When you leave Ottawa, take River Road (County Road 19). Continue along County Road 19, turn right on County Road 8, and cross the river to Manotick. Turn right when you get to County

Road 49. Go left onto County Road 10, and follow it through Franktown to Perth, an 80-km (50-mile) ride from Ottawa. One of Ontario's oldest towns, Perth is known for its old stone buildings. Many of them were built by stonemasons who settled here after completing the Rideau Canal.

Continue on County Road 10 (the Perth Road), which was built as a colonization road to help settle this area, through Westport at the head of Upper Rideau Lake. Take the Perth Road through Inverary, past the Cataraqui Creek Conservation Area, and over Highway 401 into Kingston, 80 km (50 miles) from Perth.

Ottawa to Montreal

The Ottawa River was an important route into Canada's interior. It was traveled by explorers and fur traders, and by pioneering loggers and settlers. Today the river is the boundary between the provinces of Ontario and Quebec. The valley on both sides of the river consists of rustic farmhouses and barns and French-Canadian villages. From the valley are views of the mountains of Quebec across the river. This two-day tour takes you along both banks of the river through the Ottawa Valley, along quiet country roads.

LENGTH: 180 km (112 miles) one way

START: Ottawa, served by VIA Rail and an airport

THE ROUTE: From Ottawa take Innis Road, which becomes County Road 30. Ride County Road 30 and turn left onto County Road 35 for 25 km (15 miles) to Highway 17. Turn right onto Highway 17 for 15 km (9 miles). Take the turn-off for Clarence, and ride along the Ottawa River through Wendover. Past Wendover ride Highway 17 to County Road 9, a 22-km (14-mile) ride from Clarence. Turn left on County Road 9 for 5 km (3 miles) to Treadwell. Go right onto County Road 24, through Lefaivre and along the river. Past L'Orignal the route becomes County Road 4.

Cycle into Hawkesbury, a 35-km (22-mile) ride from Treadwell, and cross the bridge over the Ottawa River and into the province of Quebec. Turn right and ride Route 344 along the north side of the river. Near Oka, 53 km (33 miles) from Hawkesbury, is Paul Sauvé Provincial Park which offers camping.

From Oka, take Route 344 to St. Eustache. Cross the Arthur Sauve Bridge onto Laval and take Route 148 to Route 117. Go right on Route 117 across the Lachapelle Bridge and into Montreal, a 40-km (25-mile) ride from Oka. (The Montreal to Oka route is described in more detail in the Quebec chapter.)

Thunder Bay to Sibley Provincial Park

From Thunder Bay, you have a view of the "Sleeping Giant," a huge rock peninsula that rises from the water. According to Ojibway Indian legend, Nanibijou, the "Great Spirit" who lived on Mount McKay, watched to keep them safe as they crossed Lake Superior. To reward the Ojibway for their loyalty, Nanibijou revealed to them a rich silver mine. He warned them that any white men who learned of it would perish, while Nanibijou himself would turn to stone. A treacherous Indian did tell the white man, but as their canoes drew near, a huge storm broke upon them, and they drowned. In the morning, Nanibijou had turned to stone. He lay sleeping, with his arms folded on his chest, across the mouth of Thunder Bay.

The Sleeping Giant is the high limestone cliff at the southwest end of Sibley Provincial Park. The park lies on the Sibley Peninsula, which is 40 km (25 miles) long and 13 km (8 miles) wide and juts into Lake Superior. The western shore of the 263-square-km (101-square-mile) park is dominated by cliffs rising 240 meters (800 feet). The park has about 80 km (50 miles) of interconnecting hiking trails, including the Kabeyan Trail which circles the tip of the Sleeping Giant.

This tour from Thunder Bay to Sibley Park is a good two- or three-day trip, with time to explore the Sleeping Giant.

LENGTH: 83 km (52 miles) each way

START: Thunder Bay, which is served by VIA Rail and an airport

THE ROUTE: From Thunder Bay, take Route 11B/17B (Memorial Street, then Cumberland Street) to Hodder Avenue. Turn right onto

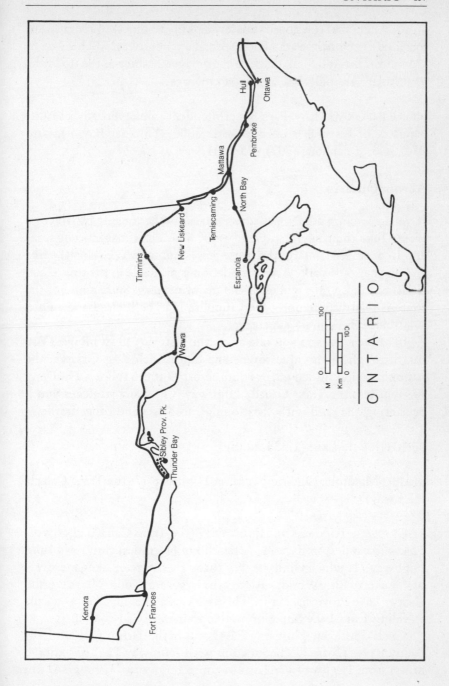

Route 11/17 and ride approximately 30 km (18 miles) to the turn-off for Sibley Provincial Park. Ride Secondary Highway 587 for 42 km (26 miles) through Sibley Park to the village of Sibley at the tip of the Peninsula. Camping is available at the park.

MORE INFORMATION: Park Superintendent, Sibley Provincial Park, Ministry of Natural Resources, Box 5000, Thunder Bay, Ontario P7C 5G6. Telephone (807) 475-1531.

Across Ontario

If you're cycling across Canada, Ontario is the longest province to cross. Take the time to stop and enjoy Ontario's magnificent scenery. In northern Ontario the route passes numerous provincial parks and one national park. Accommodation is available in the towns and cities. Stock up on supplies in the major centers. Since some of the route is relatively remote, food supplies may be limited and, when available, can be more expensive.

In eastern Ontario you ride along the historic Ottawa River. You pass through picturesque towns and cities, including Ottawa, the nation's capital. Much of the route across Ontario follows Highway 17, which is the Trans Canada Highway. On many stretches you'll be sharing the road with vacationing motorists and other traffic.

LENGTH: 2,137 km (1,328 miles)

START: Manitoba-Ontario border at Highway 17 (the Trans Canada Highway)

THE ROUTE: Ride east on Highway 17 (the Trans Canada Highway) 52 km (32 miles) to Kenora. After 20 km (13 miles) turn right onto Highway 71, which winds its way through a maze of lakes and rivers past Lake of the Woods. Along the way are Sioux Narrows and Caliper Lake Provincial Parks. This area was a vital link for voyageurs traveling from Lake Superior to the prairies.

Cycle south on Highway 71 through the farming area of the Rainy River District. The junction with Highway 11 is 157 km (98 miles) from Highway 17. Turn left onto Highway 11 and go 41 km

(25 miles) to Fort Frances, and continue east through hilly forested country. Located 22 km (14 miles) past Atikokan is the turn-off for Quetico Provincial Park, a 4,669-square-km (1,800-square-mile) wilderness famous for its spectacular canoeing. The park also offers camping and hiking.

Back on Highway 11, it's 118 km (73 miles) east to the junction with Highway 17. Another 64 km (40 miles) takes you to Thunder Bay. Along the way is magnificent 39-meter (128-foot) Kakabeka Falls. Adjacent to the falls is a provincial park offering camping.

From Thunder Bay, cycle Highway 17 along the north shore of Lake Superior. To enjoy this route fully stop often and savor the area's natural beauty. Some of the highlights are Sibley Provincial Park (described separately in this chapter) and Rainbow Falls Provincial Park. Pukaskwa National Park, 25 km (15 miles) east of Marathon, is a rugged wilderness which preserves the coast of Lake Superior and offers shoreline hiking trails, canoeing, and camping. It's 470 km (292 miles) from Thunder Bay to Wawa.

Turn off Highway 17 at Wawa and ride east on Highway 101 past The Shoals Provincial Park and Ivanhoe Lake Provincial Park through Timmins, once the largest producer of gold in the Western Hemisphere. Ride to Matheson, an agricultural center at the junction with Highway 11, a distance of 400 km (250 miles). Turn south on Highway 11 for 140 km (87 miles) to New Liskeard. It is on Lake Temiskaming and is surrounded by farmland. From New Liskeard, go east on Highway 65 for 27 km (16 miles) across the Quebec border to Notre Dame du Nord.

Go south on Quebec Highway 101 for 159 km (99 miles) to Temiscaming, then cross the Ottawa River and ride back into Ontario. Take Highway 63 for 24 km (15 miles) and then go east on Secondary Highway 533 for 54 km (33 miles) to Mattawa on the Ottawa River. This northern route is about 87 km (54 miles) longer than following Highway 17 the whole way through Sault Ste. Marie, but it has a lot less heavy traffic.

If you want to head to southern Ontario, you can ride west on Highway 17 through North Bay and Sudbury to Espanola, a distance of 257 km (160 miles). Then take Highway 6 through the La Cloche Mountains to Little Current on Manitoulin Island (a tour of the island is described separately in this chapter) and the ferry to Tobermory on the Bruce Peninsula (also described separately in this chapter) and southern Ontario.

If you are continuing east across Ontario from Mattawa, cycle east on Highway 17 through Deep River and Chalk River. Soon after passing Canadian Forces Base Petawawa, take County Road 17 through McGuire to the city of Pembroke, 150 km (93 miles) east of Mattawa.

Leave Pembroke by Highway 148 and follow it across Allumette Lake into Quebec. Follow Quebec Highway 148 along the north side of the Ottawa River which, in this area, generally has less traffic than Highway 17 on the river's south side. Ride Highway 148 for 150 km (93 miles) to Hull. Cross the Ottawa River into the city of Ottawa. From here follow the Ottawa to Montreal Tour (described separately in this chapter) and you're in Quebec.

Guidebooks

The Great Toronto Bicycling Guide, by Elliott Katz. Available from: Great North Books, Box 507, Station Z, Toronto, Ontario M5N 2Z6. Price $3.95.

Ontario Cycling Route Map Series: 1. Southwestern Ontario (Windsor/London areas); 2. Western Ontario (London/Waterloo areas); 3. Bruce Peninsula/Manitoulin Island; 4. Golden Horseshoe (Niagara/Toronto areas); 5. Muskoka/Haliburton; 6. Lake Ontario/St. Lawrence (Peterborough/Kingston areas); 7. Ottawa Valley (Ottawa/Renfrew areas). Available from: Ontario Cycling Association, 1220 Sheppard Avenue East, Willowdale, Ontario M2K 2X1. Price $4.00 each, or $22.00 for a set of seven.

Pedal Niagara, edited by Jim Couper. Available from: Freewheeling Niagara, R.R.2, Wainfleet, Ontario L0S 1V0. Price $3.95 ($4.50 postpaid).

10 Quebec

Quebec's beauty, charm, and *joie de vivre* are best experienced by bicycle. Ride along the St. Lawrence River through historic villages and see traditional woodcarvers at work. Enjoy the province's special ambience everywhere; in the lively Laurentian Mountain villages, at Percé in the Gaspé, or on the sand beaches of the Îles de la Madeleine. Quebec's French language and culture makes touring in Quebec a bit like exploring a foreign country. Most residents, however, do speak some English.

The largest province in Canada, Quebec's 1,540,595 square km (594,860 square miles) is greater than the combined areas of France, Germany, and Spain. The province's three main geological regions are the Canadian Shield stretching north of the St. Lawrence River to Hudson Bay, the Appalachian region south of the St. Lawrence, and the St. Lawrence Lowlands between the Canadian Shield and the Appalachian region.

The Canadian Shield, known in southern Quebec as the Laurentians, forms an immense rolling plateau covered with a coniferous forest and many rivers and lakes. Quebec's Appalachian region, an extension of the Appalachian Mountains of the eastern United States, is a succession of plateaus and plains. The 900-meter (3,000-foot) Chic-Choc Mountains in the Gaspé are a continuation of the 600- to 900-meter (2,000- to 3,000-foot) Sutton, Stoke, and Megantic ranges of the Eastern Townships region southeast of Montreal.

ROADS: Quebec roads generally do not have paved shoulders. The limited-access expressways have paved shoulders, but do not permit bicycles.

WEATHER: Most of Quebec experiences a temperate climate with hot summers and cold winters. Average rainfall during the summer months is around 11 cm (4 inches) per month. Quebec's mild autumn temperatures provide comfortable cycling weather at the time when the forests are a dazzling kaleidoscope of blazing colors. This is the time of year when the countryside is at its peak of beauty and should not be missed.

TOURIST INFORMATION: For general tourist information, including a road map and camping and hotel directories, contact: Tourism Quebec, Box 20,000, Quebec City, Quebec G1K 7X2. Telephone: in Montreal, (514) 873-2015; elsewhere in Quebec call toll-free 1-800-361-5405; in Ontario, New Brunswick, and Prince Edward Island, 1-800-361-6490; in the eastern United States, 1-800-443-7000.

HOSTELS: Hostels in Quebec are operated by the Quebec Hostelling Federation, 4545 Avenue Pierre du Coubertin, Montreal, Quebec H1V 3R2. Telephone (514) 252-3117.

AIRPORTS: Montreal and Quebec are served by major airlines, and have connections to smaller centers.

TRAINS: For information on VIA Rail service, call: in Montreal (514) 871-1331; in Quebec City (418) 692-3940, elsewhere in Quebec, call toll-free 1-800-361-5390. Bicycles are carried at no extra charge on trains that have a baggage car.

BUSES: Voyageur Bus Lines requires that bicycles be dismantled and boxed. They are charged at the bus parcel rate for an 11-kg (25-pound) parcel.

BICYCLING: Vélo-Quebec, 4545 Avenue Pierre du Coubertin, Box 1000, Station M, Montreal, Quebec M1V 3R2. Telephone (514) 252-3123.

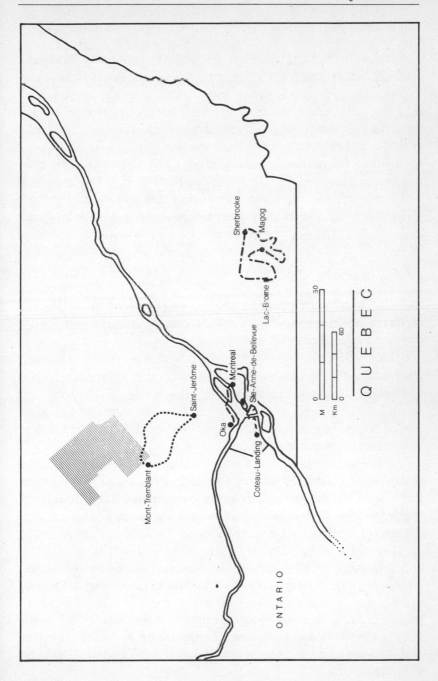

Laurentian Mountains

Known as Quebec's "Little Switzerland," the Laurentians is a beautiful district of wooded hills, glacier-worn mountains, lakes, and valleys. The region has many inns, motels, hotels, resorts, and campgrounds. Follow the winding country roads to unspoiled mountain villages, many over one hundred years old. You can swim, fish, canoe, and boat.

Fall turns the foliage into a display of blazing colors. This tour explores picturesque secondary roads east and west of Highway 117 and the Laurentian Autoroute, the main roads into the Laurentians from Montreal. The route is mountainous with some climbing and makes a good two- or three-day tour near Montreal.

LENGTH: 211 km (131 miles)

START: St-Jérôme, 56 km (35 miles) north of Montreal. St-Jérôme is served by Voyageur bus. (See the chapter introduction for its policy on transporting bicycles.)

THE ROUTE: From St-Jérôme, known as the "Gateway to the Laurentians," take the road through Lafontaine to St-Hippolyte on Lac Echo. Then head to Ste-Marguerite on the shores of Lac Masson. The route is steep and climbs constantly. Ride to Ste-Lucie where there is a public beach.

From Ste-Lucie, the route turns southwest, continues to climb and passes several lakes on the way to Lac Brulé near Ste-Agathe-des-Monts, the largest center in the Laurentians. Take Route 329 north for 6 km (3.7 miles), turn left onto a secondary road, and ride 17 km (10.5 miles) to Lac-Carré located north of St-Faustin.

Head north toward Lac-Supérieur and turn west. Go through the southern edge of Mont-Tremblant Park to the village of Mont-Tremblant. Mont-Tremblant Park, 2,564 square km (990 square miles), offers camping, hiking trails, swimming, canoeing, and fishing.

From the village of Mont-Tremblant, take Route 327 south through St-Jovite and along the winding banks of the Rouge River and the Diable River. At Arundel, 19 km (12 miles) away, you cross a covered bridge.

Go east on Route 364 through Weir to Lac-des-Seize-Îles, another 16 km (10 miles) away. Another 21 km (13 miles) farther is the English community of Morin Heights, where there is a campground. Picturesque St-Sauveur, 11 km (7 miles) from Morin Heights, is a charming village with boutiques and cafes in a valley surrounded by popular ski hills.

To get from St-Sauveur back to St-Jérôme, cross Autoroute 15 on the overpass and take Highway 117 south for several kilometers. Go right on Chemin de Lac Marois, and then left on Montée Filion to Chemin Rivière des Lacs. Take Chemin Rivière des Lacs to the village of Bellefeuille, which has camping. Return to St-Jérôme by Boulevard de la Salette, Chemin de la Montagne, and Boulevard Demartigny.

MORE INFORMATION: Park Superintendent, Mont-Tremblant Park, Box 129, St-Faustin, Quebec J0T 2G0. Telephone (819) 698-2336.

The Eastern Townships

Situated southeast of Montreal, the Eastern Townships — known in French as *l'Estrie* — is part of the Appalachian Mountain chain. The region of forests, lakes, and farms is a northern extension of the Green Mountains of Vermont. Both areas share the same magnificent mountain and rural scenery, but relatively few cyclists have discovered the Eastern Townships, compared to the throngs of cyclists touring in Vermont just across the border. This region is also known for its art and culture. During summer several theaters are open, and there are concerts at the Orford Art Centre. North Hatley is known for its handicrafts. There are numerous accommodations and campgrounds along the route.

LENGTH: 223 km (138 miles) loop

START: Sherbrooke is the largest city in the Eastern Townships. It is served by VIA Rail from Montreal on its service to Halifax, and by Voyageur bus.

THE ROUTE: From Sherbrooke, head south on Queen Sud to Lennoxville, and then take Route 108 to the town of North Hatley on Lake

Massawippi. Here you will find a summer theatre, antique shops, and the work of craftsmen and artists. Continue on Route 108 to Ste-Catherine-de-Hatley and take Chemin de la Montagne south to Route 141. Ride northwest on Route 141 and turn left at Chemin Fitch Bay. Take this road to Fitch Bay, and then take Route 247 west to Georgeville.

Cycle north on Route 247 along the shores of Lake Memphre-magog, to the town of Magog. Located at the northern tip of Lake Memphremagog, Magog offers cruises on the lake, a beach and a summer theater. Take Route 141 out of Magog to Mount Orford Park where, in addition to camping on the shores of Lake Stukely, you can go hiking or hang-gliding, or take in a concert at the Orford Art Centre.

Going south again from the park, take Route 112 for 1 km (0.6 mile). Then take Chemin du Bolton Est to Austin and a short side trip to the Benedictine Abbey of St-Benoît-du-Lac, which is known for its cheese (L'Ermite), cider, and chocolate. Head west to Bolton Centre. Go south on Route 245 to the town of South Bolton and then take Route 243 to Lac-Brome (Knowlton).

Continue on Route 243 through Waterloo (known for its mush-rooms) and Warden to Ste-Anne-de-la-Rochelle. Head east on Route 220 to the tour's starting point at Sherbrooke.

MORE INFORMATION: Park Superintendent, Mount Orford Park, Box 146, Magog, Quebec J1X 3N7. Telephone (819) 843-6233.

Montreal through St-Eustache to Oka

Winding back roads through gently rolling hills bring you to Oka, the setting of the Trappist monastery which produces the world-renowned Oka cheese.

St-Eustache has many historic sites dating from the Battle of St-Eustache during the Rebellion of 1837. The church, built in 1793, was damaged during the battle, which was fought between 150 *patriotes,* led by Dr. Olivier Chenier, who had taken refuge in the church, and 2,000 militia soldiers under Sir John Colborne. Chenier and dozens of his followers were killed in this last encounter of the Rebellion of 1837. Scars made by the cannonballs can still be seen on the church walls.

This easy tour can be done as a day trip, or you can make it a two-day tour and camp overnight at Paul Sauvé Park which also has a beach and nature trails.

LENGTH: 86 km (53 miles) return

START: Montreal

THE ROUTE: Head to Laval by going north on Route 117 to Route 148. Go west on Route 148 through farm country to the Arthur Sauvé Bridge over the Rivière des Milles Îles, and into the town of St-Eustache, founded in 1768. After crossing the bridge turn left on St-Louis to the St-Eustache church. Then turn right onto Rue St-Eustache and *"Le Vieux Saint-Eustache,"* of old houses and a mill built in 1762.

After exploring St-Eustache, ride southwest along the river on Route 344. At Ste-Marthe, take the bicycle path which goes as far as Pointe Calumet, and then rejoin Route 344. You pass the Trappist monastery and then go through Paul Sauvé Park. In the town of Oka is a ferry across Lac des Deux Montagnes to Como. To return to Montreal, retrace your route.

MORE INFORMATION: Park Superintendent, Paul Sauvé Park, Box 447, Oka, Quebec J0N 1E0. Telephone (514) 479-8337.

Montreal through Île Perrot to Coteau Landing

This is an easy trip along flat terrain, and can either be a day trip or a leisurely overnight trip from Montreal. It takes you through rural land and past several historic sites. As the route follows the shores of rivers and lakes, it can be windy. There are hotels and campgrounds along the way.

LENGTH: 62 km (38 miles) each way

START: Ste-Anne-de-Bellevue at the western tip of the island of Montreal, reached from downtown by cycling on Lakeshore Drive along Lac St-Louis. At the town of Ste-Anne-de-Bellevue, Lakeshore Drive becomes Chemin Ste-Anne.

THE ROUTE: Ride on Chemin Ste-Anne to the Ste-Anne Canal, which allows boats to bypass the Ste-Anne Rapids. Here is a park and picnic area.

Cross the Highway 20 bridge to Île Perrot. Turn left onto Boulevard Perrot and follow it to Pointe du Moulin Historical Park. The 12-hectare (30-acre) park encompasses a renovated windmill and miller's house, as well as a heritage center with exhibits on early-eighteenth-century technology.

From the park, turn left on Boulevard Perrot and follow the water's edge to Highway 20. Go west across the Ottawa River and turn left onto Route 338 to Pointe-des-Cascades, where there is a campground. From Pointe-des Cascades, follow the winding road along the St. Lawrence River to Coteau Landing, where again there is a campground. Coteau-du-Lac served as a port for importing to Upper Canada (now the province of Ontario). At Coteau-du-Lac National Historic Park are the remains of a port and canal, as well as a reconstructed octagonal blockhouse. Return by the same route.

MORE INFORMATION: Pointe du Moulin Historic Park, 2500 Boulevard Don Quichotte, Île Perrot, Quebec J7V 7P2. Telephone (514) 453-5936.

Coteau-du-Lac National Historic Park, Box 550, Coteau-du-Lac, Quebec J0P 1B0. Telephone (514) 763-5631.

Ottawa/Hull to the Gatineau Hills

Gatineau Park covers 356 square km (138 square miles) of wooded mountains and lakes at the confluence of the Ottawa River and the Gatineau River. This route is suitable for a day trip from Ottawa or Hull. Ottawa has an extensive network of bicycle paths.

LENGTH: 40 km (25 miles) each way

START: Hull, across the Ottawa River from the city of Ottawa which is served by VIA Rail. From Ottawa cross the Alexandra Bridge to Hull. The bridge gives you a good view of the Parliament Buildings.

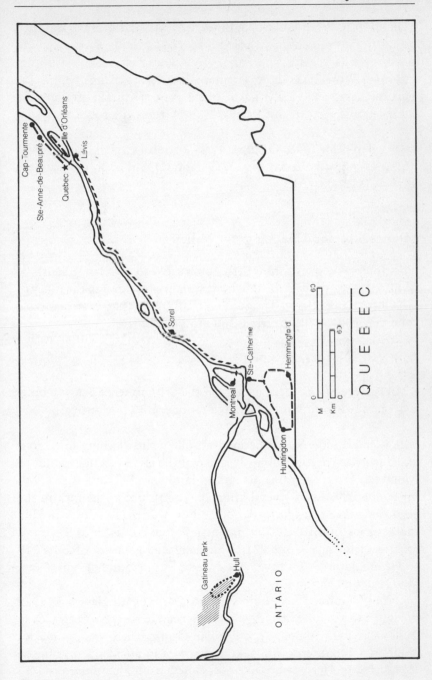

THE ROUTE: From Hull, take Boulevard Alexandre Taché and then go north on Promenade du Lac des Feés to Gatineau Park. Lac Pink offers cyclists scenic panoramas. Tour Lac Pink, and the 30-km (19-mile) Promenade de la Gatineau loop along Kingsmere Lake, Fortune Lake, and Meach Lake. In the park are picnic grounds and hiking trails. Return to Ottawa/Hull by the same route.

MORE INFORMATION: Gatineau Park, National Capital Commission, 161 Laurier Street West, Ottawa, Ontario K1Y 6J6. Or, call Gatineau Park at (819) 827-2020.

Montreal to the Chateauguay Valley

This tour takes you through the orchards and farmlands south of Montreal towards the American border, returning through the valley of the Chateauguay River. The route is relatively flat and is an enjoyable tour that you can begin from downtown Montreal.

LENGTH: 201 km (125 miles)

START: Côte-Ste-Catherine Park on the St. Lawrence Seaway bikeway, reached from Nun's Islands near downtown Montreal.

THE ROUTE: Côte-Ste-Catherine Park offers birdwatching for herons and ducks, as well as fishing. It is one of the closest campgrounds to Montreal. From the park, go east on Highway 132, and then south on Route 209. After several kilometers, go right at the fork in the road onto Rang St-Pierre Nord. Follow this road as it eventually merges back into Route 209. Ride on Route 209 as far as St-Rémi, and turn left onto Route 221 to Sherrington. Then take Route 219 to Hemmingford. You have now cycled 57 km (35 miles) from Côte-Ste-Catherine Park.

From Hemmingford, follow Route 202 west to Havelock; then go south to Covey Hills. A secondary road leads west from Covey Hills and rejoins Route 202 at Franklin Centre where you can make a side trip to St-Antoine-Abbé, known for its apple cider. Continue on Route 202 to Herdman, 43 km (27 miles) from Hemmingford. Go south on Route 202 and then west to Powerscourt, where you are

2 km (1.2 miles) from the United States border. Head north to Huntingdon, 14 km (9 miles) from Herdman. Follow the secondary road 16 km (10 miles) along the south side of the Chateauguay River to Ormstown. From Ormstown, the road follows the north side of the river for 17 km (11 miles), almost to Howick. From Howick head along a small country road 11 km (6 miles) to St-Urbain, then ride for 6 km (4 miles) on Route 205 southeast to Route 209. Turn left and ride the 12 km (7 miles) to St-Rémi, then retrace the same route from St-Rémi to Côte-Ste-Catherine Park 15 km (9 miles) away.

Montreal to Quebec along the St. Lawrence River

Called the "Route of the Pioneers," the road along the St. Lawrence River was one of the colony's first roads. It takes you through villages founded in the seventeenth century, among farms that were feudal seigneuries of colonial New France, and past many scenic and historic sites.

This relatively easy tour is one of the province's most popular cycling tours. By combining this tour with the Quebec to Mont-Joli tour, you can ride to the Gaspé tour.

LENGTH: 319 km (198 miles)

START: Montreal, served by VIA Rail, Voyageur bus and numerous airlines

THE ROUTE: Leave Montreal by the sidewalk of the Jacques Cartier Bridge. Cross the bridge and head toward Rue St-Charles north into the city of Longueuil. It's also possible to transport your bike via the Metro to the Longueuil station. (For information, call the Montreal Urban Community Transit Commission: 514-AUTOBUS.) Or take it on the South Shore Transit Commission buses. (Call the South Shore Transit Commission (514) 463-0131.)

Ride on Rue St-Charles north through Longueuil, passing the historic buildings of Vieux Longueuil. Rue St-Charles links with Boulevard Marie-Victorin. Continue on Boulevard Marie-Victorin through Boucherville, founded in 1668 and one of Quebec's oldest towns. Along the route is Maison Louis-Hippolyte Lafontaine, the residence of a pre-Confederation prime minister.

Just south of Varennes, Boulevard Marie-Victorin links with Highway 132. Varennes is a farming community with many historic homes and religious buildings. A free ferry from Varennes goes to Île Ste-Therese, which offers cycling and hiking, as well as another ferry to the east end of Montreal.

Continue on Highway 132 along the shores of the St. Lawrence River and go through Verchères, a former seignieury located where Madeleine de Verchères fought the Iroquois in 1692. Go through Contrecoeur and St-Joseph-de-Sorel, and cross the Richelieu River to the port and shipbuilding city of Sorel. Founded in 1642, Sorel is Canada's fourth oldest city. Sorel is approximately 60 km (37 miles) from Longueuil.

At Odanak, 30 km (18 miles) farther along Route 132 on the Rivière St-François, is an Indian reserve with a museum. Continue riding Highway 132 through Nicolet, 58 km (36 miles) from Sorel.

Stay on Highway 132 through Gentilly, Les Becquets, Deschaillons, and Leclercville, which is on a plateau at the mouth of the Rivière du Chene. Between Leclercville and Lotbinière is a ferry to the village of Deschambault, on the north side of the St. Lawrence River. Lotbinière was founded in 1692, part of a seignieury granted in 1672. Lotbinière is 84 km (52 miles) from Nicolet.

Continue along the river for 58 km (36 miles), through Ste-Croix, St-Antoine-de-Tilly, and St-Nicholas, into the suburbs of Quebec City. You can cross the St. Lawrence River and go into the city of Quebec via the Quebec bridge, or continue along Highway 132 to Lévis and take the ferry.

Quebec City through Île d'Orléans to Cap-Tourmente

On this tour in the Quebec City area you step back into the seventeenth, eighteenth, and nineteenth centuries. Founded in 1608 by Samuel de Champlain, Quebec City was built on high cliffs overlooking the St. Lawrence River, and is North America's only walled city north of Mexico City.

Nearby Île d'Orléans, a gem of historic Quebecois homes, old farming villages, and traditional Quebecois restaurants, is the most popular cycling tour in the Quebec City area.

Breathtaking Montmorency Falls, east of Quebec City, are higher than Niagara Falls. Farther on is Ste-Anne-de-Beaupré, a well-known Catholic shrine. Also on this tour is Mont Ste-Anne Park, and the Cap-Tourmente Wildlife Reserve, home to thousands of migrating snow geese. There is a good selection of campgrounds and accommodations along the route.

LENGTH: 151 km (94 miles)

START: Quebec City, served by VIA Rail, Voyageur bus, and several airlines

THE ROUTE: Leave Quebec City via Route 138, for the Île d'Orléans Bridge. Cross the bridge to the island, go right on Route 360 and follow Route 360 around the shores of the island, a tour of 65 km (40 miles).

On Île d'Orléans, first visited by Europeans in 1542, you experience the rural Quebec of centuries ago. Follow Route 360 through the island's tranquil and picturesque villages. Ste-Pétronille offers a panoramic view of Quebec City and Lévis. In St-Laurent the old mill is now an art center. St-Jean has a church dating from 1732, historic houses and a lighthouse. At St-François is a campground and a view of Île Madame, Île aux Ruaux, and Cap-Tourmente. At Ste-Famille, the oldest parish on the island, the church dates from 1749. At St-Pierre the church dates from 1717.

Recross the Île d'Orléans bridge and take Highway 360 to Montmorency Falls, which drop 83 meters (272 feet). Continue for 21 km (13 miles) to Ste-Anne-de-Beaupré, where pilgrims have come since 1658. The current neo-Romanesque basilica dates from 1923.

From Ste-Anne-de-Beaupré ride the 4 km (2.5 miles) to Beaupré and take Chemin du Cap-Tourmente for 15 km (9 miles), including 2 km (1.2 miles) of unpaved road, to the Cap-Tourmente Wildlife Reserve. It was created in 1969 to protect the natural habitat of snow geese; 250 other species of wild birds have also been observed here. Explore the reserve on its network of nature trails.

Return to Beaupré where you can take Route 138 for 2 km (1.2 miles) to the Grand Canyon of Ste-Anne Falls, which drop 74 meters (243 feet) in a gorge. Also from Beaupré you can ride 10 km (6 miles) on Route 360 to Mont Ste-Anne Park, which has a 6.5-km

(4-mile) cycling path, camping, hiking trails and a gondola to the 800-meter (2,625-foot) summit of Mont Ste-Anne.

Quebec to Mont-Joli along the St. Lawrence River

This tour can be a continuation of the Montreal to Quebec City tour and connects with the Gaspé Tour. Cycle Highway 132, the "Route of the Pioneers," through the farmland of the St. Lawrence Valley past many historic buildings, many open to visitors. The area has spectacular sunsets and magnificent panoramas of the St. Lawrence River. Many of the islands in the river are bird sanctuaries. Whale-watching is also possible. Highlights include St-Jean-Port-Joli, well-known for its woodcarvers and artisans.

LENGTH: 355 km (220 miles)

START: Quebec City, reached by VIA Rail, Voyageur bus, and several airlines

THE ROUTE: From Quebec City, take the ferry across the St. Lawrence River to Lévis. Lévis has many historic buildings, including Pointe Lévis Fort No. 1 National Historic Park. Leave Lévis via Highway 132, and go through Beaumont where there is camping.

From Berthier-sur-Mer, popular for windsurfing and sailing, you can see the Montmagny archipelago of sixteen islands, islets, and sandbanks. At the town of Montmagny, 54 km (33 miles) from Lévis, you can take a thirty-minute ferry trip to Île aux Grues. Leaving Montmagny, the first village you encounter is three-centuries-old Cap-St-Ignace.

St-Jean-Port-Joli, 26 km (16 miles) farther, was founded in 1721 and is known as the woodcarving capital of Canada. You can see the traditional Quebec woodcarvers, weavers, craftsmen, and artists at work and buy their works in the numerous handicraft shops.

Continue along the picturesque Highway 132 through Village-des-Aulnaies and La Pocatière, which has a scenic view of the river and many tourist facilities. Rivière Ouelle has a beach. At the village of St-Denis is the home of Jean-Charles Chapais, one of the Fathers of Confederation.

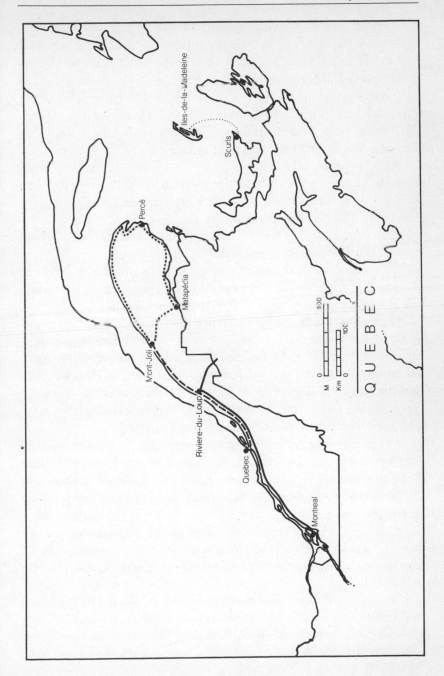

Kamouraska, an Algonquin word meaning "there are bullrushes at the water's edge," reflects three centuries of Quebec history. It is 51 km (32 miles) from St-Jean-Port-Joli. The area is known for its great beauty and for the magnificent views of both the river and the mountains on its north shore. Past St-André you have views of the Pèlerins Islands where a large number of seabirds nest. Notre-Dame-du-Portage was named after the colonial road "Le Portage du Temiscouata," a portage used by the Indians and fur traders.

At the town of Rivière-du-Loup, 43 km (27 miles) from Kamouraska, the river cascades approximately 30 meters (100 feet) into a natural basin carved in the rock. Rivière-du-Loup dates from 1683. Here also is the Museum of Bas St-Laurent. Inland at St-Modeste, the 70-km (43-mile) Grand Portage Hiking Trail follows part of the Temiscouata Portage to Cabano.

If you're heading to New Brunswick, turn off Highway 132 at Rivière-du-Loup and take Highway 185 (the Trans Canada Highway), for 100 km (60 miles) to the New Brunswick border.

Continuing along the St. Lawrence River shore from Rivière-du-Loup, avoid Highway 132 (which has heavy traffic on this section) and take Route 291 to St-Arsène. Then ride on the secondary road, along the Canadian National Railway line, back to Highway 132 and the farming village of L'Isle Verte. At the bay is a bird sanctuary. You can take a ferry to L'Isle Verte, 3 km (1.8 miles) from the shore. On the island is the oldest lighthouse in Quebec.

As you travel farther east along Highway 132, the strip of farmland narrows and is cut by rocky ledges. Trois-Pistoles, 49 km (30 miles) from Rivière-du-Loup, has become known for whale-watching from the ferry boat *Le Gobelet d'Argent*, which cruises to Escoumins on the north shore of the St. Lawrence River. In Trois-Pistoles are campgrounds, the Musée St-Laurent of antiques and the Maison du Notaire arts and crafts center. You can also take an excursion to Île aux Basques, an important bird sanctuary with seagulls, eider ducks, and blue herons.

From Trois-Pistoles, ride along the coast. At Bic is a campground and hotels. Rimouski, 67 km (42 miles) from Trois-Pistoles, has a museum and a variety of accommodation including hotels, motels, and campgrounds. Leaving Rimouski, continue on Highway 132 to Mont-Joli, where you can add on the Gaspé tour (described separately in this chapter). There is camping at Ste-Flavie and at Mont-Joli.

MORE INFORMATION: Grand Portage Trail, c/o Bas St-Laurent Tourism Association, 506 Lafontaine, 3rd Floor, Rivière-du-Loup, Quebec G5R 3C4. Telephone (418) 867-1272.

Gaspé Peninsula

Mountains plunging to the sea, panoramic ocean views, and unspoiled fishing villages make the Gaspé coast one of Quebec's most visited areas and a challenging, exciting bicycle tour.

Magnificent Percé Rock, Île Bonaventure — once a pirate hideout and now one of the world's largest bird sanctuaries — spectacular Forillon, and the Gaspésie parks are some of the Gaspé's best-known highlights. In 1534, at the site of the town of Gaspé, Jacques Cartier first stepped ashore in North America.

This tour has four parts. From Mont-Joli to Madeleine-Centre, 255 km (158 miles) along the Gulf of St. Lawrence, is the coast section. The road squeezes between the cliffs and the water in many places. At each river mouth is a cove protecting a coastal fishing village. In Gaspésie Park are the highest mountains in southern Quebec.

The Land's End area at the tip of the peninsula stretches 282 km (175 miles) from Madeleine-Centre to Newport. The most popular part of the Gaspé, Land's End encompasses Forillon National Park, the village of Gaspé, and Percé Rock.

After rounding the tip of the Gaspé Peninsula, you reach the Baie des Chaleurs, named by Jacques Cartier during the hot days of July 1534. Here are red cliffs and sandbars. You can swim, sail, and windsurf along its shores. The villages along the 226 km (140 miles) from Newport to Matapédia were settled by Acadian refugees in 1755. Two villages were established by United Empire Loyalists.

The last part of the tour goes inland for 149 km (92 miles) along the Matapédia River, known for its salmon fishing. You pass through the valley's farming and forestry villages to your starting point at Mont-Joli.

The route can be windy. There are campgrounds and accommodation along its entire length. If you're going during high tourist
season (mid-July to mid-August) and plan to stay in hotels or motels,
make reservations in advance.

LENGTH: 900 km (560 miles) loop

START: Mont-Joli, served by VIA Rail and Voyageur Bus Lines. VIA
Rail also serves the southern coast of the peninsula to the town of
Gaspé.

THE ROUTE: This tour follows Highway 132 for almost its entire
route. From Mont-Joli, overlooking the St. Lawrence River, ride
along the shore for 70 km (43 miles) to Matane, which is known for
its shrimp and salmon. The name comes from a Micmac word
meaning "beaver breeding ground."

Leaving Matane, the route is more hilly. At Grosses-Roches are
imposing lone rocks rising up out of the water. The fishing village of
Les Mechins, where each street is named after a fisherman's boat, is
47 km (29 miles) from Matane. At Capuchins and Cap-Chat are
beaches. The name Cap-Chat comes from a rock resembling a
crouching cat, near the lighthouse 2 km (1.2 miles) west of the
village. Near Cap-Chat you can see the peaks of the Chic-Choc
Mountains.

At Ste-Anne-des-Monts, 41 km (25 miles) from Les Mechins, you
can take a side trip inland via Highway 299 to scenic Gaspésie Park,
39 km (24 miles) away. The park's Chic-Choc Mountains reach
1,270 meters (4,166 feet). Part of the Appalachian Mountain chain,
the Chic-Chocs are the highest mountains in southern Quebec.
Moose, wood caribou, and Virginia deer inhabit the forest. The park
offers hiking trails, fishing, and canoeing, as well as campgrounds
and an inn.

Back on Highway 132, ride to Mont-St-Pierre, 57 km (35 miles)
from Ste-Anne-des-Monts. The route is steep at first, and skirts
picturesque bays. Mont-St-Pierre is the glider capital of eastern
Canada. You can ride the road to the top of the 430-meter (1,410-foot)
mountain which has a panoramic view and glider launching pads.

Anse-Pleureuse, which means "Crying Cove" is named for the cries of shipwrecked ghosts.

The 35 km (22 miles) from Mont-St-Pierre to Madeleine-Centre meanders beside the cliffs. At Petite-Madeleine you will find camping and hotels. At the mouth of Rivière Madeleine is a 1,300-meter (4,265-foot) long sand spit.

Continue on Highway 132 through Grande-Vallée, which, as its name implies, is situated in a wide valley. In the village is the covered Galipean bridge. Pointe à la Frégate, 30 km (19 miles) from Madeleine-Centre, has camping.

L'Anse-à-Valleau, 34 km (21 miles) away, has hotels and campgrounds. From l'Anse-à-Valleau it's 16 km (10 miles) to the entrance of Forillon National Park, located at the eastern end of the Gaspé Peninsula separating the Gulf of St. Lawrence and Gaspé Bay. Covering 238 square km (92 square miles) in area, the park's eastern coast is dominated by 180-meter (600-foot) limestone cliffs. The southern shore, facing Gaspé Bay, has pebble beaches and small coves interspersed by rocky headlands. The hills in the park's interior reach almost 540 meters (1,800 feet).

Harbor seals and several species of whales can be seen in the waters near the park. The network of over 55 km (34 miles) of trails follows the valleys and highland routes through the park's interior. If you don't want to tour Forillon Park, you can take Highway 197 across the peninsula and save a few kilometers.

From the park entrance, it's 73 km (45 miles) along Highway 132 through the park and on to the village of Gaspé. The village is situated on a headland overlooking a spectacular bay, which provides an immense natural harbor into which three salmon rivers flow. The name Gaspé comes from a Micmac word meaning "land's end."

South of the village of Gaspé are the beaches at Sandy Beach and Haldimand East, popular for windsurfing. Continue through Douglastown, a small Loyalist stronghold with a scenic sandbar, 24 km (15 miles) from Gaspé. Another 50 km (31 miles) brings you to Percé, which is dominated by Percé Rock: the Gaspé's most famous attraction for tourists and artists.

You can walk to Percé Rock at low tide, or go by boat at other times. Do take the boat to the Île Bonaventure bird sanctuary, with its thousands of gannets and seagulls. At Percé is an art center and a theater.

Leaving Percé, you ride on the southern side of the Gaspé Peninsula, and the terrain is less hilly. At Pabos, 40 km (25 miles) away, is a beach and camping. Continuing on Highway 132, you pass through many small villages. In Anse-aux-Gascons is a white sand beach. Craftsmen make little wooden boats which they sell at roadside stands. Port-Daniel, 41 km (25 miles) from Pabos, is at the end of a deep bay and has a sandy beach. Tuna fishing, unusual in the Gaspé, is carried on here.

From Port-Daniel to the old Loyalist village of New Carlisle is 36 km (22 miles) of relatively flat terrain. From New Carlisle to Black Cape, 45 km (28 miles) away, the road follows the coast of the Baie des Chaleurs. Bonaventure is an Acadian farming center. Many Acadian refugees came to settle here in 1755.

Cycling the 42 km (26 miles) from Black Cape to St-Omer you have a view of the coast of New Brunswick. Along the way you pass through several villages including Carleton, which was founded in 1756 by Acadian refugees. St-Omer offers good birdwatching and clam-digging as well as a youth hostel, hotels, and campgrounds.

From St-Omer it's 65 km (40 miles) to Matapédia, at the head of the Baie des Chaleurs and the New Brunswick border. Here you can connect with the Northeast Coast Tour of New Brunswick (described in the New Brunswick chapter). From Matapédia, the Gaspé loop tour goes inland through the valley of the Matapédia River. You pass through Causapscal 56 km (35 miles) from Matapédia, and go along Lac au Saumon and Lac Matapédia to Sayabec, a farming and forestry village at the head of Lac Matapédia, 79 km (49 miles) away. From Sayabec you continue through an agricultural area for 47 km (29 miles) to Mont-Joli, this tour's starting point.

MORE INFORMATION: Gaspé Tourism Association, 357 Route de la Mer, Ste-Flavie, Quebec G0J 2L0. Telephone (418) 775-2223.

Park Superintendent, Gaspésie Park, Box 550, Ste-Anne-des-Monts, Quebec G0E 2G0. Telephone (418) 763-3301.

Park Superintendent Forillon National Park, Box 21220, Gaspé, Quebec G0C 1R0. Telephone (418) 368-5505.

Îles de la Madeleine

An archipelago of islands in the center of the Gulf of St. Lawrence, the Îles de la Madeleine (also called the Magdalen Islands) have beaches of fine white sand, washed by warm Gulf Stream waters. They are also noted for their green rolling hills, red cliffs, sand dunes, blue ocean, and hillsides of dense, stunted forest. Over the centuries, the islands have been responsible for countless shipwrecks and many of the shipwrecked mariners settled on the islands. In the fishing villages you can meet their descendants and see lighthouses, boats, and seabirds. There is also fishing and diving.

The communities connected by sand dunes and bridges, are Havre Aubert, Cap-aux-Meules, Havres-aux-Maisons, Pointe-aux-Loups, Grosse-Île, and Grande-Entrée. Île-d'Entrée, 16 km (10 miles) from Cap-aux-Meules, is not joined to the archipelago by land. The islands are 290 km (180 miles) east of the Gaspé, 120 km (75 miles) north of Prince Edward Island and 100 km (60 miles) off the coast of Cape Breton.

The ocean has carved the cliffs, forming magnificent caves, which you can explore on foot at low tide at Dune du Sud, or by boat at Gros-Cap. You can also see how the constant winds has slowed the growth of trees and transformed the sand dunes.

During the summer months, the water temperatures reach 17°C (62°F), which is pleasant for swimming. The islands have a maritime climate with cooler temperatures in summer and milder temperatures in winter. Cycling season is from the beginning of June to mid-September. The islands experience a lot of wind. Try to do your bicycle touring on days when the wind is not strong so you won't have to deal with blowing sand.

Camping is not permitted on the beaches. Four campgrounds, as well as motels and inns, are available.

LENGTH: 134 km (83 miles)

START: Cap-aux-Meules, is reached by the ferry *M.V. Lucy Maud Montgomery*, which operates six days a week from Souris, Prince Edward Island, and by the weekly *M.V. Madeleine* ferry from Montreal. Canadian Pacific Airlines also serves the Îles de la Madeleine.

THE ROUTE: Highway 199 is the main road connecting the islands. The ferry takes you to Cap-aux-Meules near the midpoint of the islands. Here you can see a diversity of ocean vessels, sailboats, and fishing boats. Going north on Highway 199 from Cap-aux-Meules you come to Île du Havre-aux-Maisons, a charming rural village. At Dune du Sud, a roadside rest area leads to the beach, bordered by magnificent cliffs and caves sculpted by the sea. You can explore them at low tide.

Continuing north on Highway 199, go through Grosse Île, a community of fishermen of Scottish descent. Here are miles of beautiful deserted beaches. Nearby, at Pointe de l'Est Reserve you can see native flora and fauna. Île de la Grande-Entrée is a lobster-fishing port.

Going south from Cap-aux-Meules, ride along Highway 199 to Île du Havre-Aubert, the oldest of the villages on the islands. Near the marine museum are boutiques and restaurants.

MORE INFORMATION: Îles de la Madeleine Tourism Association, Box 1028, Cap-aux-Meules, Îles de la Madeleine, Quebec G0B 1B0. Telephone (418) 986-2245.

The *M.V. Lucy Maud Montgomery* ferry is operated by CTMA, Box 245, Cap-aux-Meules, Magdalen Islands, Quebec G0B 1B0. Telephone: in Cap-aux-Meules, (418) 986-4264; in Souris, (902) 687-2181.

For reservations for the *M.V. Madeleine*, contact Inter-Voyage Agency, 1253 McGill College Street, Montreal, Quebec H3B 2Y5. Telephone (514) 866-1944; in Cap-aux-Meules (418) 986-4224.

Across Quebec

If you're traveling across Quebec on your way to Atlantic Canada, ride the Montreal to Quebec City tour, and then follow the Quebec City to Mont-Joli tour as far as Rivière-du-Loup. Here take Highway 185 (the Trans Canada Highway) east for 100 km (60 miles) to New Brunswick.

Guidebooks

Great Montreal Bicycling/Montreal et les Alentours à Vélo, by Elliott Katz. Available in English or French from: Great North Books, Box 507, Station Z, Toronto, Ontario M5N 2Z6. Price $6.95.

Partir à Bicyclette (in French) by Louise Roy, includes thirty route maps of cycling tours in Quebec. Available from: Vélo-Quebec, 4545 Avenue Pierre du Coubertin, Box 1000, Station M, Montreal, Quebec H1V 3R2. Price $9.95.

The Quebec Bicyclist's Map highlights forty-two routes on the Quebec road map. Available from: Vélo-Quebec. Price $3.50.

11 New Brunswick

Fishing villages, the world's highest tides, charming historic towns, sand dunes and beaches are just some of the attractions of New Brunswick, the Gateway to Atlantic Canada. At 73,432 square km (28,354 square miles), New Brunswick is the largest of the Maritime provinces. It has 2,250 km (1,400 miles) of coastline and is surrounded on three sides by water. Over 85 percent of the province is covered by forests and by a vast array of rivers, lakes, and streams.

New Brunswick's bicycling opportunities are not as well-known outside the province as those of neighboring Nova Scotia and Prince Edward Island, but they are well worth exploring.

ROADS: Most of the main routes have paved shoulders.

WEATHER: The interior of New Brunswick has a continental climate of hot summers. The coast has more temperate weather due to the moderating influence of the ocean. Average summer temperatures range from 13 to 26°C (55 to 78°F) at Fredericton in the interior, and from 12 to 21°C (54 to 70°F) at Saint John on the Bay of Fundy.

TOURIST INFORMATION: General tourist information, including a map and an accommodation guide listing campgrounds, bed-and-breakfasts, motels, and hotels is available from Tourism New Brunswick, Box 12345, Fredericton, New Brunswick E3B 5C3.

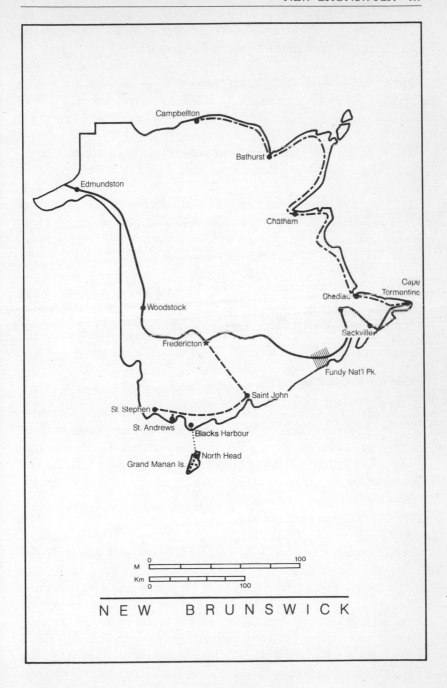

Campbellton

Bathurst

Edmundston

Chatham

Woodstock

Chediac

Cape
Tormentine

Fredericton

Sackville

Fundy Nat'l Pk.

Saint John

St. Stephen

St. Andrews

Blacks Harbour

North Head

Grand Manan Is.

M   0   100

Km 0   100

N E W   B R U N S W I C K

Call toll-free: in New Brunswick, 1-800-442-4442; in the rest of Canada and in the United States, 1-800-561-0123.

HOSTELS: For a list of hostels in New Brunswick, write to the Canadian Hostelling Association/New Brunswick, Box 6251, Station A, Saint John, New Brunswick E2L 4R7.

AIRPORTS: The main centers in New Brunswick are Moncton, Fredericton, and Saint John. All are served by major airlines.

TRAINS: For information on VIA Rail service, call: in Moncton (506) 382-7892; in Saint John (506) 642-2916; elsewhere in New Brunswick call toll-free from 6 a.m. to 7 p.m. 1-800-561-3952 and from 7 p.m. to 6 a.m., 1-800-361-7773.

BICYCLING: For information on cycling clubs, contact: New Brunswick Cycling Association, 114 Morton Avenue, Moncton, New Brunswick E1A 3H6. Telephone (506) 854-8876.

Fundy Tidal Coast

The highest tides in the world, plus seascapes, rugged shorelines, and quiet coves are seen on this tour of the southern shore of New Brunswick along the Bay of Fundy. The communities in this area were settled largely by United Empire Loyalists following the American Revolution and many of their historic homes have been preserved.

LENGTH: 247 km (154 miles)

START: Fredericton, served by VIA Rail, buses, and an airport

THE ROUTE: From Fredericton, take Highway 102 along the Saint John River for 140 km (88 miles) to Saint John, Canada's oldest incorporated city and New Brunswick's largest. Marked walking tours let you explore the city's restored historic areas. The city is also known for the Reversing Falls, which occur twice a day when the Bay of Fundy's high tides force the Saint John River to flow upriver.

Rockwood Park, in the heart of Saint John, is a good viewpoint. The park also offers camping.

From Saint John, take Highway 1 west along the Bay of Fundy coast. This road has a 0.3 to 0.6 meter (1 to 2-foot) wide paved shoulder and is very hilly in places; but it makes for great cycling as it visits many picturesque fishing villages. Blacks Harbour, situated just off Highway 1 on Route 776, is the ferry terminal for Grand Manan Island (a bicycle tour of the island is described separately in this chapter). In Lake Utopia, near the town of St. George, a monster is said to live.

Turn off Highway 1 onto Route 127 to St. Andrews, 96 km (60 miles) from Saint John. St. Andrews is a popular resort town with a charming New England atmosphere. The town was founded in 1783 by United Empire Loyalists, and many of the buildings date from that period. Whale-watching cruises are available from the St. Andrews wharf.

To get to St. Stephen, 29 km (18 miles) away, take Route 127 back to Highway 1 and continue west to the town of St. Stephen, a major border crossing from Maine.

Grand Manan Island

The largest and most remote of the Bay of Fundy Isles, situated off the southwest coast of New Brunswick, Grand Manan is 35 km (22 miles) long and 10 km (6 miles) across at its widest point. The eastern side of the island has several villages and long sandy beaches. The uninhabited western side, where the edible dulse seaweed is harvested, is characterized by craggy 90-meter (300-foot) cliffs.

More than 275 species of birds have been sighted here; ornithologist James Audubon did many of his sketches in the area. Whale-watching and hiking are popular.

LENGTH: 29 km (18 miles) each way

START: North Head, the terminal for the ferry from Blacks Harbour

THE ROUTE: Grand Manan has only one main road, which is 29 km (18 miles) long and runs along the sea for the entire length of the island. Along the way are quaint villages, country inns, lighthouses, and magnificent seascapes. Off the main road are gravel roads into the island's interior. Near Seal Cove are Anchorage Provincial Park and a bird sanctuary. A free ferry crosses a narrow channel to White Head Island.

MORE INFORMATION: Grand Manan Island ferry service is operated by: Coastal Transportation Limited, Box 26, Saint John, New Brunswick E2L 3X1. Telephone (506) 657-3306.

Park Superintendent, Anchorage Provincial Park, Seal Cove, Grand Manan Island, New Brunswick E0G 3B0. Telephone (506) 662-3215.

Northeast New Brunswick

This tour explores the northeastern coast of New Brunswick, a region of many rivers, beaches, sandbars, and historic Acadian settlements. If you want to cross New Brunswick along the coast, this is the route, especially if you're coming into New Brunswick from the Gaspé Peninsula.

LENGTH: 450 km (280 miles)

START: Campbellton, located just east of the Quebec town of Matapédia. Campbellton can be reached by VIA Rail.

THE ROUTE: Campbellton is at the western tip of the Baie des Chaleurs near the mouth of the Matapédia and Restigouche Rivers. Here is scenic Sugarloaf Provincial Park. From Campbellton, follow Route 134 along the coast through the communities of Dalhousie and Eel River Crossing. The latter has one of the longest natural sandbars in the world. Route 134 joins Highway 11 which has 0.6- to 1.2-meter (2- to 4-foot) shoulders. At Belledune, get back onto Route 134. It's narrower but has scenic views of the Baie des Chaleurs. This route takes you to Bathurst through the neighboring villages of Pointe Verte, Petit Rocher, Nigadoo, and Beresford.

From Bathurst, take Highway 11 northeast and then south along the coast, passing through fishing villages like Grande Anse, Caraquet, Tracadie, and Neguac. Highway 11 has a paved 15 to 30-cm (6-inch to 1-foot) shoulder. Between Grand Anse and Caraquet is the Acadian Historical Village, which tells the story of the early Acadian settlers in this region.

Just beyond Caraquet, Highway 11 turns south to Tracadie and Chatham. Here you can take Highway 11 through St. Margarets to Kouchibouguac National Park, or follow Route 117 around the coast and enter the park at Pointe Sapin. Situated on 26 km (16 miles) of shoreline on Northumberland Strait, this 238-square-km (92-square-mile) park has sand dunes formed by the sea and wind, secluded beaches, rivers, lagoons, and a mixed forest. Kouchibouguac Park has a 25-km (15-mile) bicycle trail system with its own campsites.

From here, follow the picturesque coastline on Routes 505 and 475 from Rexton to Bouctouche and Route 134 to Shediac. (Or you can take the Highway 11 bypass route which has a 0.6 to 1.2-meter (2 to 4-foot) wide shoulders.

At Shediac, if you want to go to Moncton, take Route 134. If you want to head to the ferry for Prince Edward Island, take Route 140 to Highway 15, which is a wide-shouldered highway, and then Route 16 to Cape Tormentine ferry terminal. To ride to Nova Scotia, take Route 132 south to Highway 2 and continue southeast.

MORE INFORMATION: Park Superintendent, Kouchibouguac National Park, Kent County, Kouchibouguac, New Brunswick E0A 2A0. Telephone (506) 876-2443.

Across New Brunswick

Known as "the Rhine of North America," the picturesque Saint John River Valley is the first part of the approximately six- to eight-day tour across New Brunswick. Along the river's course, through highlands and rolling farmlands, are the magnificent cataract at Grand Falls and the famous Reversing Falls.

First traveled by the Indians and explorers, the Saint John River was a vital communication link between the Maritime provinces and the rest of Canada. A variety of settlers, including Acadians, United Empire Loyalists, Scots, and Danes, traveled the river to their new homes and you can see their influence. Numerous historic sites are found along the river shore. Thirty-two covered bridges are found in the valley. You'll cross some of them on this route.

If you want to ride across New Brunswick as part of a cross-Canada trip or otherwise, here is the scenic route. You will encounter less traffic than if you took the Trans Canada Highway for the whole way. The Trans Canada Highway has paved shoulders, however; Highway 105 does not. The tour described here goes from west to east.

LENGTH: Approximately 505 km (314 miles)

START: The Trans Canada Highway at the Quebec-New Brunswick boundary. The nearest VIA Rail stop is at Edmundston, just east of the boundary.

THE ROUTE: Crossing the border from the province of Quebec, the Trans Canada Highway becomes Highway 2 in New Brunswick. The Trans Canada Highway through New Brunswick has a 0.6- to 1.2-meter (2- to 4-foot) wide shoulder. At the border is a provincial tourist information center.

Ride east on the Trans Canada Highway to Edmundston, at the junction of the Madawaska and St. John Rivers. It is known as the capital of the Republic of Madawaska. The republic was formed by nineteenth-century inhabitants, who were tired of being pawns in border negotiations between Canada and the United States.

Continue east past St. Leonard and Grand Falls (Grand Sault in French), where you can see its 41-meter (135-foot) waterfall, one of the largest cataracts east of Niagara Falls. At Grand Falls turn off the Trans Canada Highway and take Highway 105 along the east side of the Saint John River. The more leisurely Highway 105 has less traffic than the Trans Canada Highway, and some spectacular views of the waterway. The two highways have several junctions as they follow the course of the river.

About 14 km (9 miles) east of Perth-Andover is camping at Muniac Provincial Park. At Upper Kent you can take a short side trip on Route 565 to a covered bridge spanning the Monquart River. Rejoin Route 105 at Bath. Farther south is Florenceville, named in honor of

Florence Nightingale, heroine of the Crimean War. Hartland, located at one of the junctions of Highway 105 and the Trans Canada Highway, is the site of the world's longest covered bridge. This impressive 391-meter (1,282 foot) long structure, stretching across the Saint John River, was built in 1899. Nearby Woodstock has a summer farmers' market. The Old County Court House is open to the public.

Continue south and then east on Route 105 along the Saint John River. Crossing the river at Hawkshaw takes you to King's Landing on the Trans Canada Highway. Here is a historic settlement which recreates a Loyalist town of the period 1790-1880. There are sixty restored buildings.

Cross the river again at Longs Creek, where there is a wildlife park, a campground, and a beach. Continue east on Route 105 to Mactaquac. Mactaquac Provincial Park evolved as a result of establishing a major hydro generating station. The 567-hectare (1,400-acre) park offers camping, swimming, nature trails, and fishing for small-mouth bass.

Staying on Highway 105 takes you to Fredericton, the provincial capital. This gracious city with tree-lined streets and small-town charm has many historic buildings and museums. Be sure to visit the Beaverbrook Art Gallery and take a walking tour of the city center.

From Fredericton follow the Trans Canada Highway past Oromocto and around the southern end of Grand Lake to Sussex, an important dairy center. Near Penobsquis, take Highway 114 through Fundy National Park. (If you're in a hurry, stay on the Trans Canada Highway straight into Moncton.)

Covering 207 square km (80 square miles) on the Bay of Fundy, this park is known for its rugged coastline and abundant wildlife, and has over 100 km (60 miles) of hiking trails through its wooded interior. The Bay of Fundy is famous for having the world's highest tides, up to 16 meters (53 feet). At low tide you can explore the tidal flats and see periwinkles, barnacles, sea anemones, and sandhoppers.

Continuing on Route 114 toward Moncton, you can see the famous Flowerpot Rocks at Hopewell Cape near the mouth of the Petitcodiac River. At high tide these mushroom-like columns look like islands, but at low tide you can descend at the Rocks Provincial Park to see them from the bottom.

Moncton is the major center in southeastern New Brunswick. Its Magnetic Hill is one of nature's contradictions. Your bike seems to coast uphill. The tidal bore can be seen from Bore Park in downtown Moncton.

From Moncton, take Highway 106 to the university town of Sackville. Just east of Aulac you can take Highway 16 to the Cape Tormentine terminal for ferries to Prince Edward Island. If you're headed for Nova Scotia, continue east on Highway 2 toward Amherst, Nova Scotia.

MORE INFORMATION: Park Superintendent, Fundy National Park, Alma, New Brunswick E0A 1B0. Telephone (506) 887-2000.

12   Prince Edward Island

"The fairest land 'tis possible to see," was how sixteenth-century French explorer Jacques Cartier described Prince Edward Island. The Micmac Indians called it *Abegweit*, meaning "home cradled on the waves."

The Garden of the Gulf, as Prince Edward Island is now known, has a gentle coastline with long stretches of red and white sand beaches washed by warm ocean waves. The flat, leisurely country roads take you through red-soiled farmland, along wooded lots, and past protected harbors with brightly colored fishing boats. The terrain is low and rolling; the highest point on the island is only 152 meters (500 feet) above sea level. Prince Edward Island is Canada's smallest province, only 224 km (140 miles) long and 6 to 64 km (4 to 40 miles) wide. Cycling distances are therefore quite short.

Excellent camping facilities, bed-and-breakfasts, farm accommodations, and lobster dinners have made Prince Edward Island very popular with cyclists. Described here are tours of one day, two days, four days, and six days duration. Most of them start in Charlottetown, the island's largest town and the provincial capital. Some of the routes overlap.

ROADS: Prince Edward Island has the most miles of paved road per capita in the country. Many of the island's 3,312 km (2,058 miles) of two-lane roads have paved shoulders. The Tourism Department has signposted several scenic routes along the province's roads. These bicycling tours use part of the Blue Heron Drive and the Kings Byway routes.

WEATHER: Prince Edward Island has a temperate climate; extreme and sudden changes in temperature are rare. The island gets more summer sunshine than the other Maritime provinces, and is free of fog as it is sheltered from the Atlantic by Nova Scotia and Newfoundland. Summer days are generally warm, with an average high of 22.6°C (73°F). Breezes are light but constant, averaging 22 km (13 miles) per hour.

Nights are cool because of the sea breezes. Morning dew is heavy and keeps the grass damp until around 10 a.m. Average annual precipitation is 110.5 cm (43.5 inches). Bring clothing for cool nights and occasional rain. The cooler autumn temperatures are also pleasant for cycling.

TOURIST INFORMATION: General tourist information including a map, and the *Visitors Guide*, which lists attractions, campgrounds, and the full range of accommodations including bed-and-breakfasts, is available from: Prince Edward Island Tourist Information Center, Box 940, Charlottetown, Prince Edward Island C1A 7M5. Call toll-free 1-800-565-0243.

ACCOMMODATIONS: Prince Edward Island offers a variety of accommodation including bed-and-breakfasts, cottages, country inns, hotels, motels, and tourist homes. The bed-and-breakfasts in towns and on farms are popular with cyclists, as they offer good affordable accommodation and a true taste of the island way of life.

HOSTELS: Prince Edward Island Hostel Association, 153 Mount Edward Road, Box 1718, Charlottetown, Prince Edward Island C1A 7N4. Telephone (902) 894-9696.

AIRPORTS: Charlottetown is served by Air Canada and Canadian Pacific Airlines.

FERRIES: Two ferry services connect Prince Edward Island to the mainland. The service from Cape Tormentine, New Brunswick to

Borden, Prince Edward Island, is operated by Marine Atlantic, 100 Cameron Street, Moncton, New Brunswick E1C 5Y6. Call toll-free: in Ontario, Quebec, Newfoundland, and Labrador, 1-800-565-9411; in New Brunswick, Nova Scotia, and Prince Edward Island, 1-800-565-9470; in Maine, 1-800-432-7344; in the continental United States outside of Maine, 1-800-341-7891.

The ferry service from Caribou, Nova Scotia, to Wood Islands, Prince Edward Island, is run by: Northumberland Ferries Ltd., Box 634, Charlottetown, Prince Edward Island C1A 7L3. Telephone (902) 566-3000. From Nova Scotia, New Brunswick and Prince Edward Island, call toll-free 1-800-565-0201.

Another ferry goes from Souris, Prince Edward Island, to the Magdalen Islands of Quebec. For more information see the Magdalen Islands Tour in the Quebec chapter.

TRAINS: There is no train service on Prince Edward Island. However, VIA Rail operates a bus service between Charlottetown, Prince Edward Island, and Moncton, New Brunswick, via the Borden-Cape Tormentine ferry. This bus service does not take bicycles. To get information on VIA Rail service when on Prince Edward Island, call toll-free, 1-800-561-3952.

BICYCLING: Prince Edward Island Cycling Association, 160 Nassau Street, Charlottetown, Prince Edward Island C1A 2X2. Telephone (902) 963-2256.

Prince Edward Island National Park

Red sandstone cliffs, sand dunes, marshes, ponds, and 40 km (25 miles) of saltwater beaches dominate Prince Edward Island National Park's 32 square km (12 square miles) on the Gulf of St. Lawrence. The magnificent white sand dunes contrast with the clear blue ocean. In July and August, water temperatures average 20°C (70°F), giving Prince Edward Island beaches some of the warmest salt water north of the Carolinas.

Cycling is very popular in Prince Edward Island National Park. Along the Gulf Shore Parkway is a 2-meter (6.5-foot) wide paved shoulder offering a spectacular day tour. A 5.7-km (3.5-mile) cycling

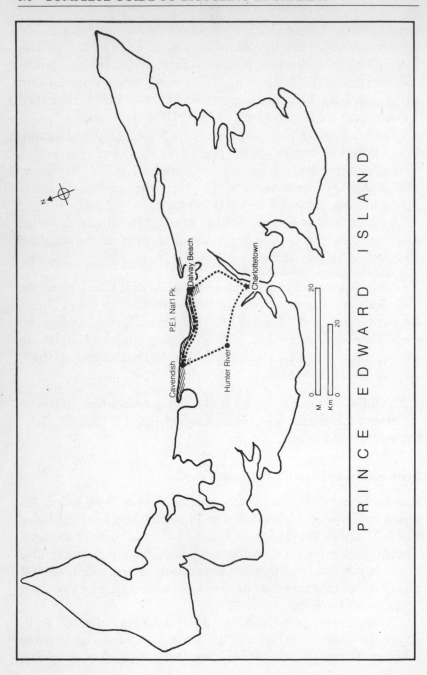

trail explores the Cavendish area. Three other tours in this chapter go through the park. The route is described here in more detail.

There are national park campgrounds at Stanhope, Rustico Island, and Cavendish. There are also several private campgrounds. The park has several nature trails. Supervised beaches are found at Cavendish, North Rustico, Brackley, Stanhope, and Dalvay.

LENGTH: 28 km (17 miles) each way

START: Dalvay Beach, headquarters of Prince Edward Island National Park, located 25 km (15 miles) from Charlottetown

THE ROUTE: Dalvay Beach got its name from Alexander MacDonald, a business associate of John D. Rockefeller. In 1898 MacDonald built a summer home here which he called Dalvay-by-the-Sea, after his ancestral home in Scotland. The residence is now a hotel near Dalvay Beach.

From Dalvay, ride west on the Gulf Shore Parkway along the beaches and sand dunes of Stanhope Beach to Brackley Beach. On the way is the Brackley Marsh, a stopover for migrating birds in August. Ride over the causeway to Rustico Island. At one time cranberries grown here were shipped all over eastern North America. Rustico Island is now home to a protected colony of great blue herons.

Exit from this section of the park via Highway 15. Go right onto Highway 6 (Blue Heron Drive scenic route) to North Rustico, one of the island's most picturesque villages. Re-enter Prince Edward Island National Park and turn left and ride on the shore of the Gulf of St. Lawrence, along some of the Island's most spectacular coastal scenery.

You pass North Rustico Beach, Cape Turner and Orby Head. On the beach you may see "mossers," people who rake the Irish moss from the beach and load it into horse-drawn carts. Irish moss is a marine red alga containing carrageenin, used as an emulsifier and thickener in toothpaste, pudding, and ice cream.

At the western end of the park is Cavendish and a 5.7-km (3.5-mile) loop cycling trail. Here also is the Anne of Green Gables House. Cavendish has been immortalized by Lucy Maud Montgomery in her "Anne" books. The Cavendish cliffs erode at a rapid pace, up to 5 meters (15 feet) per year, by the action of wind and waves.

Retrace the route to return to Dalvay Beach.

MORE INFORMATION: Park Superintendent, Prince Edward Island National Park, Box 487, Charlottetown, Prince Edward Island C1A 7L1. Telephone (902) 672-2211.

Charlottetown to Prince Edward Island National Park

This leisurely two-day tour from Charlottetown across the island goes through gently rolling terrain dotted with picturesque farm buildings perched on the rich red soil, to Prince Edward Island National Park. Ride along the park's sand dunes, white sand beaches, and redstone cliffs. Return to Charlottetown through the Island's rural interior.

LENGTH: 90 km (56 miles)

START: Charlottetown

THE ROUTE: From Charlottetown, leave by St. Peter's Road which becomes Highway 2 (signposted as the Kings Byway scenic route). After 14 km (9 miles) turn left onto Highway 6 for 10 km (6 miles) to an entrance of Prince Edward Island National Park. (See the Prince Edward Island National Park Tour for a more detailed description.) Enter the park and ride along Dalvay Beach, Stanhope Beach, and Brackley Beach on the Gulf of St. Lawrence. Be sure to stop and enjoy a swim.

National park campgrounds are located at Brackley Beach, and private campgrounds at Stanhope Beach. After exploring the park, turn onto Highway 15 toward the community of Brackley Beach. It's a 13-km (8-mile) ride from the eastern park entrance to Brackley Beach.

Go right onto Highway 6 (the Blue Heron Drive scenic route) to North Rustico. Here is another part of Prince Edward Island National Park. Ride along North Rustico Beach and Cavendish Beach on the Gulf of St. Lawrence to the town of Cavendish. There are numerous campgrounds along this part of the route.

From Cavendish, go inland on Highway 13 for 16 km (10 miles) to Hunter River. Then go left onto Highway 2 for 22 km (14 miles) to Charlottetown.

Central Beach Tour

This four-day tour takes you through central Prince Edward Island. You can explore the Island's red shores in the south and the white sand beaches and dunes of Prince Edward Island National Park along the north shore. While crossing the island, you ride through rolling fields where the famous Prince Edward Island potatoes are grown, and on winding roads through the wooded Bonshaw Hills.

Part of this tour follows Blue Heron Drive where, as its name suggests, you can see blue herons in the tidal marshes. Along this route is the Borden terminus for the ferry from Cape Tormentine, New Brunswick. If you're arriving by this ferry, you can start this loop tour from there.

LENGTH: 197 km (122 miles)

START: Charlottetown

THE ROUTE: Leave Charlottetown via University Avenue, which becomes Highway 1 (the Trans Canada Highway, and here part of the Blue Heron Drive). Ride Highway 1 for 11 km (7 miles) to Cornwall. Follow Highway 19 (Blue Heron Drive) another 15 km (9 miles) to Fort Amherst National Historic Park, on the site of the French settlement of Port LaJoie, which was founded in 1720. Fort Amherst was built by the British after they won control of the island in 1758.

After visiting Fort Amherst Park, continue cycling on Highway 19 along the shores of Hillsborough Bay to Canoe Cove on Northumberland Strait. At DeSable, go left and follow Highway 1 (the Trans Canada Highway and Blue Heron Drive) to Hampton. At Hampton, turn left to the picturesque seaside village of Victoria, a 34-km (21-mile) ride from Fort Amherst. Nearby are private campgrounds. Sailing excursions can be arranged from Victoria.

From Victoria, continue on Highway 1 (the Trans Canada Highway

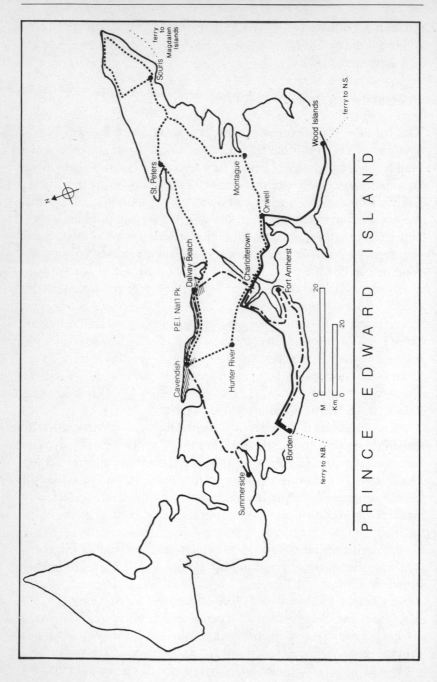

PRINCE EDWARD ISLAND

and Blue Heron Drive), to Tryon, 7 km (4 miles) away. At Tryon follow Highway 10 (Blue Heron Drive) another 11 km (7 miles) to Carleton. Here Highway 1 goes south 3 km (2 miles) to Borden, the terminus for the ferry to Cape Tormentine, New Brunswick.

Continue on Highway 10 (Blue Heron Drive) for 13 km (8 miles) from Carleton to Central Bedeque. Then ride for 11 km (7 miles) on Highway 1A into the town of Summerside, where ocean-going vessels are loaded with Prince Edward Island potatoes for export. Here also is the Acadian Museum depicting the nineteenth-century life and culture of the island's Acadian people.

From Summerside, go 5 km (3 miles) on Highway 1A (Blue Heron Drive) to Travellers Rest, and turn right onto Highway 2 for 8 km (5 miles) to Kensington. From here take Highway 6 for 11 km (7 miles) to New London. Along the way are several artists' communities.

Continue on Highway 6 (it rejoins the Blue Heron Drive), for 11 km (7 miles) to Cavendish. Ride into Prince Edward Island National Park and along Cavendish Beach and North Rustico Beach on the Gulf of St. Lawrence. (See the Prince Edward Island National Park Tour for a more detailed description of this part of the route.) There is a national park campground at Cavendish Beach and several private campgrounds along the way. It's 10 km (6 miles) from Cavendish to the village of North Rustico.

At North Rustico, you leave the western section of Prince Edward Island National Park, and ride 10 km (6 miles) on Highway 6 (Blue Heron Drive) to Oyster Bed Bridge. Continue on Highway 6 for 3 km (1.8 miles) to Highway 15 and turn left to Brackley Beach and the eastern part of Prince Edward Island National Park. Ride along Brackley Beach, Stanhope Beach, and Dalvay Beach.

Exit from the park and turn left onto Highway 6 (part of the Kings Byway scenic route). Ride Highway 6 and then turn right onto Highway 2 and cycle into Charlottetown, 24 km (15 miles) farther.

Eastern Kings Tour

Explore the tall capes, long white beaches, and deep inlets and harbors of the eastern part of Prince Edward Island on the first part of this six-day tour. You ride through charming towns with an old-world flavor, lively fishing ports, and villages settled by Scottish and French pioneers. Along this route is Souris, the terminus for the ferry to the Magdalen Islands of Quebec (described in the Quebec chapter).

At East Point you can see Nova Scotia. The tour then turns west and goes along the spectacular beaches of Prince Edward Island National Park on the Gulf of St. Lawrence.

LENGTH: 302 km (188 miles)

START: Charlottetown

THE ROUTE: Leave Charlottetown by going east on Highway 1 (the Trans Canada Highway and the Kings Byway scenic route), across the Hillsborough Bridge. Travel for 5 km (3 miles) to Cross Roads. Continue on Highway 1A (Kings Byway), to Tea Hill. At the top of Tea Hill you have a spectacular view of Northumberland Strait and Governor's Island. Turn left and follow Highway 1A through strawberry country to Highway 1 near Mount Mellick, a ride of 12 km (7 miles) from Cross Roads.

Go right and follow Highway 1 (the Trans Canada Highway and Kings Byway) for 12 km (7 miles) to Orwell. Here is Orwell Corner Historic Site, a community restored to depict nineteenth-century Prince Edward Island life.

From Orwell, take Secondary Highway 210. Go right on Highway 24 at Kinross and then left on Secondary Highway 210 through Lyndale and Victoria Cross to Montague. The third largest town on Prince Edward Island, Montague is the home of the Garden of the Gulf Museum. If you're camping, the nearest provincial park with camping is Brudenell River Provincial Park, 5 km (3 miles) along Highway 4, then right for another 5 km (3 miles).

Ride north from Montague along Highway 4 for 34 km (21 miles) to Rollo Bay West. Take Highway 2 (Kings Byway) to Souris, 10 km (6 miles) farther. Souris, the island's fourth largest town, is the terminus for the ferry to the Magdalen Islands of Quebec (see the Magdalen Islands Tour in the Quebec chapter).

The tour does a loop around East Point and returns to Souris. You can use Souris as base to leave some of your gear and ride with less weight.

Leave Souris and ride Secondary Highway 305 to Hermanville on the Gulf of St. Lawrence. Turn right and follow Highway 16 (Kings Byway) along the north shore to North Lake, a distance of 30 km (18 miles) from Souris. North Lake is known for its tuna fishing.

Ride another 10 km (6 miles) to East Point, from which you have a view of Cape Breton Island, 56 km (35 miles) away. At the tip of the point is the East Point Lighthouse, warning ships of the dangerous rock reef and turbulent waters below. Head west along Highway 16 to Basin Head. Then go past Red Point Provincial Park back to Souris, 25 km (15 miles) from East Point.

From Souris, ride for 10 km (6 miles) on Highway 2 (Kings Byway) to Rollo Bay West. Follow Highway 2 west for 19 km (12 miles) to St. Peters, which was founded by shipwrecked French sailors. St. Peters Provincial Park offers a good beach and campground.

Continue on Highway 2 (here it rejoins Kings Byway). At Tracadie Cross, turn right onto Secondary Highway 219 to Mill Cove, a 39-km (24-mile) ride from St. Peters. Go right on Highway 6 to the Dalvay Beach entrance of Prince Edward Island National Park, and ride the park road along the Gulf of St. Lawrence to Stanhope Beach, 8 km (5 miles) from Mill Cove. (See the Prince Edward Island National Park Tour for a detailed description of this part of the route.) At Stanhope Beach is a national park campground, as well as a selection of private campgrounds.

From Stanhope Beach ride along the shore for 13 km (8 miles) to Brackley Beach. Take Highway 15, turn right onto Highway 6 and ride to North Rustico, another 13 km (8 miles). Here ride 8 km (5 miles) to North Rustico Beach, and go along the beaches on the Northumberland Strait to Cavendish Beach. A national park campground is situated here. There are also private campgrounds nearby.

From Cavendish, take Highway 13 for 16 km (10 miles) to Hunter River. Then turn left onto Highway 2 and ride 22 km (14 miles) into Charlottetown.

Across Prince Edward Island

If you're crossing Prince Edward Island from its western ferry terminus at Borden to its eastern ferry terminus at Wood Islands, as part of a cross-country cycling tour, the quickest way across the island is the Trans Canada Highway. You should, however, definitely consider spending more time exploring the picturesque island.

LENGTH: 115 km (71 miles)

START: Borden, terminus of the CN ferry from Cape Tormentine, Nova Scotia

THE ROUTE: From Borden, follow Highway 1 (the Trans Canada Highway) for 54 km (33 miles) through farmland to Charlottetown. From Charlottetown, ride east for 61 km (28 miles) on Highway 1 along Hillsborough Bay and Northumberland Strait to Wood Islands, the terminus for the ferry to Caribou, Nova Scotia.

13   Nova Scotia

In Nova Scotia you cycle beside sandy beaches, and ride along rocky shorelines where the waves crash against the cliffs. You visit picturesque fishing communities in quiet coves that represent centuries of history. The magnificent scenery, along with plentiful campgrounds and accommodations, including charming bed-and-breakfasts, have made Nova Scotia one of the continent's most popular cycling areas. Known as Canada's Ocean Playground, Nova Scotia's 55,487 square km (21,425 square miles) are almost completely surrounded by water. Its western shores are washed by the Bay of Fundy, which has the world's highest tides. To the north are Northumberland Strait and the Gulf of St. Lawrence, and to the south and east is the Atlantic Ocean.

Although no part of Nova Scotia is more than 56 km (35 miles) from the sea, the province is more than just shoreline. The province's interior contains rugged hills, rolling farmlands, and orchards.

ROADS: Most of the province's roads are narrow, winding, picturesque, and paved. Traffic on these roads is generally light. The 100 series highways are straight and have wide, paved shoulders, but they carry faster traffic and are not recommended for bicycle touring. The signposted routes, such as the Sunrise Trail and the Glooscap Trail, are keyed to the Nova Scotia tourist guide and maps.

WEATHER: The weather is maritime and subject to the frequent changes the sea can bring. Average annual precipitation is 89 cm (35 inches). Expect and be prepared for rain. Have fenders on your bike. Summer temperatures range from 12°C (53°F) at night, occasionally dipping to 5°C (40°F), to a daytime high of 30°C (86°F). Sea breezes keep summer daily temperatures averaging around 21°C (70°F). In summer, banks of fog drift inland an average of thirty-eight days during June, July, and August, but they rarely remain all day. Spring arrives late in Nova Scotia, but the autumn season is long.

TOURIST INFORMATION: For general tourist information contact: Nova Scotia Tourism, Box 456, Halifax, Nova Scotia B3J 2R5. Call toll-free in Nova Scotia, New Brunswick and Prince Edward Island, 1-800-565-7105; in Halifax-Dartmouth, (902) 425-5781; in Newfoundland and Quebec, 1-800-565-7180; in central and southern Ontario, 1-800-565-7140; in northern Ontario, Manitoba, Saskatchewan, and Alberta, 1-800-565-7166; in British Columbia, 112-800-565-7166; in the United States, 1-800-341-6096; in Maine, 1-800-492-0643. Nova Scotia Tourism also operates Check Inn, a reservation service for hotels, motels and campgrounds.

ACCOMMODATIONS: The whole range of accommodation from campgrounds and bed-and-breakfast inns to luxury hotels is generally available in every part of the province. Use the Nova Scotia tourist guide to select accommodations and campgrounds in the places along these tours. Information on bed-and-breakfast homes is available from the local and regional tourist associations.

HOSTELS: Information on hostels can be obtained from Nova Scotia Tourism or from the Canadian Hostelling Association, 5516 Spring Garden Road, Box 3010, South Halifax, Nova Scotia B3J 3T3. Telephone (902) 425-5450.

AIRPORTS: Nova Scotia is reached by air service to its international airport at Halifax as well as airports at Sydney and Yarmouth. The airports handle bicycles at an extra charge.

FERRIES: Ferry service to Nova Scotia is available from Bar Harbor and Portland, Maine, to Yarmouth, and from Saint John, New

Brunswick, to Digby. All ferries take bicycles at a small or no additional charge.

The service from Bar Harbor is operated by Marine Atlantic. In the United States, contact Marine Atlantic, Bar Harbor, Maine 04609, or call toll-free: in the northeast United States, 1-800-341-7981; in Maine, 1-800-432-7344. In Canada, contact Terminal Supervisor, Marine Atlantic, Yarmouth, Nova Scotia B5A 1K0. Call toll-free: in the Maritime provinces, 1-800-565-9470; in Newfoundland, 1-800-563-7701; in Quebec and Ontario, 1-800-565-9411.

For information on the Portland to Yarmouth service, write Box 609, Yarmouth, Nova Scotia B5A 4B6, or Prince of Fundy Cruise Limited, P.O. Box 4216, Station A, Portland, Maine 04101. Call toll-free: in Maine, 1-800-482-0955; in Nova Scotia, New Brunswick, and Prince Edward Island, 1-800-565-7900; nationwide in the United States, 1-800-341-7540.

TRAINS: VIA Rail mainline service in Nova Scotia has baggage cars and will transport bicycles. The Halifax-Yarmouth dayliner does not take checked baggage; it may take bikes on a space-available basis, but don't depend on it. Telephone: in Halifax, (902) 429-8421, elsewhere in Nova Scotia, call toll-free 1-800-561-3952.

BUSES: Acadian Bus Lines serves most of the larger towns in the province but will take bikes only if there is room. Don't depend on taking your bike on the bus during peak travel times. For more information, contact Acadian Bus Lines, 6040 Almon Street, Halifax, Nova Scotia B3K 1T8. Telephone (902) 454-9321.

BICYCLING: Bicycle Nova Scotia, Box 3010 South, Halifax, Nova Scotia B3J 3G6. Telephone (902) 425-5450.

Sunrise Trail

On the relatively flat shore of the Northumberland Strait, the Sunrise Trail takes you to picturesque seascapes and some of the warmest saltwater beaches north of the Carolinas. Average water temperature in the summer is 21°C (70°F). In the summer months, Scottish heritage festivals are held in towns and villages along this route.

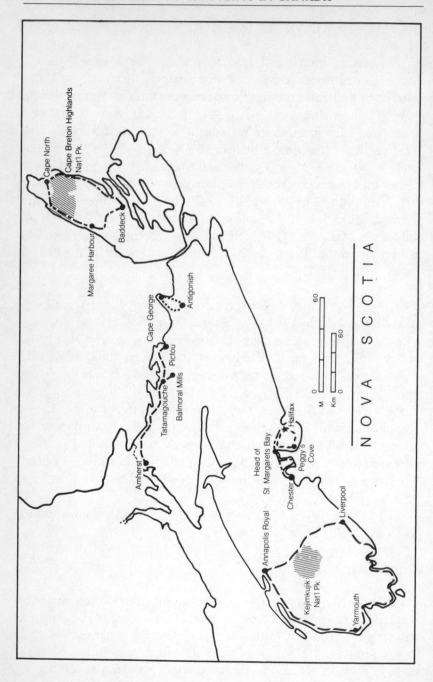

The Sunrise Trail extends from Amherst to Auld Cove on the Strait of Canso. This cycling tour, however, ends at Pictou, the approximate midpoint of the trail. The tour generally follows flat roads with few hills, and has ocean views and many long sandy beaches. Lorneville, Amherst Shore, and Northport are summer colonies on some of the finest beaches north of Cape Cod. ·

Also along this route is the Caribou ferry terminal for Prince Edward Island.

LENGTH: Approximately 190 km (118 miles)

START: Amherst, on the Trans Canada Highway just east of the New Brunswick boundary. Amherst can be reached by VIA Rail.

THE ROUTE: Leave Amherst on Highway 6 east, and turn off onto Highway 366, which meets the Northumberland Strait 18 km (11 miles) away at Tidnish, an Indian name meaning "a paddle." Here are the remains of the uncompleted Chignecto Ship Railway, begun in 1890 and intended to haul schooners and boats across the isthmus to the Bay of Fundy. From Tidnish, follow the shore, which has many ocean views and beaches and usually strong inshore breezes, 25 km (15 miles) to Pugwash.

Pugwash is a popular tourist spot on the Sunshine Trail. Its harbor handles both fishing boats and large freighters carrying lumber and salt. A Scottish festival called the "Gathering of the Clans" is held annually in July.

About 15 km (9 miles) farther is Wallace, a fishing and farming community on Wallace Bay, once a source of the sandstone used to build Province House in Halifax and the Parliament Buildings in Ottawa. A few kilometers beyond Wallace is the North Shore Road, which detours around the Malagash peninsula, site of abandoned salt mines.

Continue 20 km (12 miles) along Highway 6 to Tatamagouche, which was an Acadian settlement until 1755, when a detachment of New Englanders sacked the town and expelled its residents. The Sunrise Trail Museum, which has exhibits on the region's history, is located here.

An interesting 10-km (6-mile) side trip from Tatamagouche is Balmoral Mills, just off Highway 311, where you can see one of the few water-driven grist mills still in operation in Nova Scotia. At nearby Drysdale Falls a branch of the Waugh River drops through a gorge to form a waterfall 5 to 6 meters (16 to 20 feet) high.

Then follow Brule, Seafoam, and Toney River, with their long beaches. At Toney River you can see Prince Edward Island 22 km (14 miles) away. Campgrounds are located in or near Tidnish, Northport, Pugwash, Wallace, Tatamagouche, Brule, Seafoam, and Caribou.

This tour's endpoint is Pictou, the largest community on the Northumberland Strait and 53 km (33 miles) from Tatamagouche. Pictou is called "the Birthplace of New Scotland." In 1773, Scottish Highlanders arrived here to begin the wave of Scottish immigration that has built the province. The town is famous for its church lobster suppers.

From Pictou you have several options. If you have to catch the train to Halifax, ride to Truro via Highways 376 and 104. If you have the time, you can take the more leisurely route to Truro via Highway 256 from Lyons Brook, turning onto Highway 311 at East Earltown.

If you want to continue to Prince Edward Island, take Highway 106 to Caribou, where ferries provide frequent daily service to Wood Islands, Prince Edward Island. (See the Prince Edward Island chapter for more information on the ferry service.)

To continue riding along the Sunrise Trail, follow the scenic Highway 245 at Sutherlands River 8 km (5 miles) east of New Glasgow, passing through Merigomish and Arisaig. At Malignant Cove you connect with the Cape George Tour described separately in this chapter.

Cape George Tour

This challenging one-day tour follows the coast of the Northumberland Strait and can be part of a continuation of the Sunrise Trail. Described as a mini Cabot Trail, the Cape George tour traverses hilly terrain and is considered strenuous. The descent from Cape George is exhilarating.

LENGTH: 71 km (44 miles)

START: Antigonish, the major center in this region of Nova Scotia, is the start and endpoint of this loop tour. The town can be reached by VIA Rail.

THE ROUTE: Ride out of Antigonish on Highway 245. An almost flat 20 km (12 miles) brings you to the sea at Malignant Cove, 19 km (12 miles) away. The town took its name from the British man-of-war *H.M.S. Malignant*, wrecked here on its way to Quebec during the American Revolution.

Turn right onto Highway 337. Here the scenery changes dramatically. Houses perch precariously on round, sometimes treeless hills, or nestle in quiet coves. Bicycling alternates between strenuous climbs and exhilarating glides.

The tour follows the shore of St. George's Bay through the communities of Ballantynes Cove, Cape George, Lakevale, Morristown, Crystal Cliffs, and Antigonish Harbour. The lighthouse at Ballantynes Cove, first built in 1895, is situated 300 meters (1,000 feet) above St. George's Bay. From this vantage point on a clear day you can see Prince Edward Island and Cape Breton Island.

Cabot Trail

"I have travelled around the globe. I have seen the Canadian and American Rockies, the Andes and the Alps and the Highlands of Scotland, but for simple beauty, Cape Breton outrivals them all," observed Alexander Graham Bell.

The famous Cabot Trail, on Nova Scotia's Cape Breton Island, is the province's best known cycling route. The spectacular three- or four-day tour gives you vast panoramas of blue ocean as you ride through mountainous terrain and rolling meadows. You pass along cliffs, lakes, river gorges, sand beaches, rocky coves, and rugged coastline. Picturesque vistas unfold before you from the top of each hill. The Cape Breton villages are known for their traditional fiddlers and folk singers.

LENGTH: 294 km (183 miles)

START: Baddeck. The nearest VIA Rail station is Orangedale, approximately 50 km (30 miles) from Baddeck. The description here goes in a clockwise direction on the Cabot Trail.

THE ROUTE: In Baddeck is the Alexander Graham Bell National Historic Park, on a hill overlooking Bras D'Or Lake. The building is a unique structure—its design incorporates tetrahedra, a favorite shape of Bell's. The museum displays many of Bell's inventions and artifacts relating to his work in communications, aviation, and medicine.

From the Bell Museum, go 8 km (5 miles) south on the Trans Canada Highway 105, turn north onto the Cabot Trail. The road follows part of the Middle River valley. At Northeast Margaree, 32 km (20 miles) from the Trans Canada Highway, is the Salmon Museum, where exhibits describe the Margaree River, known among fishermen as one of Eastern Canada's finest salmon rivers.

Continue 18 km (11 miles) through farmland to Margaree Harbour on the coast. Here you can get a view of the Northumberland Strait. Turn north and cycle the 27 km (16 miles) to Cheticamp, a French Acadian fishing village where the tricolor is often seen. Inquire locally about whale-watching boat trips. At Petit Etang is the Acadian Trail, a four-hour hiking trail to the top of the Highlands where you have a panoramic view of the Cheticamp area.

The entrance to Cape Breton Highlands National Park is 5 km (3 miles) north of Cheticamp. Admission is free for people entering on bicycles.

Inside the park you enter a narrow valley, then climb up Cap Rouge, with good views of Cheticamp and the surf below. On French Mountain, the road climbs steeply inland from the ocean. Ride along the high plateau and gradually descend to the top of MacKenzie Mountain at its end. Along the way you can stop and explore a bog with native flora, which has a boardwalk winding through it.

The road from MacKenzie Mountain descends steeply, via a series of switchbacks, to the village of Pleasant Bay, 44 km (28 miles) from Cheticamp. A few kilometers beyond Pleasant Bay is the Lone Sheiling, a replica of the stone huts used by the Scottish crofters, the region's first settlers, to protect themselves against the blast of the North Sea while tending their sheep in northern Scotland and the Hebrides. Beyond this is the ascent up North Mountain, the hardest climb of the entire Cabot Trail, followed by another breathtaking descent. The road hugs the cliffs that line the gorge of the North Aspy River valley. You then come to the famous view, seen on all the tourist brochures, of the Sunrise Valley.

Cape North, 29 km (18 miles) from Pleasant Bay, is the northern-most point on the Cabot Trail. From here turn east and cycle 19 km (12 miles) to Neil Harbour, then south to Black Brook, where there are campgrounds and an attractive and popular beach.

Ride through Ingonish, a popular resort area. Ingonish is one of the oldest settled areas on the Atlantic seaboard. Portuguese fishermen wintered here as early as 1521. Here are beaches, parks, hiking trails, and scenic lookouts. Ingonish Beach offers swimming in the ocean and at a nearby freshwater lake. The provincially owned Keltic Lodge is located here.

The road gradually climbs Cape Smokey, a towering 360-meter (1,200-foot) promontory often capped by white mist. The Cape Smokey ski area has Atlantic Canada's only double chair lift. During summer it takes visitors to an unforgettable view of the Atlantic and the rocky Cape Breton coast.

From Cape Smokey the road descends to sea level again in less than 3.2 km (2 miles) and then straightens out and continues along the rugged coastline. It passes through small fishing villages such as Skir Dhu (Gaelic for "black rock"): population ten. At North Shore is Plaster Provincial Park, a picnic area with a short but steep walking trail to the cliff that has views of the Bird Islands, where many seabirds nest from early June to late July.

At picturesque St. Ann's, 63 km (39 miles) from Ingonish Beach, is the Gaelic College, which preserves the region's Highland heritage with courses on such things as bagpipe playing, clan lore, and Gaelic singing. Visitors are invited to observe classes held both outside and inside the college. Continue on the Cabot Trail to the Trans Canada Highway 105 and then to Baddeck, 31 km (19 miles) from St. Ann's.

An alternative and quicker route back to Baddeck is to take the ferry to Englishtown. Here you can see the burial place of Angus MacAskill, "the Cape Breton Giant." Standing 213 cm (7 feet

9 inches) tall and weighing 192 kg (425 pounds), MacAskill was famous as a strongman with the P.T. Barnum Circus during the nineteenth century.

If you took the ferry, continue on Highway 312 to the Trans Canada Highway. Then proceed to Baddeck to end your tour.

MORE INFORMATION: Park Superintendent, Cape Breton Highlands National Park, Ingonish Beach, Cape Breton, Nova Scotia B0C 1L0. Telephone (902) 285-2270.

Peggys Cove Tour

Peggys Cove is one of Nova Scotia's best-known tourist attractions. A picturesque fishing community centred around a narrow ocean inlet, the village is dominated by the famous lighthouse, perched on a huge granite outcrop.

LENGTH: 110 km (68 miles)

START: Halifax, reached by VIA Rail train, international airport, and bus.

THE ROUTE: Leave Halifax via the Armdale Rotary, and take Route 3. Just beyond Second Chain Lake, take Highway 333 through Goodwood, Whites Lake, Shad Bay, and the Dovers. From Whites Lake, you can take side trips to Terence Bay or to Prospect. Peggys Cove is 45 km (28 miles) from Halifax. When you have seen the village, continue on through Glen Margaret and Seabright to Upper Tantallon. From here you can either return to Halifax quickly via Highway 103, or take a more leisurely and more interesting ride on Highway 3 through Five Island Lake and Timberlea.

Halifax to Chester

This is a two-day tour, starting in Halifax and taking you past beautiful scenery and beaches. It can be done in one day but take at least two to have time to enjoy it all. It's great for a hot summer weekend.

LENGTH: 158 km (98 miles)

START: Halifax, reached by VIA Rail train, international airport, and bus.

THE ROUTE: Leave Halifax via the Armdale Rotary, and take Highway 3, the St. Margaret's Bay Road. You encounter the steepest hills on your way out of Halifax. The route goes inland and passes through Lakeside, Beechville, and Timberlea. At Upper Tantallon, 20 km (12 miles) from Halifax, the road starts to follow the bays and inlets of the South Shore.

Near Head of St. Margaret's Bay is the start of the Bowater Mersey Hiking Trail. Popular beaches are found at Queensland, Black Point, and Hubbards.

Just past Hubbards, about 21 km (13 miles) from Upper Tantallon, turn left onto Highway 329. Here the route detours around the Aspotogan Peninsula. Near the tip of the peninsula is Bayswater Beach Provincial Park, offering a sand beach and a picnic area. Next is the town of Blandford, the former site of a whaling industry. From the shoreline you can see the Tancook Islands in Mahone Bay. The detour around the peninsula is about 35 km (22 miles).

Rejoin Highway 3 at East River. Nearby is Graves Island Provincial Park, a particularly beautiful campground and picnic site. Chester, 8 km (5 miles) from East River, offers swimming, sport fishing, and sailing. Boat trips to Big and Little Tancook Islands can be arranged.

To have time to enjoy the beaches and scenery, camp at Hubbards or on Graves Island, or stay in one of the many accommodations in the area. Return to Halifax the following day.

Southwestern Nova Scotia

Rugged coastline, white sand beaches, crashing surf, lighthouses, and colorful fishing villages with wharves piled high with lobster traps are some of the sights you see as you begin this tour along Nova Scotia's south coast. From the Atlantic coast you ride through the interior of the province to Kejimkujik National Park. On the shores of the Bay of Fundy you explore through historic Acadia. Along the way are places with stories of buried treasure and ghost ships.

As this tour is a loop you can start anywhere and ride in either direction, but if you go counter-clockwise you miss the long steep climb from Annapolis Royal to Milford. Although you could do this tour in five days, plan to take ten days to two weeks so you can explore the many attractions.

LENGTH: Approximately 500 km (310 miles)

START: Anywhere along the loop is a good place to start. The route description here starts at Yarmouth, which can be reached by road, VIA Rail dayliner from Halifax, or ferry from Bar Harbor or Portland, Maine. Another ferry terminus along this route is at Digby, on the Bay of Fundy, where the ferry service connects with Saint John, New Brunswick.

THE ROUTE: Yarmouth has a shipping tradition dating from the days of wind and sail. Exhibits at the Yarmouth County Historical Society Museum reflect this tradition. Just outside Yarmouth is Cape Forchu, named by Champlain in 1604, and site of the Yarmouth Light, built in 1840.

The tour from Yarmouth to Liverpool follows the scenic Lighthouse Route along the Atlantic coast, with many bays and points to explore. The signs for the Lighthouse Route follow Route 3. Just beyond Doctors Cove, about 76 km (47 miles) from Yarmouth, take a side trip to Cape Sable Island, Nova Scotia's southernmost point, on Route 330. If you want to save time, take Highway 103 just beyond Crowell to Shelburne, a short cut of about 40 km (25 miles). A major tourist center on the Lighthouse Route, Shelburne was settled by United Empire Loyalists, and is now a shipbuilding and fishing community. Liverpool, 70 km (44 miles) beyond Shelburne, is a pretty town with tree-lined streets and many historic buildings. Deep-sea fishing trips can be arranged locally.

From Liverpool, go north on Highway 8 inland through farm and forest land for 67 km (42 miles) to Kejimkujik National Park. Here you can swim in the freshwater lakes, rent a canoe for a wilderness trip on rivers once used by the Micmac Indians, or hike along some of the more than 100 km (60 miles) of wooded trails. From Kejimkujik Park to Annapolis Royal is 50 km (30 miles).

Annapolis Royal, founded in 1605, is the oldest English settlement in Canada. Here is Fort Anne National Historic Park, dating from 1643, and the Port Royal Habitation — the oldest permanent settlement by Europeans north of the Gulf of Mexico. Nearby is the unique Fundy Tidal Power Project and the Lequille hydroelectric plant housed in a seventeenth-century-style building.

Leave Annapolis Royal on Highway 1. Just over the bridge at Clementsport turn left toward Clementsvale. At Clementsvale, take the road for the pretty village of Bear River, known as "the Switzerland of Nova Scotia." Take the road that runs beside the Bear River and rejoin Highway 1, which merges with Highway 101 after a few kilometers. Digby, the terminus for the Marine Atlantic ferry to Saint John, New Brunswick, is just off Highway 101 on Route 217. The town is about 15 km (9 miles) from Bear River. At Digby is the provincially owned resort, The Pines.

Continue on Highway 101 to Weymouth, 30 km (19 miles) from Digby, then rejoin Highway 1. The longest main street in Canada starts at Weymouth and ends at Yarmouth and passes through many little coastal villages. This is the center of the French Acadian culture in Nova Scotia. Try some native Acadian cuisine, especially "rappie pie," at one of the family-run restaurants.

There may be heavy traffic on Highway 1 in areas where Highway 101 has not yet been completed. If you encounter heavy traffic take a break in one of the many small villages along the route. Stay on Highway 1 as far as Yarmouth.

MORE INFORMATION: The ferries from Bar Harbor, Maine, to Yarmouth, and from Saint John, New Brunswick, to Digby, are operated by Marine Atlantic. The ferry from Portland, Maine, to Yarmouth is operated by Prince of Fundy Cruises Limited. Details on ferry services are given at the beginning of this chapter.

Park Superintendent, Kejimkujik National Park, Box 36, Maitland Bridge, Annapolis County, Nova Scotia B0T 1N0. Telephone (902) 242-2770.

The Annapolis Valley

The famous fruit-growing region of the Annapolis Valley is sheltered by mountains on both sides from heavy winds and fog. The

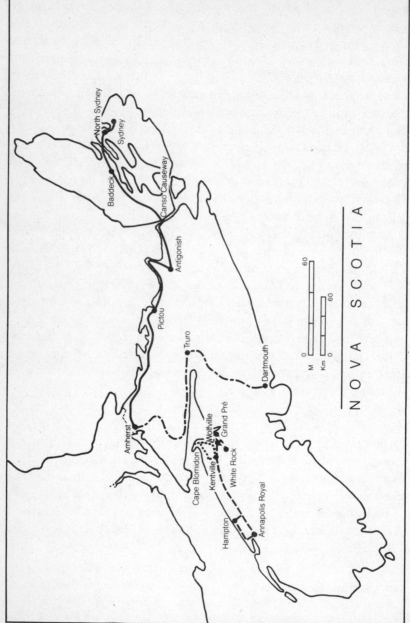

steep North Mountain separates the valley from the Bay of Fundy. On the other side of the valley is the South Mountain. This tour is fairly level unless you cross North Mountain.

In late May you can see the apple blossoms. In summer there are seasons of strawberries, raspberries, plums, and cherries. October is apple-picking season, and the woods blaze with fall colors.

Annapolis Royal, where this tour begins, is one of Canada's most historic regions. In addition to Fort Anne National Historic Park and the Port Royal Habitation, there are many other restored buildings and historic gardens, as well as a theater. There are approximately ten bed-and-breakfasts in the area.

LENGTH: Approximately 120 km (75 miles)

START: Annapolis Royal can be reached by VIA Rail train from Halifax to Yarmouth. This is a dayliner with no checked baggage. Bikes are permitted on a space-available basis, and your chances are better if your bike is in a box, but don't depend on it during busy season.

THE ROUTE: After visiting Annapolis Royal, ride east on either Highway 1 or Highway 201. Highway 1 has more traffic but is flatter and passes through the attractive towns of Bridgetown, Paradise, and Lawrencetown.

For a hilly side trip over the North Mountain, take Highway 1 past Granville Ferry. Ride north to Parker Cove, and along the coast road beside the Bay of Fundy to Hampton. You may notice a drop in temperature between the Valley and the Fundy Shore. Turn right just past Hampton to return to Highway 1 at Bridgetown. Bridgetown is 24 km (15 miles) from Annapolis Royal. Above Bridgetown is Valleyview Provincial Park, a picnic park with a panoramic view of the Annapolis Valley.

North of Bridgetown, you can take the Clarence Road east along the base of the North Mountain. At Middleton, 22 km (14 miles) farther on, take Highway 221. This route extends 56 km (35 miles) to Canning at the east end of the Annapolis Valley. North of Canning, the North Mountain comes to a dramatic end at Cape Blomidon.

Another option near Middleton is to take Route 362 over Mount Hanley. Ride east along the Bay of Fundy to Margaretsville, and then south to Kingston. South of Middleton, at Nictaux Falls, is a pond above the dam on the Nictaux River where you can swim. From Middleton, continue on Highway 201 past the air base at Greenwood to Morristown. A paved road up the South Mountain leads to Lake George Provincial Beach Park at Lake George. Take this road back to Highway 1 and ride into Berwick. Berwick is 35 km (22 miles) beyond Middleton. East of Berwick, take Highway 360 north and turn right onto Highway 221. A small lake at Lakeville is another place to swim.

From the scenic village of Canning you can take the Blomidon-Scots Bay Tour (described separately in this chapter). In the Canning area are many paved roads on which to explore farm areas. Take Highway 358 to reach Wolfville, a university town that was settled in the 1760s. Wolfville is 28 km (17 miles) from Berwick. There is a VIA Rail station in Wolfville, served by a dayliner.

Blomidon Peninsula

The Blomidon Peninsula was the home of the Micmac god Glooscap. This tour can be done on its own or as a continuation of the Annapolis Valley Tour. You pass farmlands and orchards and reach the cliffs, trails, and beaches of Blomidon Provincial Park. There are several steep hills on the tour.

LENGTH: 85 km (53 miles)

START: Kentville, which can be reached by VIA Rail from Halifax or Yarmouth. This is a dayliner with no checked baggage. Bikes are permitted on a space-available basis, and your chances are better if your bike is in a box.

THE ROUTE: From Kentville, take the road for Port Williams through the dykelands of "Glooscap Country," past farms with apple orchards. Go through Port Williams where freighters loading barrels of fresh apples sit high and dry beside the wharf at low tide. Follow the coast road to Blomidon past the wide red mudflats of Minas Basin — if the 8- to 12-meter (26- to 39-foot) tide is out.

Blomidon Provincial Park, a few kilometers past Blomidon, offers picnic grounds, hiking trails and beaches. There is a 3-km (1.8-mile) gravel road, which climbs up North Mountain to the Scots Bay Road. Turn right and cycle through Scots Bay to the end of the road. In Scots Bay is the start of the 13-km (8-mile) hiking trail to a spectacular cliff at Cape Split, known for its strong tides, fierce winds, and thousands of seabirds.

Return along the Scots Bay Road to the village of The Lookoff, where there is a famous view of the Annapolis Valley and the Minas Basin. From here you can either go south on Route 358 to Canning and retrace your route to Kentville; or you can ride west along the North Mountain to Glenmont. From Glenmont, an exhilarating, winding road descends beside Sleepy Hollow Brook, through Sheffield Mills and Centreville back to Kentville, the starting point of the tour.

Evangeline Country Tour

Grand Pre National Historic Park commemorates the British expulsion of the French Acadians in 1755, an event that was immortalized in Longfellow's poem *Evangeline*. This is a loop route starting and ending at Grand Pre, and it has only one hill. In late May the apple blossoms turn the orchards along this route a snowy white. In late September the boughs are bent with rosy fruit.

LENGTH: 24 km (15 miles)

START: Grand Pre National Historic Park, which can be reached by VIA Rail service between Halifax and Yarmouth. This is a dayliner with no checked baggage. Bikes are permitted on a space-available basis, and your chances are better if your bike is in a box.

THE ROUTE: From Grand Pre Historic Park, ride up the slight rise to Highway 1, turn right and continue on into Wolfville. In Wolfville, turn left onto Gaspereau Avenue. After a steep climb, you are rewarded by a panoramic view of the valley. You then have an exciting descent. Turn right before you reach the river onto the White Rock road, a quiet road beside the Gaspereau River. At White Rock you can see the hydro station from the road. Turn left across the river and left again to follow the river back to Gaspereau. Continue through the villages of Melanson and Wallbrook, where signs lead you back to Grand Pre.

Glooscap Trail

The Glooscap Trail follows the shores of the Minas Basin to Cape Blomidon. This tour follows the Glooscap Trail to Shubenacadie before branching off to Dartmouth. You can explore beaches with semi-precious stones, the traditional Micmac hunting and fishing grounds, and a historic port of call.

Glooscap, the Micmac Indians' legendary man-god who lived on Blomidon, claimed this land hundreds of years ago. According to Micmac legend, when the beaver taunted his people, Glooscap threw five handfuls of mud at him. These clumps of mud became the Five Islands near Parrsboro.

LENGTH: 275 km (170 miles)

START: Amherst, which is situated on the Trans Canada Highway just east of the New Brunswick-Nova Scotia border. Amherst can be reached by VIA Rail.

THE ROUTE: Start on Highway 2 out of Amherst, and turn right onto Route 302 to the communities of Nappan and Maccan. At Nappan Station is a federal Agricultural Experimental Station open to visitors on weekdays. Near Athol, Little Forks Road turns east to reach Highway 2 near Springhill Junction.

Springhill, 24 km (15 miles) from Amherst, is situated on the northeastern slope of a rounded hilltop. Large-scale coal mining began here in 1872. The 1,230-meter (4,000-foot) deep No. 2 mine was once the deepest in Canada. Tragedy struck Springhill three times: in 1891, when an underground disaster took the lives of 125 miners; in 1956, when an explosion took 39 more; and in 1958, when a massive earth disturbance in No. 2 mine claimed 76 lives.

The mines are now closed, but a Miner's Museum perpetuates the memory of the miners, with underground tours and exhibits.

Continue on Highway 2 to Mapleton, a center for maple sugar and maple syrup production. The ride from Southampton to Parrsboro is especially beautiful in the autumn when the maple trees turn scarlet and yellow. Near Halfway River East the road goes along Newville Lake between the Canaan Mountains and the Boar's Back Ridge, which contains interesting rock formations. Continue on Route 2 to Parrsboro, 26 km (16 miles) from Southampton.

An alternative route for adventurous cyclists is to ride from Maccan to the coastal town of Joggins on Highway 242. Take the 40-km (25-mile) section of unpaved road between the coast and the Chignecto Game Sanctuary to Apple River. Highway 209 from Apple River follows the coast of the Minas Channel through Advocate Harbour to Parrsboro. The route is hilly, rising and falling from sea level to elevations of 230 meters (750 feet). This scenic winding route is often compared to the Cabot Trail. From Maccan to Parrsboro on this route is about 116 km (72 miles).

Parrsboro is the largest town on the northern shore of Minas Basin and a major tourist center. On the town's beaches and cliffs you can find amethysts, agates, and other semi-precious stones. You can also see them in the Geological Museum. Around the corner from the museum is a giant statue of Glooscap, the Micmac god whom legend says created the Fundy tides and scattered his grandmother's jewellery along the Minas shore.

Highway 2 continues east through the Moose River district and winds through a narrow gorge between high wooded hills. Five Islands is a popular tourist destination. The best view of the five offshore islands is from Five Islands Provincial Park, a campground and picnic area 24 km (15 miles) east of Parrsboro.

Economy Mountain, the only major hill on the tour, rises 215 meters (705 feet) above the Minas Basin and provides a panoramic view of the countryside. The name is from the Micmac word *kenomee*, meaning "a long point jutting out into the sea."

Continue on Highway 2 to Bass River, where you can fish for striped bass near the mouth of the river. Ride on through Great Village, an important shipbuilding community and port of call during the nineteenth century. Many fine old sea captains' mansions remain. Continue through the farming communities of Glenholm and Masstown to Truro, 87 km (54 miles) from Parrsboro.

Truro is at the junction of Highways 102, 2, 104, and 4, and is on the VIA Rail main line. Take a break from bicycling and stroll through the 405-hectare (1,000-acre) Victoria Park, where there are hiking trails and a deep gorge with two waterfalls. The Salmon River in the north end of town experiences a tidal bore. This wall of water, up to half a meter (18 inches) high, moves upstream against the current and can be seen from several viewing places. For tide times call DIAL-A-TIDE at (902) 426-5494.

South of Truro, continue on Highway 2 toward Halifax. Along the way you go through the fertile Stewiacke River Valley, a traditional Micmac fishing and hunting territory. Near Shubenacadie is a provincial wildlife park where you can go birdwatching.

Near Enfield is Halifax International Airport, which can be reached by Highway 102. Highway 2 crosses Highway 102 on an overpass. At Grand Lake, Oakfield Park provides picnic facilities, while Laurie Park offers camping, swimming, and fishing for salmon, trout, and striped bass in Grand Lake.

Highway 2 passes through Wellington, Fall River, and Waverley. At Highway 318, turn left. Highway 318 is a tree-lined road that winds along the chain of lakes that make up what was once the Shubenacadie Canal. This road takes you into Dartmouth.

Across Nova Scotia

If you're crossing Nova Scotia en route from New Brunswick to North Sydney and the ferry to Newfoundland, you can take the Trans Canada Highway for the entire route, or, for a longer and more scenic route, combine some of the tours here.

LENGTH: 500 km (300 miles) approximately

START: Amherst, just east of the New Brunswick-Nova Scotia border.

THE ROUTE: From Amherst, ride the Sunrise Trail Tour (described separately in this chapter) to Pictou, and then continue on the

Sunrise Trail to the Cape George Tour (also described in this chapter). Take that route to Antigonish. Continue on the Sunrise Trail to Auld Cove on the Strait of Canso.

Cross the Canso Causeway, which at a depth of 67 meters (217 feet) is the world's deepest causeway. From the causeway it's 151 km (94 miles) on Highway 105 (the Trans Canada Highway) to the North Sydney ferry terminal. The road winds along the base of the Creignish Hills, and crosses several brooks and rivers coming down from the mountains. The highway then proceeds along the shore of Bras d'Or Lake, a vast inland sea connected to the Atlantic by the fjord-like channels Great Bras d'Or and Little Bras d'Or to the northeast, and by St. Peters Canal to the south. At the town of Nyanza is a Micmac Indian reserve. At Baddeck, you connect with the Cabot Trail Tour (described separately). Stay on Highway 105 to North Sydney, and the terminal for the ferry to Newfoundland.

An alternative route across Cape Breton follows Highway 4 from Canso along the southeastern shore of Bras d'Or Lake to Sydney.

Guidebooks

Bicycle Tours in Nova Scotia. Available from: Bicycle Nova Scotia, Box 3010 South, Halifax, Nova Scotia B3J 3G6. Price $3.50.

14 Newfoundland and Labrador

A rugged rocky island in the Atlantic Ocean, Newfoundland lies 130 km (80 miles) off the Canadian mainland. The 112,293-square-kilometer (43,359-square-mile) island has been isolated for much of its history, and many of the outport communities were cut off from each other until relatively recently. Many areas still have an old-world atmosphere.

The island of Newfoundland is a continuation of the Appalachian Mountain chain. The Long Range Mountains on the northern peninsula rise abruptly from the west coast. Newfoundland's rugged southern and eastern coasts are laced with islets, filigree bays, and coves.

Newfoundland's unique touring opportunities have yet to be discovered by many cyclists. There is a lot more to cycling in Newfoundland than crossing the island via the Trans Canada Highway. The cycling tours here explore secondary roads, taking you to picturesque outport communities and spectacular scenery. In many settlements are Hospitality Homes offering accommodation with a Newfoundland family. If you are planning to go across Newfoundland, take a side trip on one of these tours.

ROADS: Most of the highways on the Island of Newfoundland are paved two-lane roads, but not all of them have paved shoulders. The rugged and isolated coast of Labrador has approximately 80 km (50 miles) of road, about 40 km (30 miles) of which are paved.

WEATHER: In early summer floating ice moves southward producing fog and cool weather on the island. Newfoundland experiences frequent high winds, and on the east coast precipitation is heavy. St. John's experiences rain or snow an average of 201 days per year and has an average total precipitation of 137 cm (54 inches) per year.

TOURIST INFORMATION: For a current accommodation guide which includes a road map and lists of campgrounds, contact: Department of Development and Tourism, P.O. Box 2016, St. John's, Newfoundland A1C 5R8. Telephone toll-free 1-800-563-6353.

HOSTELS: Newfoundland Hostel Association, Box 1815, St. John's, Newfoundland A1C 5P9. Telephone (709) 754-0210.

AIRPORTS: Air Canada, Canadian Pacific Airlines, Air Nova, Air Atlantic, and Labrador Airways serve Newfoundland.

FERRIES: Marine Atlantic provides ferry service from North Sydney, Nova Scotia, to Port aux Basques and Argentia, Newfoundland, as well as serving Newfoundland outport communities. Some cycling tours incorporate ferries as part of the trip.

If you want to take the ferry, make reservations well in advance. Use Marine Atlantic's toll-free numbers. Be sure to ask the extra cost of transporting your bike.

For more information and reservations, contact: Marine Atlantic, Box 250, North Sydney, Nova Scotia B2A 3M3. Call toll-free: in Ontario and Quebec, 1-800-565-9411; in Newfoundland and Labrador, 1-800-563-7701; in New Brunswick, Nova Scotia, and Prince Edward Island, 1-800-565-9470; in Maine, 1-800-432-7344; in continental United States, 1-800-341-7981; in the terminal area at North Sydney, Nova Scotia, (902) 794-7203; at Port aux Basques, Newfoundland, (709) 695-2124; in Argentia, Newfoundland, (709) 227-2311.

TRAINS: There is no passenger train service in Newfoundland. For information on VIA Rail service when in Newfoundland, call toll-free from 6:30 a.m. to 7:30 p.m., 1-800-561-3926, and from 7:30 p.m. to 6:30 a.m., 1-800-361-6180.

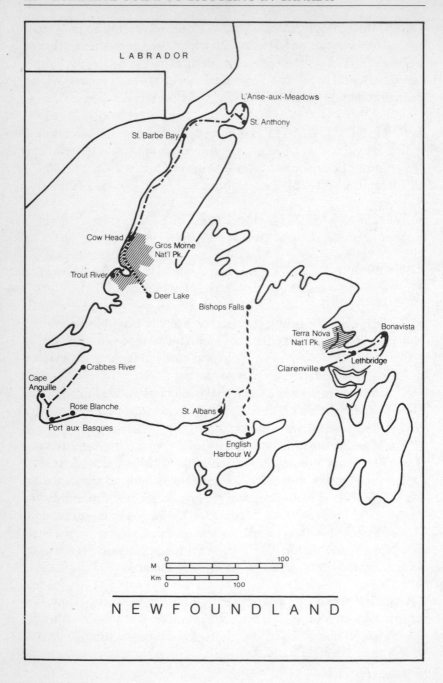

LABRADOR

L'Anse-aux-Meadows

St. Anthony

St. Barbe Bay

Cow Head

Gros Morne
Nat'l Pk.

Trout River

Deer Lake

Bishops Falls

Terra Nova
Nat'l Pk.

Bonavista

Crabbes River

Clarenville

Lethbridge

Cape
Anguille

Rose Blanche

St. Albans

Port aux Basques

English
Harbour W.

M 0   100

Km 0   100

NEWFOUNDLAND

BUSES: Bus service on the island is provided by Terra Transport Roadcruiser Services, 495 Water Street, Box 310, St. John's, Newfoundland A1C 5K1. Telephone (709) 737-5912.

BICYCLING: The Newfoundland and Labrador Cycling Association, Box 2127, Station C, St. John's, Newfoundland A1C 5R6. Telephone (709) 576-2513.

Port aux Basques to Crabbes River

The southwestern corner of Newfoundland is the first part of Newfoundland that many visitors see. The rugged coast here has dark cliffs pounded by waves.

LENGTH: 200 km (125 miles)

START: Port aux Basques, the Marine Atlantic ferry terminus.

THE ROUTE: Port aux Basques was named by Basque fishermen as long ago as the sixteenth century. The town has motels and stores.

A side trip can be made east along the coast of Cabot Strait before starting on the Trans Canada Highway. Approximately 27 km (16 miles) east on Route 470 is Otter Bay Provincial Park with campsites and a swimming area. Along the way is Isle aux Morts, French for "Island of the Dead," so named because of the many shipwrecks that occurred in this area. More than forty shipwrecks lie in the waters of Cabot Strait. At Rose Blanche, another 18 km (11 miles) east of Otter Bay, you can see a stone lighthouse, dating from 1856, with a good view of the Cabot Strait.

From Port aux Basques, start riding on the Trans Canada Highway. Only 2.5 km (1.5 miles) away is John Cheeseman Provincial Park. There is a sandy beach here as well as at the Cape Ray Sands. At 518-meter (1,700-foot) Table Mountain, part of the Long Range Mountains, is a hiking trail to a scenic viewpoint. Mummichog Provincial Park, with 15 km (9 miles) of beach, is another 18 km (11 miles) from John Cheeseman Park. It is a good spot for birdwatching.

Approximately 6 km (3.7 miles) northeast, at Tompkins, you can take Route 407 to the Codroy Valley, a picturesque farming area, approximately 45 km (28 miles) from Port aux Basques. Continue through Millville, Codroy, and other communities to reach Cape Anguille, Newfoundland's westernmost point.

Return to the Trans Canada Highway by Route 406. Along the way is Grand Codroy Provincial Park (day use only), 3 km (1.8 miles) off Route 1, and 2 km (1.2 miles) from the community of Doyles. The park has a beach.

It is 55 km (34 miles) from Doyles to Crabbes River Provincial Park, which has camping. You can swim in the river before going 5 km (3 miles) into St. Fintan's on Route 405. You can buy lobster, salmon, or cod from the local fishermen.

Near Crabbes Park, you can take Route 404 to the scenic fishing and farming communities of McKays and Heatherton.

Deer Lake to Gros Morne National Park

The highest and most spectacular portion of the Long Range Mountains is found in 1,812-square-km (700-square-mile) Gros Morne National Park on Newfoundland's west coast, one of the province's most scenic areas. Gros Morne's coastal Long Range Mountains are cut by huge fjords with cliffs rising 600 meters (1,968 feet) above the water. The shoreline has almost every type of beach, from those covered with large boulders to fine sandy beaches. The coastal tidal pools support crabs, starfish, chitons, mussels, barnacles, periwinkles, hermit crabs, sea urchins, and sea anemones.

LENGTH: 100 km (62 miles)

START: Deer Lake is the junction of the Trans Canada Highway and Route 430 leading to Newfoundland's northern peninsula and southern Labrador. It has an airport with interprovincial flights. Terra Transport Trans Island Motorcoaches also make routine stops but carry bicycles on a space-available basis only.

THE ROUTE: Take Route 430, known as The Viking Trail, out of Deer Lake and ride 23 km (14 miles) to Wiltondale. Here are a museum and a restored "company" house. You are now at the entrance to Gros Morne National Park. Continue on Route 430 to Rocky Harbour, a fishing village and headquarters of Gros Morne National Park. Gros Morne Park's main campground, the Berry Hill campground, is 4 km (2.5 miles) north of Rocky Harbour.

At Lobster Cove Head, just north of Rocky Harbour at the entrance to Bonne Bay, is a lighthouse with marine displays. Route 430 follows the rugged shore 10 km (6 miles) to Green Point, where there is a campground near the ocean.

Approximately 5 km (3 miles) from Green Point is Sally Cove, where lobster fishing is carried on. Ride 5 km (3 miles) to the spectacular Western Brook Pond, a 19-km (12-mile) inland fjord set between 600-meter (2000-foot) cliffs. To explore the pond, walk 2 km (1.2 miles) along the trail to the nearest shore, where boats take you to the end of the pond.

Another scenic spot is 5 km (3 miles) north of the trail at the mouth of Western Brook. Here the river twists through high dunes and runs out by beautiful sandy beaches.

Follow Route 430 north to St. Pauls Inlet, 76 km (47 miles) from Norris Point. Approximately 16 km (10 miles) farther is Cow Head, with fine views of the coast. Another 7 km (4 miles) is Shallow Bay, off Highway 430 through Cow Head. There are a campground and a driftwood-strewn beach here. You can walk to Gros Morne Park's northern boundary, just beyond the north tip of the bay. The Viking Trail Tour (described separately in this chapter) begins nearby.

The Viking Trail: Gros Morne National Park to St. Anthony

The site of the only known Viking colony in North America, L'Anse aux Meadows, is along this tour of Newfoundland's Great Northern Peninsula. To cycle this tour as a circuit without having to retrace your route, take the Marine Atlantic ferry from St. Anthony at the tip of the Northern Peninsula to Lewisporte. Make reservations in advance and schedule your trip so you won't have a long wait for the ferry in St. Anthony.

L'Anse aux Meadows, one of the most historically significant areas in North America, is believed to be the site of Leif Eiricsson's colonization of the New World around the year 1000. Sod buildings erected here recreate the earliest-known European structures in North America. In 1978, L'Anse aux Meadows was named the first UNESCO World Heritage Site.

LENGTH: 410 km (254 miles)

START: Parson's Pond, near the northern boundary of Gros Morne National Park.

THE ROUTE: From Parson's Pond, take Route 430 north. Just 10 km (6 miles) north and to the left is a short road leading to "The Arches," two massive arches carved by the action of the sea. Another 12 km (7 miles) brings you to Daniels Harbour, a fishing, lumbering, and mining town offering a variety of stores and two motels.

Ride 35 km (22 miles) north from Daniels Harbour to River of Ponds Provincial Park, which offers camping and swimming areas. The park has several upstream trout pools. Approximately another 15 km (9 miles) away is Hawkes Bay, midway between Deer Lake and St. Anthony. The river is popular for salmon fishing. A little farther on, at Port Saunders, are general stores and a hospital. Port aux Choix, 10 km (6 miles) from Port Saunders, has a national historic park with archaeological artifacts from a prehistoric Dorset Inuit community. A short ride on an unpaved road takes you back to Route 430.

Continue north on Route 430 for 45 km (28 miles), past Castors River and Bartletts Harbour, to Plum Point, where many buildings and traditions remain of the French occupation. At St. Barbe, 15 km (9 miles) from Plum Point, is the terminal for the ferry across to Labrador (a Labrador cycling route is described separately in this chapter). Another 30 km (18 miles) on Route 430 brings you to Flowers Cove, a fishing community with the Grenfell Mission nursing station.

Ten km (6 miles) north of Flowers Cove, Route 430 turns inland off the coastal Viking Trail. After another 17 km (10 miles) is the junction of Route 436, which leads to L'Anse aux Meadows, reached by 30 km (18 miles) of unpaved highway.

After visiting L'Anse aux Meadows, return to Route 430 and continue for 22 km (14 miles) to St. Anthony, the largest northern town and the headquarters of the International Grenfell Association which still provides some medical services to Newfoundland's isolated communities. Grenfell Handicrafts is known for its hand-embroidered parkas. The town has a hospital, a grocery store, and hotels.

St. Anthony is a port of call for the Marine Atlantic ferry serving coastal communities between Lewisporte and Goose Bay. Take the ferry to Lewisporte and continue cycling on Route 340 for 15 km (9 miles), to the Trans Canada Highway.

From St. Anthony you can retrace your route or take Labrador Airways which has flights within Newfoundland and Labrador.

MORE INFORMATION: Labrador Airways, Box 13485, Station A, St. John's, Newfoundland A1B 4B8. Telephone (709) 753-9370.

Marine Atlantic coastal ferries: in Newfoundland call toll-free 1 000-563-7336.

Bishops Falls to English Harbour West

Route 360 links with the Trans Canada Highway near Bishops Falls, and goes through the unspoiled interior wilderness to the remote communities on Newfoundland's south coast. The road is paved, although subject to occasional washouts.

Cycling the south coast of Newfoundland is a journey back into a rich unspoiled part of the province's traditions and folklore. The people here depend on the sea off one of the roughest coasts in North America for their livelihood.

LENGTH: 190 km (118 miles)

START: Bishops Falls, near the junction of the Trans Canada Highway and Route 360.

THE ROUTE: From the Trans Canada Highway ride south to Jipujikuei Kuespem Park (Little River Pond Park), a distance of 80 km (50 miles). This area is part of the traditional hunting grounds of the Micmac Indians, whose ancestors were brought to Newfoundland from Nova Scotia by the French in the eighteenth and nineteenth centuries. A few kilometers north of the park you pass the junction of Route 361 to Conne River and St. Albans.

Continue south on Route 360 to the junction with Route 362. From here, ride approximately 35 km (22 miles) of gravel Route 362 through several settlements on ruggedly beautiful bays, to English Harbour West, a port of call for the Marine Atlantic coastal service. From here you can travel by ferry (make inquiries and reservations well in advance) to Terrenceville and Fortune, both located on the Burin Peninsula. From either of these ports you can explore the Burin Peninsula (described separately in this chapter). From Fortune another ferry takes you to the French islands of St. Pierre and Miquelon. (Tours of the islands are described separately in this chapter.)

Terra Nova National Park and the Bonavista Peninsula

Canada's easternmost national park, Terra Nova is situated on the Appalachian mountain range. The park encompasses 400 square km (155 square miles) of deep rocky fjords, rolling crested hills, inland ponds and a deeply indented coastline on the shores of Bonavista Bay and the Labrador Sea. It offers hiking, swimming, canoeing, scuba diving, and sailing. The scenery is typical of Newfoundland's east coast. From the park, this tour explores the Bonavista Peninsula.

The cold Labrador current gives the area cool wet summers. Icebergs, and a variety of whales and seals can be seen occasionally off the coast during the summer. Fishing for brook trout and Arctic char in the ponds, streams, and lakes is excellent. Saltwater fish in the area include cod, mackerel, herring, lumpfish, and caplin. Blue mussels, barnacles, and periwinkles can be found on coastal rocks, while crabs and lobsters thrive in deeper water.

LENGTH: 240 km (150 miles)

START: Terra Nova National Park, on the Trans Canada Highway 78 km (48 miles) southeast of the town of Gander, North America's easternmost international airport.

THE ROUTE: The Trans Canada Highway extends for 41 km (25 miles) through Terra Nova Park. The road is hilly but moderately graded and it has a paved shoulder. This part of the Appalachian mountain system has spectacular views. The park's two main campgrounds are at Newman Sound and Malady Head.

Take a side trip to Charlottetown, a tiny community on the Atlantic coast where you can observe varied bird life — you may even see a bald eagle. You can sometimes see whales, too.

After exploring Terra Nova Park, head toward the Bonavista Peninsula by riding 10 km (6 miles) past the park boundary to Route 233. This has about 25 km (15 miles) of gravel road, but the rest of the tour is paved, except for side routes off the main road. The communities along this route are situated so close together that you are seldom cycling long stretches of lonely highway. Follow Route 233 to Musgravetown, which offers a Hospitality Home.

Take Route 230 at Southwest Brook and travel 48 km (30 miles) through Lethbridge, past the Rattle Falls viewpoint and Southern Bay, to Trinity. Dating back to 1500, the village of Trinity is considered to be the oldest European settlement in North America. It was named by the Portuguese explorer Gaspar Corte-Real, who sailed in on Trinity Sunday. In addition to the historic buildings here, you can find boating, whale-watching, and scuba diving. Accommodation is available in nearby Goose Cove.

Lockston Path Provincial Park offers sheltered campsites and a freshwater beach, and is only 6 km (4 miles) from Port Rexton. At Port Rexton you are 64 km (40 miles) from the Trans Canada Highway. The park is a good base camp from which you can visit the nearby historic communities of Port Union and Catalina 27 km (16 miles) farther.

The last community on the peninsula is Bonavista. You have now traveled approximately 144 km (90 miles) from the Trans Canada Highway. Nearby Cape Bonavista is believed to be the place where John Cabot first saw the New World on June 24, 1497. Bonavista is the largest community on Newfoundland's east coast, and entirely dependent on the fishing industry. Places of interest include the museum, the restored lighthouse, and White Rock, which offers a panoramic view of the surrounding countryside and ocean. Accommodation is available in Bonavista.

An alternative to retracing your route from Bonavista back to the Trans Canada Highway is to take Route 235 along the coast of

Bonavista Bay, through Amherst Cove, 18 km (11 miles) from Bonavista, then 13 km (8 miles) to Knights Cove, on a mostly unpaved road. You ride on paved highway again for 19 km (12 miles) to Plate Cove, and another 21 km (13 miles) to Southern Bay. Connect here with Route 230 and travel 45 km (23 miles) through Lethbridge and Southwest Brook to Milton. You arrive at the Trans Canada Highway at Clarenville, a distribution center for the Bonavista Peninsula where there are hotels, restaurants, banks, and a shopping center.

Burin Peninsula and St. Pierre-Miquelon

The picturesque Burin Peninsula has its history tied to the fishery on the Grand Banks. A rich fishing ground, the Grand Banks attracted Europeans to these shores as early as the 1500s, when the French, English, and Portuguese came in the summer to fish and dry their catch before returning home in the fall. The islands of St. Pierre and Miquelon, French territories, offer an enchanting taste of France, just a two-hour ferry ride from Fortune.

This tour follows Route 210 south from the Trans Canada Highway. The road is open and exposed to wind and rain, but the scenery is spectacular.

LENGTH: 235 km (146 miles)

START: The junction of the Trans Canada Highway and Route 210. For a shorter trip, start at Marystown for a circuit of the lower Burin Peninsula.

THE ROUTE: Go south on Route 210 from the Trans Canada Highway. You pass through the community of Swift Current and then Pipers Hole River Provincial Park, which is 35 km (22 miles) south of the Trans Canada Highway.

Ride the 110 km (73 miles) from Pipers Hole River Provincial Park to Marystown on Placentia Bay. Along the way are gravel roads leading to outport communities. Marystown is a shipbuilding and fishing community with motels, restaurants, banks, and a shopping mall.

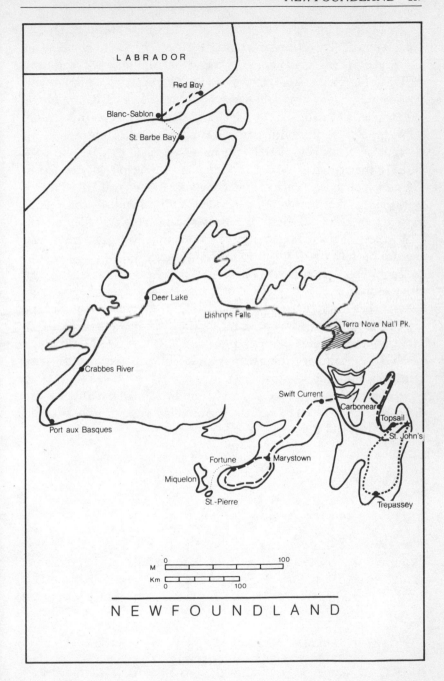

LABRADOR

Red Bay

Blanc-Sablon

St. Barbe Bay

Deer Lake

Bishops Falls

Terra Nova Nat'l Pk.

Crabbes River

Swift Current

Carbonear

Topsail

St. John's

Port aux Basques

Fortune

Marystown

Miquelon

St.-Pierre

Trepassey

M 0 100

Km 0 100

N E W F O U N D L A N D

At Marystown, start the circuit of the historic Burin Peninsula. Take Route 210 to Winterland, then Route 213 west to Frenchmans Cove Provincial Park, where there are camping and swimming facilities. The park is approximately 40 km (25 miles) from Marystown. At Grand Bank, 54 km (33 miles) from Marystown on Route 210, is the Seaman's Museum about the Grand Banks. Then on to Fortune, a fishing community with hotels, restaurants, and stores.

From Fortune you can take the ferry (operated by Lake and Lake Ltd.) to the French islands of St. Pierre and Miquelon, located 18 km (11 miles) offshore. Once off the ferry you are in a real French town with French cuisine, wines, perfumes, clothes, and, of course, the French language. St. Pierre is a busy fishing port with only 3 km (1.8 miles) of road. Miquelon is a picturesque island where several hundred people live by fishing and farming.

From Fortune, continue on Route 220. The road goes through the picturesque coastal villages of Lamaline and Lawn to reach St. Lawrence, a distance of 80 km (50 miles). St. Lawrence was once the site of a large fluorspar mine. Here you can visit the Miner's Museum. Continuing on Route 220 for approximately 35 km (22 miles), you reach Burin, another fishing center built along a series of cliffs, with a fish plant and docking facilities for trawlers.

Another 10 km (6 miles) and you are back at Marystown. Make this a base from which to visit the surrounding settlements of Mortier, Tides Point, and Creston.

MORE INFORMATION: Lake and Lake Ltd., Box 98, Fortune, Newfoundland A0E 1P0. Telephone (709) 832-1950.

St. John's and the Avalon Peninsula

This circuit, four days long at a leisurely pace, explores the Avalon Peninsula, the easternmost part of Newfoundland. The area has some of the oldest European settlements in North America. This tour follows Highway 10, known as the Southern Shore. Many tales of shipwrecks are told here.

LENGTH: 300 km (186 miles)

START: St. John's, the capital of the province of Newfoundland

THE ROUTE: Start with the 31-km (19-mile) ride from St. John's to the fishing community of Bay Bulls. It is one of Newfoundland's oldest settlements, dating from 1638. In the deep waters of Bay Bulls lies the wreck of the *H.M.S. Sapphire*, sunk in battle in 1696.

The road is hilly but has good views of the coast. At Tors Cove, 40 km (25 miles) along this route, is an offshore bird sanctuary which extends to the LaManche Valley. LaManche Valley Provincial Park has swimming and a hiking trail. Ferryland, 34 km (21 miles) from Tors Cove, is a good stop for the night. A battle site and an early settlement are found here.

Ride the 70 km (43 miles) from Ferryland to Trepassey, much of it across some bleak barrens. You cross traces of the old railway track that once served the coast to Trepassey.

Trepassey means "the dead" or "dead souls"; it was settled by the Welsh in the 1620s, and was the starting point for trans-Atlantic flights in the 1920s. Trepassey is a good place to spend the night.

Cycle west from Trepassey Bay across the highlands. There are a lot of hills on this stretch of road, and a section of 10 km (6 miles) is unpaved. There is a provincial park with camping at Holyrood Pond, and a beach at Point La Haye. Hospitality Home accommodations are available in St. Josephs, Newbridge, and Salmonier. Ride the 78 km (48 miles) along Route 60 (the Conception Bay Highway) along the Salmonier Line, past the Salmonier Nature Park, and back to St. John's.

Conception Bay and Trinity Bay

If one single area could portray Newfoundland, it must be Conception Bay, west of the city of St. John's. From Cape St. Francis, at the tip of Conception Bay's Eastern Arm, to Grates Cove on the western tip is 200 km (124 miles) by road. This tour continues to the Trinity Bay coast.

LENGTH: 345 km (214 miles)

START: Topsail, located 12 km (7.5 miles) west of St. John's. From St. John's take the Topsail Road, which is Route 60, to the village of Topsail.

THE ROUTE: Start your tour with a view of Conception Bay and its islands by climbing Topsail Head. From Topsail, take Route 60 south along the Conception Bay coast. The 25 km (15 miles) to Holyrood is along fairly even terrain. You pass several communities including Kelligrews, celebrated in the Newfoundland ballad "The Kelligrews Soiree."

The road is busy at times, and rough pavement edges are to be contended with frequently. At Holyrood are a municipal park and Butter Pot Provincial Park with camping facilities. To get to the provincial park you must take the Trans Canada Highway, which intersects with Route 60 south of Holyrood. From Holyrood, Route 60 turns north along the coast.

Keep to the road that borders the sea around the Arm and over a series of hills through Harbour Main, Avondale, and Conception Harbour. Ride over the Barrens to historic Brigus, and to Cupids, the first settled place in Newfoundland. Rejoin Route 60, ride to South River and take Route 70 to Bay Roberts, 80 km (50 miles) from St. John's, which offers plenty of accommodation in hotels and Hospitality Homes. Continue north on the hilly road through several communities to the town of Harbour Grace. Here is Newfoundland's oldest stone church, and a museum in the old Customs House.

At Carbonear, a few kilometers beyond Harbour Grace, you have a choice. You can continue north along Conception Bay, Route 70, right to the cape at Grates Cove; or you can ascend the steep hill and head along Route 74 to Hearts Content on Trinity Bay.

Along Route 70 are Salmon Cove Beach and Northern Bay Sands Provincial Park, which has camping. Grates Cove is at the windy western tip of Conception Bay. Round trip from Northern Bay Sands Park to Hearts Content is almost 100 km (60 miles), so allow sufficient time. Hearts Content is the site of the first successful trans-Atlantic telegraphic communications. The old cable station is now a museum.

Go through Hearts Desire and Hearts Delight, farther down the coast, to Cavendish. A little farther is Backside Pond Park with camping and swimming. At the Trans Canada Highway junction at Whitbourne, 58 km (35 miles) from Hearts Content, you can continue touring toward the Southern Avalon, or return to St. John's on 80 km (50 miles) of the Trans Canada Highway.

Labrador Coast from Blanc Sablon to Red Bay

The Labrador coast, the part of Newfoundland on mainland Canada, is an adventure for cyclists who want to explore a remote region of rugged, unspoiled terrain. Labrador is separated from Newfoundland by the 17-km (11-mile) wide Strait of Belle Isle. In the communities of Forteau, West St. Modeste, and Red Bay are the descendants of fishermen who first travelled from the Island of Newfoundland to the lucrative fishing grounds off Labrador centuries ago.

You can see whales, icebergs drifting southward from the Arctic, and a variety of birds. There is also hiking and fishing. Local arts and crafts are available.

LENGTH: 80 km (50 miles)

START: Blanc Sablon in Quebec, just 5 km (3 miles) west of the Labrador boundary. Take the ferry from St. Barbe in northern Newfoundland, across the Strait of Belle Isle to Blanc Sablon.

THE ROUTE: From Blanc Sablon, take Route 510 for 5 km (3 miles) east to the Labrador boundary. From Blanc Sablon to Pinware the road is paved. The route from Pinware to Red Bay, approximately 40 km (25 miles), is unpaved.

Anglers will find good salmon fishing at Forteau and Pinware. At L'Anse Amour is a Maritime Archaic Indian burial site that is 7,500 years old. Around Pinware in August you can pick ''bakeapples'' or cloudberries, considered a delicacy by the locals. Red Bay is the site of a sixteenth century Basque whaling station.

Accommodations along this route include Pinware River Provincial Park for the overnight camper, and a Hospitality Home in Forteau as well as one in L'Anse au Loup. Retrace your route back to Blanc Sablon.

MORE INFORMATION: The Strait of Belle Isle ferry is operated by Puddister Trading Company Ltd., 23 Springdale Street, Box 38, St. John's, Newfoundland A1C 5H5. Telephone (709) 722-4000.

Across Newfoundland

Following the Trans Canada Highway, Route 1, takes you across the Island of Newfoundland from Port aux Basques to St. John's. There are provincial parks and private campgrounds an easy day's ride apart, and motels and hotels in the larger towns. The route ranges from hilly to mountainous.

LENGTH: 905 km (565 miles)

START: Port aux Basques ferry terminal

THE ROUTE: From Port aux Basques to Corner Brook, the Trans Canada Highway follows the coast. From Corner Brook to Lewisporte the terrain is more hilly and it becomes mountainous between Deer Lake and South Brook. Climbs tend to be long and gradual. From Lewisporte to Argentia is rolling coastal to hilly terrain.

The other tours described in this chapter are segments of the Across Newfoundland Tour, but they include secondary roads leading to coastal areas and smaller communities.

Guidebooks

Newfoundland by Bicycle, by Audrey Porter and Tom Sandland. Available free from: Newfoundland and Labrador Cycling Association, Box 2127, Station C, St. John's, Newfoundland A1C 5R6.

Index

Printed in Canada